A MUG-UP WITH ELISABETH

A Mug-up with
Elisabeth

A COMPANION FOR READERS OF ELISABETH OGILVIE

Melissa Hayes & Marilyn Westervelt

Down East Books

"Last Waltz on Criehaven" and excerpts from "Profile: Grand Dames of Criehaven"
are from *Island Journal,* used with permission from the Island Institute.

Excerpts from Edie Lau, "On Criehaven, Visitors Worthy of Big Welcome" used
with permission from the *Portland Press Herald / Maine Sunday Telegram.*

Excerpts from George Putz, "This New England: Criehaven, Maine"
used courtesy of Yankee Publishing, Inc., all rights reserved.

Excerpts from Katy Perry, "Award to Elisabeth Ogilvie Highlights Spring
Conference" used with permission from *The Maine Line,* Maine Media Women.

Map of Gay's Island, by Dawn Peterson, reprinted from
My World Is an Island, Down East Books.

Map of Bennett's Island, by Anthony Bacon Venti,
reprinted from *An Answer in the Tide,* Down East Books.

Cover illustration by Beverly Lawson

ISBN 0-89272-532-X
Library of Congress Catalog Card Number: 2001094145
Printed at Versa Press, Inc.

2   4   5   3   1

Down East Books
www.downeastbooks.com
Orders: 1-800-766-1670

For my husband, John,
and our children, Maggie, John, and Liz,
with love and gratitude.

M. II. –

For my husband, Jim,
who made it possible for me to live
my dream of life in Maine.

– M. W. –

Contents

Photographs follow page 84.

Acknowledgments

We wish to express our gratitude to the following people for their invaluable assistance: Our editors Karin Womer and Jane Crosen, and Neale Sweet and Terry Brègy of Down East Books, for their hard work and unfailing support of this project; Martha Reed of The Personal Book Shop in Thomaston, Maine, as it was through her that we met Elisabeth and each other; Jan and Ken Ogilvie and Beverly and Warren Lawson for their help with Elisabeth's family tree and history; Beverly Lawson for the beautiful book cover art; Barbara Ogilvie Mosher for assistance with obtaining photos; Luthera Dawson for her encouragement and invaluable help with the Maine terms glossary; Jean Crie Hodgkins for generously sharing her family history of Criehaven; Barbara Lawrence for sharing several articles about Elisabeth; Frank Moffett, Linda Cibotti, and Corinne Mitchell of North Quincy High School; Vance Bunker for island transport, and Sari Bunker for her wonderful photographs, research assistance, and friendship; Georgeanne Davis; Paula Bousquet; friends at the Jonathan Trumbull Library in Lebanon, Connecticut; and all of our *A Mug-up with Elisabeth* newsletter subscribers, who have enthusiastically supported this project.

Special thanks go to Elisabeth Ogilvie for her gracious cooperation and for her precious friendship; it has been our privilege to work on this book.

Finally, we want to express appreciation to our families for their love and support.

✿ Prelude

The Gut between Pleasant Point and Gay's Island was swathed in fog as the men were getting ready to go out to haul. She carried her first mug of coffee to the table and placed it carefully next to the stacks of books and the yellow pad already thick with words. The sun hadn't yet made its appearance, but her mind was already racing with thoughts and bits of dialogue. As she picked up her pen to begin, she smiled at her cat, curled up on the couch and purring like an engine. The sound merged with the first boats leaving the harbor. Her eyes closed as she envisioned similar mornings on Criehaven:

> The men were leaving the harbor, and she was up—senses tingling, eyes bright—she grabbed her coat and went out. As the sun rose over the golden rocks of the island, she walked to Sou'west Point to pick berries. The sun made a path of glittering diamonds on the water, the cry of gulls her only orchestra as she strode briskly along. The beauty of the island morning made her throat ache with barely suppressed joy. She knew that to contain this ecstasy would be impossible. She ran back to the house to grab her pad and pen, her fingers itching to capture this glory.
>
> She sat on a high perch of granite ledge, opened her notebook, and began to write. Time dissolved as her pen flew over the pages. She pushed her dark hair off her face and pondered the endless ocean stretched in front of her. She was just fifteen, but she knew with a certainty that took her breath away that she had found her truth, the very essence of life.

The older woman, hair now white and softly curling around her face, opened her eyes and took a sip of coffee. She picked up her pen as she took one more glance out the window. The boats had all gone now, and the sun was dancing on the water. A lone gull perched on the wharf. She smiled again, and began to write.

PART 1

Elisabeth's Beginnings

1 ❧ HER ANCESTRY

THE SPRING OF 1917 BROUGHT momentous change to the Ogilvie household of Dorchester, Massachusetts. A family with three sons was about to welcome a new baby daughter. On May 20, 1917, Elisabeth May was born to Frank and Maude Ogilvie, joining brothers Allan, age nine, Kent, age seven, and five-year-old Gordon. Maude had been expecting to have a fourth boy—she knew well that the Ogilvie clan "went into lots of boys"—but Elisabeth arrived instead. About her birth and welcome into the family as the only girl, Elisabeth has remarked, "I guess I was quite a success."

Her three brothers were careful in looking out for their baby sister. Gordon, the youngest, resented Elisabeth at first for displacing him from his status as baby of the family. Elisabeth has said that Gordon was perfectly content before she was born, and "saw no need of me whatsoever; he said so, often. Loudly!" They called him Boanerges, which means "son of thunder." (Probably from the ancient Greek, Boanerges is found in the Bible, with one reference saying, "James, as a Boanerges, would thunder God's grace.")

Ironically, the older boys had always thought Gordon had it soft, because, as the youngest before Elisabeth's arrival, he would often run to their father and return gleefully clutching a few pennies. Even so, Gordon never took his displacement out on Elisabeth. If Gordon was loud and boisterous, Kent was known as the easygoing one; he was very popular and lovable, and grinned at people in public when he was a baby. Allan, the oldest, was quieter and more introspective. An early photo of the children shows an ebullient group of boys, holding kittens aloft, surrounding a serene baby Elisabeth.

Elisabeth was born during a time of great historical significance. The sinking of the *Lusitania* occurred on May 7, 1915, ending the United States's isolationist stance regarding World War I. America was deeply involved in World War I by the time Elisabeth was born two years later. The war directly affected the Ogilvie family through Frank Ogilvie's Army Reserves status. As a soldier in the Reserves, Frank was serving in the Coast Artillery, the branch of the service that manned the big guns at Fort Revere on Boston Harbor.

THE OGILVIES

It was only natural that Frank Ogilvie should serve his country. He came from a long line of fighters, including James Ogilvie, who fought for Bonnie Prince Charlie in the Battle of Culloden in 1745. It is thought that James may have been imprisoned for his involvement in this famous Scottish battle, before he came to the state of Georgia in 1751, along with sons Peter and John. According to the Colonial Records of Georgia, James Ogilvie was granted land in Burke County, Georgia, between 1759 and 1766.

Elisabeth includes references to this family history, in fictionalized form, in *The Devil in Tartan*. Her fictional character Angus Mor was no doubt modeled on her Ogilvie ancestors. Elisabeth writes of Angus, "He'd have been fifteen at the time of the rising for Prince Charlie in 1745; quite possibly, if he were a big enough boy, he'd have been out for the Prince like the rest of the Kendrum [Ogilvie] men. Most of them had been massacred at Culloden as they tried to hold the line against Butcher Cumberland's dragoons. Their chief, the fifth Earl, had been killed, and those who'd escaped back to their valley expected to be hunted out and killed or sent into slavery. It was the same ghastly story all over the Highlands." Clearly this Ogilvie ancestry captivated Elisabeth—and her brother Gordon (also a writer of historical fiction).

James Ogilvie began to raise his family in Georgia. His sons Peter (referred to as Peter Senior) and John continued the Ogilvie soldierly tradition by fighting as Loyalists in the Revolutionary War. Fearing for their safety at the war's end, the brothers made plans to go to Nova Scotia in 1783. Peter Senior, as a Loyalist soldier with the rank of ensign, was entitled to live under the British flag on a soldier's land grant in Nova Scotia. Their journey began in St. Augustine, Florida, which at that time still belonged to Spain. Setting sail on the refugee ship *Argo* in October, the brothers arrived in Nova Scotia in December 1783. Grants of land were waiting for them in Manchester Township, in the Canso area, but Peter Senior instead chose land along the Musquodoboit River, now called Elderbank. He and his wife raised their four children on this property: Peter (who would come to be called Captain Peter), James, Jane, and Agnes. It was on this homestead, one hundred years later, that Frank Ogilvie—Elisabeth's father—was born to James's son Allan and his wife Catherine.

Peter Senior is buried in the Pioneer Cemetery in Middle Musquodoboit, Nova Scotia. The inscription on his headstone, although dim with age, appears to read: "Peter Ogilvie Senior, died May 6, 1837, in the 88th year of his age." Peter Senior's brother John ended up settling in a nearby alder swamp called Meagher's Grant, where he and his wife brought up a large family. The offspring of these Ogilvies spread out all over Canada, and sites of many of their first cabins can still be found.

Elisabeth incorporates this family history into *The Devil in Tartan*, writing of the character Angus Mor, "[he] was well-documented [in Brierbank] by the recording of his crown grant in Halifax; his stone in the churchyard, his name in town and church records, the names and dates of his children's births in various old family Bibles." And she refers to the genealogical exploring that must have been done by members of her family when she writes, "To us he was a young adventurer. My cousins and I played in the cellar hole of his cabin. We had an old skiff on the river and used to act out the story of his arrival by canoe, following the river up from Oquiddic Harbor eighteen miles away. All that we knew of him before that day was that he'd come from Scotland by way of Georgia."

Captain Peter, Frank Ogilvie's great-grandfather, was born in December 1792. He married Ann Bruce, daughter of James Bruce, who had come from Scotland in 1812. Captain Peter inherited the lands that were granted to Peter Senior; he later shared them with his sons. Captain Peter died in April 1865 and Ann in December 1887.

The Ogilvies were both fighters and explorers, fighting for the causes they believed in and not afraid to venture out into new territories. Elisabeth has said that the Ogilvies were travelers, willing to go far for freedom and new experiences. Both the Ogilvies in the United States and Canada went out west. In a conversation with the authors, she recalled, "That's where my father's youngest brother went. My father came to the States, and another uncle stayed in Nova Scotia to farm the home place. All the other brothers went west and did very well."

FRANK

Frank Everett Ogilvie was the eldest son of Allan and Catherine, born in 1884. Frank's childhood was a happy one. He was raised in a good home with a churchgoing family of high standards. Elisabeth recalls her grandparents as kindly people who couldn't abide gossip at the supper table. If the children talked about things that went on in the town, they were firmly told that there was to be no gossiping. She remembers something of her grandmother Catherine from when she was about five years old: "She was a tall, quiet lady. She managed to raise ten children without ever raising her voice—quite a feat!"

Frank was an avid reader and benefited greatly by the excellent education system of Nova Scotia. Most of the children in their family went through school just as far as the parents could afford to send them. Elisabeth says of her father, "He could quote at length from poems learned in school, and his grandfather taught him to read from the Bible. Two of his sisters and one of his brothers were schoolteachers."

Elisabeth describes her Uncle Jamie, one of her father's brothers, as "one of the relatives that stood out the most, though they're all stand-outs. He was typical of the Ogilvie fire and spirit." In order to get his education, Jamie would teach school for a year, then attend college for a year, continuing this way until he received his law degree from the University of Alberta. Elisabeth tells us, "World War I came along, and many of my Canadian relatives, wearing kilts, went to serve. Jamie went to London, and they found out he had a law degree. They put him in the Judge Advocate's office, and he never saw any action. When he came back, the first night he was home, he burned his uniform in the furnace."

While Frank and his nine siblings all grew into adulthood, the flu epidemic of 1918 took its toll on the family. Frank's youngest sister Winifred, along with her husband and child, died in the epidemic, as did Frank's father.

Frank went to Massachusetts as a young man, the only one of his family to emigrate to the United States. He worked at a variety of jobs, taking whatever work he could find. The job that would prove important to his future was working as a market teamster, delivering goods for Edgar Rhodes's grocery business. There, fate would bring him together with his future wife.

MAUDE

Maude Elizabeth Coates was a bookkeeper in one of Edgar Rhodes's grocery stores. Edgar was her brother-in-law as well as her boss, married to her older sister, May. This may have played a part in convincing Maude to take the job. Working as a bookkeeper was not her first choice; she had wanted to take courses in teaching woodcrafts. But Edgar needed a bookkeeper for the store, so she took the job—and soon found that it provided her with good training and the opportunity of meeting her future husband.

Frank was tall and handsome, and he caught Maude's eye right away. A relationship soon developed, which led to a marriage proposal. Maude's adoptive mother, Hannah, was against their marriage at first, but marry they did, when they were both just twenty-one years old.

Like her husband, Maude shared a distinctly Scottish lineage, with a little Welsh and French mixed in. Her ancestors may not have participated in the bloody battle of Culloden like Frank's did, but they experienced their share of hardship in Scotland. Elisabeth explores her mother's history in her first Jennie book, *Jennie About to Be*, where she tells of the Highland Clearances. In this heartless process, tenant cottagers were forcibly evicted from their homes by progressive lairds, to make way for more profitable sheep.

Maude's ancestors from the Isle of Lewis, part of the Outer Hebrides, were cleared from their land, albeit in a more humane fashion. The man who owned the land where they lived wanted to turn all the small subsistence plots of the tenant farmers into one successful big farm. He promised land in Canada to all of these tenants if they would emigrate. Not only did he pay their fare, he agreed to buy their livestock as well.

This is what happened to Elisabeth's great-grandmother Peigi MacLeod. Peigi (pronounced "Peggy") came to Canada in 1851 with her parents and several other siblings, settling in the Quebec area. Peigi went on to marry Thomas Penney and raise a family, and eventually her daughter, Emily MacLeod Penney, was born.

Emily was a simple, Gaelic-speaking girl who went to work in the mills of Lowell, Massachusetts, in the 1880s, where she met the dashing Arthur Kennedy, a man of English descent who worked as an electrician in the mills. Arthur Kennedy had been born in 1857 in Manchester, England, to William Kennedy and Elizabeth Galliard. William's father, Thomas Kennedy (Elisabeth Ogilvie's great-great-grandfather), was born in Dumfries, Scotland, so the Scottish heritage was evident in this branch of the family as well.

Arthur was twenty-five when he married Emily in Lowell on November 15, 1882. Elisabeth knows from family members that Arthur was a "hale fellow, well met," friendly kind of man who enjoyed sitting outside on the steps of a Sunday evening, talking with everyone who walked by. Emily was most likely a quieter sort, perhaps shy and hesitant since she spoke no English.

No doubt there was separation between the Kennedy and Penney families because of these cultural differences. Years later, a relative searching for the graves of Arthur and Emily Kennedy found Emily's grave set apart from the rest of the Kennedy clan—she was buried alone. Apparently, the Kennedy family, being of middle class English descent, must have felt they were better than the Gaelic-speaking Emily. "They might have been a bit snobbish," Elisabeth concludes.

Emily and Arthur had been married for a few years and had a two-year-old son, Robert, when Emily gave birth to their second child, Maude, in 1884. Emily died shortly after Maude's birth, leaving her husband solely responsible for their two small children. Arthur—bereft, bewildered, and unprepared—did not feel equipped to deal with his new role as single parent. He promptly looked for help from his unmarried sister Elizabeth.

Aunt Elizabeth Kennedy was a strong and prominent figure in Lowell, where she served as teacher and Playground Commissioner. Elisabeth describes her as the grand lady of the family, a bright, accomplished, and self-sufficient woman with a natural dignity. Aunt Elizabeth held a high position in the world of education, and the many professional demands placed on her made it impossible to care for her young niece and nephew. Nevertheless, Arthur left them in her care and moved to upper New York State, where he began a new life.

Knowing she could not care for both children, Aunt Elizabeth arranged for baby Maude to be adopted by an acquaintance, Hannah Coates. Originally from New Hampshire, Hannah had been a farmer's wife, but was now widowed and living in Boston with her eighteen-year-old daughter, May. Hannah worked as a dressmaker and also ran a lodging house. Years before, her son, Henry, had died of tuberculosis as a young man. Hannah had adopted May when Henry was in his teens.

Aunt Elizabeth may have discussed this adoption proposal with Arthur, but Elisabeth has no way of knowing for sure. In fact, it is possible that Elizabeth Kennedy had little contact with her brother for a very long time after his rather abrupt departure. In any case, Aunt Elizabeth made the necessary arrangements, and a new life began for the child, now named Maude Elizabeth Coates.

Maude was instantly welcomed by this warm-hearted family, who treated her as one of their own. The Coateses boasted quite an impressive Yankee lineage, including a great-aunt who had married Daniel Webster. From the start, the relationship between Maude and her adoptive sister May was a close one, with May acting almost as a second mother to Maude.

Elisabeth Ogilvie feels that her mother had a wonderful time growing up in Boston in the 1890s, with frequent visits to New Hampshire. In later years, Maude would tell intriguing stories about her childhood in the lodging house, and Elisabeth, already the budding writer, would say, "Wouldn't that make a great book!"

Elisabeth has said, "The lodging house in Boston always seemed to be full of interesting people- visitors from New Hampshire, and even some Civil War veterans." Hannah would feed anyone who needed a meal, not just her boarders. Many members of the local repertory theater boarded there in the winter months. It must have been a stimulating environment for young Maude, and these theatrical folk no doubt inspired her in later years when she showed a talent for writing plays and skits. Some of these actors belonged to the Emerson College of Oratory. They gave Hannah tickets to their theatrical productions, and often Maude would accompany her to the theater.

Maude was also exposed at an early age to the supernatural. Some friends once came to visit from New Hampshire, and the one thing the woman wanted to do was to visit a "clairvontey"—a clairvoyant. Hannah obliged, taking her to see one in Boston. The medium told Hannah that she "attracted phenomena"—apparently Hannah had quite an artistic and sensitive spirit. It is easy to see why Elisabeth was intrigued by stories of her mother's colorful upbringing.

Aunt Elizabeth never forgot her niece. She traveled from Lowell to Boston each year to visit her, bringing gifts. As a young girl, Maude didn't know who this kind, elegant stranger was, but things changed when Maude was in her early teens. She noticed a family resemblance between herself and Aunt Elizabeth, and wondered if this woman might possibly be her mother.

Her older sister May told Maude the truth—that Maude was adopted and this generous visitor was her aunt. The sisters didn't let their mother know they were discussing this, as Hannah was possessive and protective of her girls. But the sisters were close, and May felt compelled to answer the many questions surrounding Aunt Elizabeth. Eventually Aunt Elizabeth herself told Maude the whole story of their family connection, and their bond was strengthened.

After a time, Aunt Elizabeth had been able to juggle her many obligations so that she could bring Maude's brother, Robert, back to live with her following a short stay in a children's residence. Robert learned about his sister Maude from Aunt Elizabeth, but he was too shy to get acquainted with her until much later. They didn't meet until Maude was working at Edgar's store.

At work, Maude noticed that a certain young man would frequently come to the store and linger to look at her. She didn't find out until later that it was her brother. Having discovered from Aunt Elizabeth where Maude was living, Robert had gone to visit her as soon as he overcame his shyness. By the time Maude was married and had her first child, Robert had also gotten married and become a father. They exchanged baby pictures of their children and were close from that time on.

In sharp contrast to this reunion, Maude never got to know her father, who had remarried after moving to New York State. Years later, when Maude was married, Arthur Kennedy came home to visit. Aunt Elizabeth asked Maude if she'd like to meet her father, and Maude answered with an unequivocal "No." She had no desire to meet the man who had abandoned them so many years before.

Nine-year-old Elisabeth supported her mother's decision, having seen a photograph of her grandfather, complete with beard, and pronouncing him "sinister-looking." Arthur Kennedy died in 1931, just a few years after his visit, so Maude did not have an opportunity to see him again.

In 1890, May played a pivotal role in another facet of Maude's life by introducing her to a new world—the island of Criehaven, Maine. Maude was just six years old when May first took her to Criehaven for a summer visit with her brother-in-law's family.

May had married Boston grocer Edgar Rhodes, who was connected with Criehaven through his brother Fred. Fred Rhodes, of Glen Cove, Maine, had married Charlotte Crie (known to later generations as Aunt Lottie), daughter of Captain Robert Crie, the original settler of the island. (See Chapter 5 for a history of Criehaven and its founding family.) Fred had gone out to the island to serve as schoolmaster.

Another link to the island was formed when Maude became close friends with Agnes Anderson (later Agnes Knowlton Simpson) when they were both teenagers during those Criehaven summers, as her daughter Elisabeth would become close, lifelong friends with Agnes's daughter Dot.

May's husband, Edgar, "always made a special pet of Maude," and he used to hand out three-dollar gold pieces to all of Maude's children, including Elisabeth. His grocery business and some wise investing had made him a wealthy man, but he was also a generous one. He always shook hands graciously when meeting a new acquaintance, many of whom ended up holding a silver dollar in the palm of their hand.

Fred Rhodes turned out to be quite an entrepreneur in his day. Not only did he own Hillside Farm on Criehaven, but he was a partner in Edgar's four large grocery stores in the Boston area. He also worked to create a summer resort on Criehaven during the early part of the twentieth century, building several summer cottages and drilling a well that was quite impressive (and still in use). Although the island never became a tourist haven, his involvement helped make Criehaven a bustling place in the early 1900s.

ELISABETH

After Maude met and married Frank Ogilvie, Aunt Elizabeth continued to visit her in Quincy, where they settled. Maude was so fond of both her aunt and her sister, she named her daughter Elizabeth May Ogilvie, in their honor. (When she was a teenager, Elisabeth began spelling her name with an *S* as a matter of personal preference.)

Elisabeth was a real favorite with her aunt and namesake. Supportive of her niece's writing, Aunt Elizabeth paid the fee for a university extension course on writing that Elisabeth attended at Harvard following high school graduation. Undoubtedly Aunt Elizabeth inspired Elisabeth with her determination and drive, her encouragement, and her independent spirit.

Maude didn't find out until she was well into her teens that her heritage was Scottish. Her favorite book as a child had been *The Scottish Chiefs,* by Jane Porter. In fact, she had always been mad about bagpipes and all things Scottish. Unbeknownst to her, she had Scottish blood running in her veins. Maude was exhilarated to discover that her mother, Emily MacLeod Penney, was the daughter of Peigi MacLeod, whose family had emigrated from the Isle of Lewis in 1751.

Maude passed down this love of Scottish heritage to her children, who were pleased that their ancestors came from such a "wild and romantic place as the Hebrides." Elisabeth and her brothers were well indoctrinated with the Ogilvie family history, and Elisabeth translated this interest into a passion for Scotland, second only to her love for Maine.

Even though Elisabeth's father never seemed very impressed with his own colorful family history, her mother used to like to listen to stories told by her father-in-law. Although Maude never traveled to Scotland, she and Frank were acquainted with many Scottish immigrant families. Elisabeth writes that during her childhood, the familiar Scottish accent "was music to us."

2 ❧ HER FAMILY

MAUDE AND FRANK STARTED their family in 1908, when their first son, Allan, was born. Sons Kent and Gordon followed, all born about two years apart. Frank began working in the insurance industry and was in the Army Reserves when World War I broke out. He was a sergeant, the highest-ranking officer at Fort Revere, and his duties included sending young soldiers through the fort for officer training. Maude would often take Elisabeth and her brothers to visit their father, traveling by boat to Hull, Massachusetts, where the fort was located.

Frank was never sent overseas, though Maude always promised she wouldn't stand in his way if he had to go. Despite her brave front, she acknowledged that her heart would always skip a beat whenever Frank came home unexpectedly, thinking he was home to pack for overseas transport.

Frank's belief in service to his country was heartfelt, and both he and Maude soon became involved in the American Legion, which was organized at that time. Frank was named the first commandant of the local post. Fellow legion members were constantly coming and going at their home in Dorchester. As a small child, Elisabeth attended many Armistice Day services remembering the soldiers killed in World War I. This early exposure to patriotism clearly influenced her, as shown in a story ("The Power and the Glory") she later wrote for her high school literary magazine.

Elisabeth and her family lived on Ashmont Street in Dorchester until she was nine years old, when they moved to Wollaston, a suburb of Quincy. She lived in Quincy until 1944, when she settled in Maine permanently.

Throughout her childhood and high-school years the family made many summer visits to Criehaven. Maude continued her pattern of summers on Crichaven even after she and Frank were married with children. The family went to the island almost every summer, taking a boat from Boston to Rockland, than another ferry out to Criehaven, and staying in either a Crie family cottage or Aunt May's cottage. In later years, Elisabeth's brother Kent would drive the family by car from Boston to Rockland, traveling through the night. After breakfasting in Rockland, they would take the ferry over to the island. Maude and the children would stay for the entire summer, while Frank (and later Kent) came just for their two weeks of vacation.

The Ogilvie children were very close while growing up and as adults. Elisabeth writes fondly of her "very pleasant little-girlhood in Dorchester, doing what most little girls of my background were doing; my days were taken up with school, dancing lessons, Sunday school, roller-skating on those lovely, wide, old-fashioned sidewalks, making Valentines, hanging May baskets, and playing dolls. I don't believe anybody expected me to be a writer, though I read a good deal and very easily from the age of five. A family of extroverts in many ways, we were also a reading family."

Along with this love of literature, the family shared a clever and enthusiastic sense of humor. Elisabeth remembers her father as a dignified person, and both Frank and Maude had serious guidelines and expectations of behavior for the children, *de rigueur* for that generation. However, one of Elisabeth's most vivid memories is of her father leaning back in his chair at the supper table and laughing away at the antics of his four children. Elisabeth's own sense of humor remains strong and is evident in all of her books.

There was a creative spark in each family member, given expression in a variety of ways. Although much of the creativity was literary, it was not limited to the world of books. Elisabeth says of herself and her brothers, "We were not show-offs like some kids, but we never had to be coaxed or bribed into anything. It was matter-of-fact, no fooling around—just do it, and enjoy it."

Elisabeth began ballet lessons at age four, and immediately responded to the glamour and excitement of performing. She "loved the footlights—the recital was all!" During her debut performance, she was struck with "the first realization of the meeting between audience and performer over the footlights—'La Paloma' and a tambourine." Never one to enjoy the mundane routine of practice, Elisabeth preferred the glory of the recital: "It wasn't until I started to learn to be a writer that I realized the uses of drudgery."

After the thrill of the recital, at age five, came a chance to perform in a Sunday school program. Elisabeth knew she didn't want to rehearse her

13

"piece" on a plain old floor. She wanted to practice in the church itself, but it was being decorated at the time and was therefore unavailable. "So they stood me on the pool table to declaim. Too bad I can't remember what the piece was!" Elisabeth says. Her wise parents didn't allow the little actress to get too full of herself. (One can imagine that her three brothers helped out in this regard as well.)

Dance lessons continued until Elisabeth was fourteen, both ballet and Scottish Highland dancing. One of her finest memories is of her first kilt and "a real grown-up ceremonial sword, part of the regalia of some organization. You could get the things at a theatrical costumer in Boston. Ballet slippers, materials, and trimmings for the costumes—a gorgeous place to wander around in." Even at this young age, Elisabeth was grooming her talents for observation.

Life on Ashmont Street was good. "Our neighborhood in Dorchester was pleasant and suburban, with nice grassy yards and trees, wide sidewalks for roller skating and wheeling doll carriages. Not especially fancy like it was a few streets over—but we had the benefit of wide-open spaces beyond one side of the street, where streetcars used to be stabled in car barns—nothing left of them now. [We had plenty] of wildflowers and birds and space to chase each other around with our cap pistols (always used without caps!)."

The children of the neighborhood were a tight-knit group. "It was hard to move away when I was nine," Elisabeth has said, "but I could go from Quincy to visit the old gang on Ashmont Street, and different ones were brought to visit me in Quincy." The friendships Elisabeth developed in Dorchester were some of her closest; although she made new friends in Quincy, it was never quite the same.

Elisabeth had favorite dolls that she remembers to this day. Every toy was named, and all were carefully put to bed at night. "They always had lots of equipment because my mother liked making doll clothes. There was also an ancient teddy bear, I'm sure he was one of the originals. I still have him, wrapped up and put away for the winter so the mice won't nibble him." Elisabeth herself also enjoyed making doll clothes for one little doll that had a cloth body, a bisque head, and movable arms and legs. She would take material and fold it, stitch it, run a thread around the top, and put it over the doll's head, pulling the thread to make it fit.

All the Ogilvie siblings played a bit of piano, and Elisabeth had a small accordion on which she could pick out a few tunes. Her brother Allan played ukulele and guitar. Music was always appreciated in their home, and would be a continuing theme throughout Elisabeth's adult life, both on Criehaven and Gay's Island and in her novels.

Animals are important in Elisabeth's writing and in her personal life. A true animal lover, she has never been without a pet. The Ogilvie family always had cats. All the pets she had in childhood belonged to the whole family, not to one certain child; they were all treated well, "just like one of the kids."

However, Elisabeth does remember a certain black Airedale, Jock— "purebred but a throwback, the vet explained to me, [to one] of the many dogs from whom the Airedale evolved"—that was truly a "soul brother" to Gordon while he was in grammar school.

As the Ogilvie children grew up and started their own families, they continued the tradition of owning cats and dogs. Elisabeth has owned both over the years, and has chronicled many of their stories in *My World Is an Island*, as well as in some of her novels. In fact, she has used real-life pets in her books, something she doesn't do often with human characters. She currently owns a cat named Joppy, whose companionship she greatly enjoys.

A SHARED LOVE OF WORDS

Elisabeth believes her writing skill runs in the family, and credits her three imaginative brothers with inspiring her to become a writer. Gordon was not only a talented painter, specializing in children's portraits, but a writer of historical fiction, and Allan wrote very good poetry. Although her middle brother Kent wasn't an author in the strict sense, he nevertheless wrote very funny letters that were passed around the family and greatly enjoyed. A love of language and reading was passed down as a legacy from both parents.

Elisabeth's mother shared not only her son Gordon's talent for painting but her daughter's love of words. Maude was a born storyteller whose creativity was expressed in poetry, short stories, plays, and skits.

Elisabeth has a school notebook of Maude's dating from the early 1890s, full of descriptions of things she had seen. To improve their writing skills, Maude and her grammar-school classmates were to write for ten minutes each day about something they had observed.

Maude went on to write for her school magazine at Girls' High School in Boston, and even for the *Boston Post*. At one time, the *Post* sponsored a long-running short story contest, the prize being a couple of dollars if they printed your story. Maude was just fourteen, and very proud, when she won the contest. Maude gave the prize money to her mother for safekeeping, and afterward would often ask to see it. Maude used to say that she received those two dollars many times over through the years.

Maude's love of the theater may have been fostered through her childhood experience with theater folk in Hannah Coates's boardinghouse. An early photo from 1907 shows her dressed up as a Salvation Army lassie, complete with tambourine, standing beside Captain Crie, on Criehaven.

In later years, Maude wrote skits and comic plays for the children of Criehaven during her summer visits, beginning around the time the island clubhouse was built shortly after World War I. Some of these productions were quite extensive, incorporating anyone who had talent and was willing to participate. Anyone who could play the guitar was added as an instrumentalist, often to accompany Maude's new lyrics set to popular tunes. One summer, Elisabeth joined in, teaching some young boys a special waltz clog dance to fit a specific production.

For those readers familiar with the Bennett's Island series, it's easy to imagine the island children practicing their roles in the clubhouse, and putting on a production for their families. The kids even had a special name for the event. Maude and family would arrive for the summer, and the kids would greet them, shouting, "Are we going to have 'A Time'?" Usually, the event would consist of a supper, then the entertainment, followed by dancing, all at the clubhouse. People would come over from Matinicus, paying twenty-five cents each, the proceeds of which would go to a charity such as the Maine Seacoast Mission. (When the people of Matinicus hosted a dance, the Criehaven islanders would attend in turn.)

This experience of writing plays for the islanders served Maude well later on, when she wrote sketches and plays for several organizations in Massachusetts. One such group was an adult dramatic club. When there was a role for a young person in a play, Elisabeth or one of her brothers would often get the part. "We weren't bashful," says Elisabeth. "We were often real show-offs."

Maude even got her husband into the act, a credit to her persuasive enthusiasm. Elisabeth speculates that her father must have enjoyed the "play" of participating in these productions, as in regular life he was a dignified, somewhat serious man. One of his roles was as Petruchio's friend in *The Taming of the Shrew*.

Maude also wrote poems for Allan, her oldest son, to recite. Allan attended the Boston Latin School, where Declamation was a standard subject. As part of their grade, students had to recite verse in a formal fashion in front of the class. Maude wrote several poems for Allan, and even though he was slightly more reserved than his siblings, he nevertheless learned the poems and recited them successfully.

Elisabeth remembers the time he recited Macauley's thrilling "Horatius at the Bridge" in their kitchen. Allan knew the whole poem by heart, as did their mother, but Elisabeth remembers the phrase "By the nine gods he swore" being intermingled with "Oh, fudge!" as Allan paused and lost his train of thought. In later years, Allan proved how much his grounding in the arts of literature and writing had influenced him, by writing, among others, a poem as the epigraph for one of Elisabeth's books, *The Dreaming Swimmer:*

> *I think the danger of the ocean lies*
> *Not in the storm, but in the mermaid's eyes;*
> *She closes them for kisses, unaware,*
> *Enfolds the dreaming swimmer, and he dies.*

Allan was often called "the bright one," but Elisabeth says, "I guess we were all bright." When Allan was thirteen, he decided to build a radio. Frank and Maude met him at the streetcar after his day at the Boston Latin School, and took him to buy radio components with his own pocket money. He successfully built a radio, which became a family conversation piece. The family would often invite friends in to listen to radio programs.

Just nineteen months apart, Allan and younger brother Kent were very close, but nevertheless had different interests. Where Allan wasn't involved in sports at all, Kent loved them. Quite an adventurer, Kent was particularly fond of ice hockey, and with a group of friends formed an ice hockey team. They called themselves the Montclair Owls, and skated often on an ice pond near their home.

Although Gordon was the youngest, he soon grew to be the tallest of the brothers. He is perhaps the brother most closely matched to Elisabeth in creativity. He shared both his mother's talent for painting and his sister's aptitude for writing. He was also perhaps the one most entranced with the family's Scottish ancestry, becoming deeply involved in genealogical research as he grew older.

In 1998 Elisabeth acknowledged Gordon's inspiration in an interview with Katy Perry published in the Maine Media Women's newsletter, *The Maine Line* (May/June 1998), on the occasion of her having received that organization's President's award. The article quotes from Elisabeth's acceptance speech: "I guess I knew I was going to be a writer even before I got to school.

. . . My brother [Gordon] was some older than me and may have been my inspiration because he was always writing historic stories."

She went on to recall a bit of dialogue from her brother's play about George Washington (GW) and Betsy Ross (BR):

> GW: We ain't got no flag for our new country. Isn't that a fright?
> BR: Well, I just got finished sewing this here quilt, and I have some leftover thread, so let me see what I can do about making a flag.

"Not only did he write the play (which was more involved than my short cut)," writes Perry, "but the neighbor kids portrayed that brief bit of history."

Elisabeth's father may not have been a writer, but he shared his family's passion for reading. In Nova Scotia, where Frank Ogilvie was raised, the subject of reading was taken very seriously. Elisabeth and her brothers all owned schoolbooks bought for them in Nova Scotia by their parents, and Elisabeth remembers that even the fourth-grade material was at quite a high level.

Frank tended to express his creativity more with his hands, through his real avocation of carpentry. From him Elisabeth inherited a love of language and a strong sense of humor, along with his strong work ethic, patriotism, and sense of common decency. There is no doubt that her quiet, strong, handsome male characters have been greatly influenced by this most significant of models, her father.

ELISABETH'S BROTHERS

Elisabeth remained close to her three brothers all their lives. Her brother Gordon, "romantic-minded" and creative, pursued many interests, including writing, painting, and exploring the family's ancestry. He investigated their Scottish heritage, working closely with their aunt Lillian P. Ogilvie Fancy of Elderbank, Nova Scotia, to write the genealogy of the Ogilvie family.

A natural outgrowth of Gordon's interest in their ancestry came to fruition in 1981, when Avon Books published his novel *Jamie Reid*, which tells the story of a swashbuckling painter from England who comes to America. An author's note at the beginning clarifies that much of the novel is biographical, containing references to Peter and John Ogilvie, who settled in Georgia.

Gordon's editor wanted him to write a sequel featuring the same characters. But as often happens in the publishing industry, Elisabeth says, "When your editor finally leaves or is fired, it's like in the old days with the palace guard in Rome. When a new person took over as emperor, the soldiers went through and killed everyone connected with the old emperor. So it went with Gordon's editor—he left, and the new editors didn't pursue the project."

Gordon's talent as a painter clearly aided him in the creation of the fictional Jamie Reid. He had been drawing and painting all his life, encouraged by his mother. It seemed natural after his service in the Marine Corps to take an art course on the GI Bill, which led to a prolific career in painting children's portraits.

Allan's interest in radio technology continued throughout his life. In later years, an aunt offered to pay for Allan to attend the Massachusetts Institute of Technology, but he declined, choosing instead to go to Eastern Radio High School. Upon graduation, he worked for Western Electric, and then RCA. While with RCA, he traveled in the Midwest, installing talking movies. During World War II, he was in infantry weapons in New Jersey. After 1945 Allan went back to work for RCA and also did some work for a company that made underwater television cameras.

Kent worked for Hayden and Stone, a firm of stockbrokers in Boston, for several years. He held a number of varied jobs before going to work as a salesman for Best Foods. He had back trouble, so was unable to get into active service. During World War II, he enlisted, serving as a recruiter and an instructor in weaponry. He married, and had a daughter, Barbara Ogilvie Mosher, Elisabeth's niece and closest relative today (see page 45).

3 ❧ HER EDUCATION AND EMERGENCE AS A WRITER

Eʟɪsᴀʙᴇᴛʜ's ʟɪꜰᴇ ʜᴀs ʙᴇᴇɴ a love affair with words. From the age of five, she read voraciously, feeding her fast-growing imagination and ever increasing her scope for learning. This early passion for words matured as she did, leading to her career in writing.

One of her family's favorite pastimes was visiting the library, and as a young child Elisabeth made good use of its resources. She enjoyed reading *The Five Little Peppers* series, the *Anne of Green Gables* series, and Charles Perrault's *Fairy Tales,* illustrated by Gustav Doré. In the latter book, it was the beauty of the illustrations that determined her favorite stories—"Puss in Boots with a wide-brimmed hat and the boots, and the wonderful pictures of Sleeping Beauty in the woods. These are the old-fashioned kind of stories—they don't always have a happy ending—[after all,] the wolf ate Little Red Riding Hood."

Other favorites included the Blue Bonnet series, introduced to Elisabeth by her mother, along with *What Katie Did*. She loved Kipling's *Just So Stories* and *The Jungle Book*, and the books of British children's writer Evelyn Nesbit (which she now collects), appreciating her "witty writing" and "delightfully delinquent" characters. Elisabeth also remembers enjoying *Master Skylark*, about a boy in Shakespeare's time, and books by William M. Sweet.

She also read the Elsie Dinsmore books, even though she disliked the title character. "Elsie was a pain, sitting all one hot day on the piano bench because it was a Sunday and refusing to play 'Annie Laurie' for her father. She fainted, and he was sorry. Elsie was a pain, but her cousin Enna was okay. Elsie's papa wore white tussore [silk] suits and was handsome. What I remember about those books are the dolls' trunks stuffed with gorgeous pieces for sewing for dolls." Undoubtedly she enjoyed this last part because of her own enjoyment in sewing doll clothes.

Elisabeth's first venture into the world of education was a joyful one. Her experiences at the Dorchester elementary school were exciting, especially for a budding author. Quoting from her write-up in the reference book *Something about the Author:* "I began writing when I was quite small, because I enjoyed making up stories as much as reading them. One of my best memories concerns the second grade, when the teacher used to pass out pictures cut from magazines for us to write stories about."

Elisabeth's delight in storytelling was not limited to schoolwork:

> I made up stories to put myself to sleep, and to help me through long boring tasks, and during my walks to and from school. I used to describe what I was doing and seeing as if I were talking about somebody else. "Elisabeth was walking along Safford Street on one beautiful spring day when she happened to see. . . ." Well, it could be anything that occurred to my imagination, and I'd take off from there.

Elisabeth recalls disliking only one teacher during all her years of education. The combination of a solid family life and close-knit neighborhood made for a contented childhood, and she formed many loyal friendships. She recounts an experience at a North Quincy High School dance that illustrates how, even as a young girl, she valued friendship over appearances.

In the eighth grade, Elisabeth was one of the taller girls, and remembers being reluctant to attend a certain dance that year. Her mother insisted that she go, as Elisabeth's class was sponsoring it. Walter, the shortest boy in class, asked her to dance that night. He was known for being a talented singer, with a lovely clear voice that brought chills to his audience. Elisabeth liked and admired him, and of course she danced with him, despite the difference in their heights and signature awkwardness of those middle-school years.

In contrast, at dances on Criehaven during her high-school summers and into her twenties, everybody danced, regardless of height, age, or any other quality. This early exposure to joyous clubhouse celebrations, free of the pressures of school dances, contributed a great deal to Elisabeth's affection for the island culture.

One of the ways Elisabeth worked to develop her own style of writing was to explore different genres of fiction. Of her early teen years, Elisabeth has said that she "wrote and wrote. Finding authors I liked, I read everything the library had of theirs and tried to write like them, all the way from whimsy to romantic adventure to sentimental tragedy." Some of the authors she most enjoyed during this period were Ann Parrish and Edward Frederic Benson (who wrote the popular Queen Lucia stories published in the 1920s—"purely pleasure reading"). The Queen Lucia stories were social satires of the affectations and weaknesses of provincial middle-class life in Britain in the 1920s and '30s. Benson's six novels chronicle the rise and fall of Mrs. Emmeline Lucas of Riseholm, including the battles among society matrons scrabbling for a foothold in upper-class society. "The Lucia novels form a kind of epic portrait of striving gone mad," wrote one critic. Elisabeth's own awareness of comedy was probably influenced by this early introduction to satire.

Another author she liked very much during high school was Maude Diver. Diver's heroes were white people living in India during the British Raj, and her plot lines were somewhat glamorized and unrealistic. This didn't matter to Elisabeth.

When I was about fourteen, I read a series of romantic novels about India that set me off on a long writing kick. Since my private life was anything but exciting, I made up for it by writing thousands of words about Somewhere Else, known to me only through the public library. In writing descriptions of places, I developed fluency, a very worthwhile exercise in itself. And I learned how to put together long, complete stories with plots. I found out early that for me, finishing a story is possible only if I know at the start how it is supposed to end. The Indian phase passed, and I began writing regional prose about Maine. . . ."

A writer who had a huge influence on Elisabeth was Hugh Walpole. Born in 1884 in Auckland, New Zealand, British novelist Walpole is known for his ability to tell engaging stories in a flowing, descriptive style. (This could equally well describe Elisabeth's writing style.) His book *The Cathedral*, written in 1922, reflects his affection for the nineteenth-century English novelist Anthony Trollope. He also wrote critical works on Trollope, Sir Walter Scott, and Joseph Conrad.

Since her high school years, Elisabeth has reread *The Cathedral* more than once; she calls it "timeless." After a recent re-reading, she commented, "I was . . . wondering if I got all the dry humor the first times I read it. I tend to read too fast, so I may have lost a lot. I particularly love Walpole's use of colors, his descriptions of place, the way he creates an atmosphere, the colors and the words he uses—the interplay of personalities. I love the way he handles language."

Although the characters of her own novels, many of them fishermen and their families, would not have much in common with the world of the English cathedral town during the 1800s, she gained a great deal of insight into the craft of writing by reading Walpole's work.

Another particular favorite of Elisabeth's was the *Jalna* series, by Mazo de la Roche, which focuses on a Canadian family. Someone sent her the whole set, and this family saga might have given her some inspiration when she later wrote about the Bennett family.

Elisabeth wrote in *Something about the Author*: "I had favorite writers whom I imitated, and they were always on the adult side of the library. This earnest imitation was the best training I could have possibly had, because I tried so hard."

NORTH QUINCY HIGH SCHOOL

The education she received at North Quincy High School, (grades seven though twelve) was exemplary, especially in the area of writing. Elisabeth was one of the first students to attend the new facility when it opened in 1927, entering as a seventh grader in 1928 and graduating with honors in 1934. North Quincy provided her with capable teachers, excellent tools, and a chance to use them often.

The curriculum included weekly theme writing for every student, regardless of their course of study. Elisabeth thrived under these requirements, and produced many excellent short stories, sharpening her skills with each assignment. "The English department of my high school was tough, demanding, and everyone, no matter what course, was expected to do a good deal of writing—no mercy was shown for poor spelling and punctuation."

One of the first educators who played a part in nurturing Elisabeth Ogilvie, the writer, was Frank Smoyer, her English teacher. The first teacher who truly impressed her mother, he had come to North Quincy following his retirement as a university professor. He was an imposing figure—bald, with eyes greatly magnified behind his glasses—and was known to intimidate more than a few of his students. Elisabeth remembers one particular phrase he was fond of using: "I thought I had plumbed the depth of adolescent ignorance, but I was wrong."

Mr. Smoyer's manner could be disquieting. Elisabeth describes an average day in his classroom this way: "He walked up and down the aisles very silently . . . he smelled heavily of tobacco. He had a blue pencil, and you'd feel him standing behind you looking over your shoulder; I didn't get the blue pencil, but some people did."

Mr. Smoyer was the first to teach her how to delve into novels and analyze their content and themes. For her biography in *Twentieth Century Authors*, Elisabeth wrote, "we had to write fairly adult analyses of the books we read, taking apart their structure and their methods of characterization. I believe my first lessons in technique for writing novels were learned in those days." Another advantage of North Quincy was its top-caliber literary magazine, *The Manet* (from the Latin meaning "It remains"). "I have never [since] seen a high school publication with such near-professional material in it," Elisabeth recalls. "In a six-year high school, all grades were encouraged to contribute." Elisabeth contributed many poems, articles, and short stories to the magazine, exploring different styles and genres. Her affinity for environment was developed early on, as well as her ear for dialogue.

By the twelfth grade, Elisabeth was comfortable writing both fiction and nonfiction, as demonstrated in an interview she conducted with fellow student Noyes Farmer. As part of an assignment, Elisabeth and Noyes interviewed British heartthrob Dennis King at the Ritz-Carlton. Elisabeth had written the questions but became so embarrassed and tongue-tied in the presence of the famous singer that Noyes had to read the questions to Mr King while Elisabeth wrote down the answers.

Elisabeth went on to become an editor in charge of submissions from the junior school. As an editor she had to learn how to be critical of others' work in a constructive manner. She also had to learn to write for a deadline, an important skill that served her well in later years.

Mr. Smoyer believed in Elisabeth's ability and encouraged her to write for *The Manet*. Knowing how high his standards were added to her feeling of accomplishment. Mr. Smoyer would mention certain alumni who had become writers, and said once to Elisabeth, "contrary to most of them, you seem to know what you're talking about." This was high praise for the fledgling writer. He also remarked, "She should go to Barnard, but she'll do all right without." With the support of Mr. Smoyer, Elisabeth admits, she was "a gone goose." After her first story appeared in *The Manet*, she turned out a short piece every two weeks. It was an ideal outlet for her creative energies during this crucial stage, and she wrote poems and stories for *The Manet* from eighth grade through her senior year. (Summaries of some of her early short stories are included in Chapter 20). Elisabeth felt so grateful for Mr. Smoyer's influence that in later years she sent him a copy of each of her books for as long as he lived.

Elisabeth's legacy continues at North Quincy High School. In the 2000–2001 school year, ninth-grade English instructor Corinne Mitchell taught a unit on Elisabeth Ogilvie's books. Mitchell's students read several of Elisabeth's stories from *The Manet*, along with excerpts from *High Tide at Noon*, and her young adult novel *Beautiful Girl*. They researched Elisabeth's life and work for submission to a "Literary Map," part of a website developed by the National Council of Teachers of English along with the Mobil Corporation, PBS, WGBH Boston, and ALT Films. This website (www.ncteamericancollection.org), devoted to the preservation of the American literary tradition, is supported by submissions from teachers and students across the country.

Elisabeth's senior yearbook portrait shows a lovely, somewhat serious young woman wearing a white lace collar, her thick, dark hair pulled back, and a thoughtful expression on her face. Next to her name is a list of her activities and accomplishments, including acting in the class play during her senior year and participating in plays that were performed at assemblies. Other activities include her involvement with *The Manet* staff in 1934, and having been on the High Honor Roll in 1932, 1933, and 1934.

THE CALL OF CRIEHAVEN

At the age of fifteen Elisabeth discovered her muse—the one place that would inspire her writing like no other. Her mother, who had first traveled to Criehaven at the age of six, continued the tradition with her own husband and children. Elisabeth first visited the island when she was two. She writes in *My World Is an Island*, "Those earliest memories are as much a part of me as the color of my eyes, my white lock that appeared when I was ten, the shape of my fingers, the sound of my voice. They have played almost as big a part in making me the person I am—Myself."

During the summer of her fifteenth year, Elisabeth returned to Criehaven after an absence of several years. Upon returning to Quincy that fall, she wrote her first story for the school magazine. She loved the way her story looked in print, and knew unequivocally from that moment on that she wanted to be a writer—a published one.

Elisabeth wrote about this time in *My World Is an Island:*

> It is a major event for a shy, impressionable, imaginative fifteen-year-old to come to a place which hitherto she has tenanted only in wisps of memories. . . .
>
> Such a happening in a young life can be in the nature of an up-heaval, an explosion. It was for me. I knew, all at once, what was going to become of me. Conveniently, I had two choices; I would either write about the island, or marry a lobster fisherman. I haven't married a lobster fisherman. I have spent too much time instead trying to get down some small part of the essence of Criehaven. Someone has said that Maine is a state of mind; for me, Criehaven is an island not so much in a geographical sense but in a spiritual sense, for I can carry it with me wherever I go. The Criehaven that became Bennett's Island on paper, and which became when I was two years old an integral part of my existence, will never go away from me.

This love of the island is translated into the deep power of place that is present in all of Elisabeth's books. Just four years later her first short story was published in a Sunday supplement of a Massachusetts newspaper. (She was paid twenty-five dollars.) The story was about a family who lived on Criehaven—specifically, a woman who married a Bennett. Although none of the characters in this first short story reappeared in later Bennett's Island books, and Elisabeth no longer recalls the exact title of the story or the name of the paper that published it, this was truly the beginning of Bennett's Island.

The effect Criehaven had on Elisabeth cannot be underestimated. The island had a visceral impact on her, as well as serving as her literary muse. The tumult of emotions was stirred from a very young age. In *My World Is an Island* Elisabeth describes eating apples on the island, with a little boy (her friend Dot Simpson's brother Russell). The images of an "Indian-dark" Elisabeth and the especially delicious apples she enjoyed are so vivid and poignant, they fairly jump off the page. When Elisabeth described how she finally realized she didn't need to search for this island paradise anymore—because she held it within herself—she put to paper some of her best lyrical writing:

> I have stopped looking for those very special apples, because I know that the apple in the hand of the four-year-old girl with the gypsy tan and the wriggling bare toes is the best apple of all, and I don't need to look for one if I already possess it. The little boy with

the bang is married, but somewhere in Time he plays with the girl be-side a tidewater pool and they gather periwinkles, very solemnly, like jewelers matching pearls.

In just these few words Elisabeth summed up her ability to keep the island in her heart. She *has* managed to find a way to forever inhabit Crie-haven—and for the island to live in her. This miracle, of always being able to put herself there, explains why Elisabeth does not feel lonesome for the island—it is with her always. It is this ability of hers that allows her readers to inhabit the island as well—to see, smell, hear, touch, and taste everything there.

Her writing is powerful partly because she has internalized this experi-ence and place so totally that she is able to "channel" it at will. In her heart and mind, she has fulfilled the promise Joanna made in *High Tide at Noon*, when she said, "I'll never live anywhere else but here. This is Bennett's Island and we're the Bennetts. We'll live here forever."

It is this gift that her readers treasure. It helps to explain her wide appeal, and why her reading audience feels such a part of the world she cre-ates—so much so that many of them long to go to Criehaven to experience this joy firsthand. Criehaven almost acquires a Brigadoon-like quality, as it is a difficult place to reach, one that most of her readers will probably never visit.

Elisabeth's books, however, give us a passport to this exceptional place. Through her vivid descriptions, we can link arms with Joanna and walk to the harbor, with the crying of the gulls as our constant accompaniment. We can sit in the orchard, taste wild strawberries, smell the strong odor of bait near the fish house. We can row to a cove for an afternoon of beachcombing and climb to the top of the hill with a strong breeze on our face—we can experi-ence all the glories of this island existence through Elisabeth's beautiful, evocative words.

Elisabeth writes about many Criehaven memories in "Last Waltz on Criehaven" (page 66), but clearly the inner core of these memories lies un-revealed, and as yet undepleted, in her soul. It serves as a constant source of inspiration for her writing.

FIRST STEPS INTO THE LITERARY WORLD

Elisabeth graduated from high school during the Depression, and fi-nances were tight. She was not able to attend college, earning her only pocket money by babysitting. Her determination to become a writer had not waned, however. With the support of her family, especially great-aunt Elizabeth Kennedy, she took a course in "Writing for Publication" at Harvard University's extension service in 1936. Her instructor there would change her life.

Donald MacCampbell was a young man, just twenty-five years old, when he began teaching the writing course. He was energetic and ambitious, working for the *Atlantic Monthly*, teaching, and making plans to open a literary agency—all at the same time. Elisabeth was just nineteen years old when she signed up for his class, and shortly thereafter her first Bennett's Island short story appeared in the Massachusetts newspaper Sunday supplement.

She had already determined that she would be a writer; there was no other path for her. All she needed now was some guidance and direction. When asked how she knew that this dream was within her grasp, Elisabeth answers, "Well, I wanted to be a writer, but it was as if I didn't think about the future; just like jumping in, sink or swim. . . . I couldn't imagine doing anything else." In other interviews, Elisabeth has spoken of her writing as almost a compulsion or addiction—she literally can't imagine a life without writing at its center.

MacCampbell provided direction for the eager young student. Elisabeth has always remembered the basic tenets he taught: "It's like when you learned to drive with the driving instructor, you always remembered to look over your left shoulder. I always think of what he said to me when I commented, 'I'm just going to write and see where it goes.' He said, 'You want to know where it is you are going before you begin, or you'll never get there.'"

MacCampbell also helped her edit her writing. "He helped me to develop an objective attitude toward my own work and to stop feeling that to cut out one sentence was to lop off one of my fingers. This is the most difficult lesson for a writer, for the nature of the critter is to be sensitive. . . . I give him all the credit for starting me off. He was a great teacher."

When the class ended, MacCampbell told Elisabeth there were only two people in all the classes he'd taught who knew what they were doing: a newspaper writer, and Elisabeth. He promptly offered to be her agent. It wouldn't cost her anything up front. He would serve in this capacity, and as friend and supporter, for many years to come. His lessons helped form the foundation of her writing style and the way she structured her outlines, particularly his words: "At least a dozen big scenes, and know where you are going." This rule was flexible, but has served as Elisabeth's basic blueprint during her entire career.

It wasn't all rosy, of course; they had their arguments. One in particular was about Elisabeth's short stories. After her first one was published, she wrote all the time, believing an author must write many short stories before attempting a novel. MacCampbell acted as an intermediary between Elisabeth and the magazine editors, and sometimes felt that if a story didn't interest him, it wouldn't interest anybody. When Elisabeth later shared this with editor Betty Finnin of *Woman's Day* magazine, Finnin simply said, "I'm going to tell his office that I want to see everything you write."

Finnin liked a wide variety of stories, especially if Elisabeth wrote them. *Woman's Day* had a strong fiction section in those days, and the staff was very particular about what they published. Betty taught a class on short story writing at Columbia University, and routinely used Elisabeth's stories as examples for the class. She and her husband, Arthur, became quite good friends of Elisabeth's and visited her frequently on Gay's Island in later years.

As a result of Betty's enthusiasm, shared by various other editors, Elisabeth saw about ten of her short stories published in magazines such as *Woman's Day, Redbook,* and *Good Housekeeping.* One of her first short stories, "Summer Girl" (page 177), was published in *Woman's Day* in 1944, the same year as *High Tide at Noon,* and was also set on Bennett's Island. Her short story "Scobie," originally published in *Woman's Day* in 1951, was selected to appear in *Maine Speaks: An Anthology of Maine Literature* (1989). "Scobie" was one of those lengthy stories called "novels" that were popular features in magazines during those years. (A complete listing of her short stories appears in the Bibliography.) About them, Elisabeth has commented, "[I] don't sell short stories as often as I'd like to. The successful ones have come to me by inspiration and must be done all at once, like a good watercolor."

It was soon after she began writing short stories for magazine publication that she began work on *High Tide at Noon.* With MacCampbell as her agent, Elisabeth signed the contract for *High Tide at Noon* in 1938 when she was just twenty-one years old. She was living in Quincy, Massachusetts, during the six years it took her to write and revise the book.

It took longer in those years to get a book published, and she spent a great deal of time writing and rewriting the manuscript for *High Tide at Noon.* Elisabeth called this experience "a most valuable apprenticeship," knowing that it would serve her well in future years.

Despite their occasional disagreements, Elisabeth remained grateful to Donald MacCampbell for his teaching and guidance, and for his role in furthering the Bennett's Island series. After *High Tide at Noon* was published, MacCampbell said to Elisabeth, "Now everybody's going to be interested in these people. You ought to keep writing about them." With her agent's wise foresight and her own passion to continue writing about the family and their island, the Bennett's Island series was born. It is appropriate that Elisabeth dedicated the first novel to her teacher and friend.

Nevertheless, after nineteen years of their agent/client relationship, which grew into a real friendship, Elisabeth and MacCampbell would part ways in 1956. Elisabeth said in a later interview that she "grew disenchanted when [MacCampbell] became more interested in business than literature. 'He had people writing romances. . . . He'd put them under contract and they would write one a month. . . . This is just not literature.'" Indeed, this romance classification is one that Elisabeth would resist in future interviews, including one with *Down East* magazine in 1985, when she commented, "As far as putting my books in categories goes, like 'gothics' or 'romances'—I don't care much for that. I have done a few things that people might call gothics, but they didn't *feel* like gothics when I was working on them . . . . Really, there was more to them than that."

Elisabeth kept in contact with MacCampbell long after he ceased to serve as her agent. "Even though we had our ups and downs, I used to call him up once in a while and talk to him. Naturally I wanted to call him up when *The Day Before Winter* came out; I thought he ought to know. He had just died . . . I felt very bad about that."

One can imagine that MacCampbell would have been very proud of his first client, forty-six successful books later. Elisabeth's readers owe him a debt of gratitude.

PART II

Islands in Her Life

"The power of place"

4 ❧ GAY'S ISLAND

ELISABETH MET DOT SIMPSON, of Criehaven, when she was quite young, and their friendship was reinforced by the fact that their mothers had been friends for years. Fourteen years her senior, Dot was a mentor to Elisabeth. Their mutual love of islands and writing further strengthened their bond.

Elisabeth had enjoyed visiting Dot's family during her childhood, and as she grew she wanted to spend more time on Criehaven. After graduating from high school, Elisabeth was determined to spend as much time as possible in Maine, and often stayed with Dot and her husband, Guy. (N.B.: Dot's stepfather and her husband were both named Simpson.)

By then, Elisabeth knew she would write about life on Maine islands, and a desire for authenticity added to her fascination with Criehaven. In order to experience the whole scope of island life for a lobstering family, Elisabeth spent the winter of 1935–36 with Dot and Guy. This research provided a strong foundation two years later, when she began writing *High Tide at Noon*. Elisabeth recalls that the winter weather on the island was not all that cold; being surrounded by salt water made it much warmer than the mainland. "It was the wind!" she says. "Terrible winds made it feel much colder—we didn't dare go outside. The supplies were still brought over . . . via the mailboat, which still ran at that time."

Beginning in 1938, Elisabeth worked on *High Tide at Noon* for six years. It was a stormy period for the young author and her family because of World War II. Two of her brothers and three of Dot's served in the armed forces during the war; concern for their men cast a shadow over both families.

She worked hard on her first novel despite the wartime conditions and was thrilled when *High Tide at Noon* was published in 1944. Proceeds from the novel allowed her the opportunity to make some decisions about her future, including the purchase of property on Gay's Island, off Cushing, Maine. These events are chronicled in her memoir, *My World Is an Island*, so a full history is not necessary in this volume. Some reflections on her life there must be mentioned, however, particularly the fact that her time on this small island in Muscongus Bay, far from the rugged open-ocean setting of Criehaven, has been filled with much inspiration, creativity, and happiness. Gay's Island proved to be the ideal location for her to create her considerable magic.

It was the summer of 1944. The Thomas Y. Crowell Publishers had just published *High Tide at Noon*, and "Summer Girl" (also set on Bennett's Island) had appeared in *Woman's Day*. Elisabeth, now twenty-seven, was staying on Criehaven with Dot and Guy, and she had decided it was time to buy some land of her own—a place where she could write. Although there were properties available on Criehaven, prices were too steep. As much as it pained Elisabeth and her friends, they knew their future did not lie on their beloved island.

On a visit to Rockland, Elisabeth, Dot, and Guy mentioned their quest to friend Freeman Young, a man from Matinicus who had moved to the mainland and become a successful real estate agent. Freeman took them to see a property on Gay's Island, just off Pleasant Point, twelve miles south of Thomaston. Freeman convinced a local boy, Roland Stimpson, to row them out to the three-hundred-acre island. Elisabeth and Dot couldn't help but notice that one could actually walk between the mainland and the island when the tide was low—vastly different from the dramatic and rugged shores of Criehaven, twenty-five miles off the coast.

Although Elisabeth and her friends were unimpressed at first, the singular beauties of Gay's Island slowly revealed themselves. Changes on Criehaven—the end of the store, school, and post office—had made it a lonelier place than in the old days. Dot and Guy were willing to give Gay's Island a try, and so was Elisabeth. A deal was made, and they were soon the proud owners of thirty-three acres of land, which included a classic yellow farmhouse on a knoll overlooking Pleasant Point Gut.

They bought the place from Harry Thompson. Harry and his brother, Frank, had made their fortune producing Moxie, one of America's first widely popular soft drinks. Paul Baguss bought the rest of Thompson's property on the island. Guy, Dot, and Elisabeth became good friends with him and with many other families who had homes there.

Christened "Tide's Way," their new house on Gay's Island was ninety-one years old when they purchased it, and it needed a great deal of work. They were up to the task, and with the help of family and friends, they soon had it readied for habitation, as detailed in *My World Is an Island*.

Although Elisabeth and Dot originally felt that they were betraying Criehaven by living so close inshore, it soon became clear that this was their home. They grew to treasure its small miracles. Even the mud flats were special in their own way. Elisabeth has often said that you stay strong living on an island—there's no other choice, with all the carrying water, rowing, and walking. In fact, they lived much the way the Bennett's Islanders do—drawing water from a well, and enjoying only the most basic outhouse facilities.

Guy Simpson fell in love with Gay's Island just as the women did. He made an effort to talk with area fisherman to ensure he would be made welcome. He was, and he fished from Gay's Island and settled into life at Tide's Way. Guy was responsible for many of the bigger jobs on the island, such as filling oil tanks and picking up supplies.

Guy also served as Elisabeth's technical advisor for many years, filling her in on all the gritty details of lobstering, as Elisabeth explained to journalist David Anderson of *Lewiston Sunday* in 1989: "He had a lot of stories, and knew every hair-raising thing that had ever happened to a lobsterman. He helped keep me accurate on details, things like long and short warps, and how many traps a thirty-foot boat can carry."

If Guy was a perfect technical adviser on lobstering, Dot was the island expert. Elisabeth has described her as "the true child of the island," and wrote in *My World* that "Dorothy, who has an equally light hand with a guitar, a boat, and an apple pie, passed on to me the history of Criehaven from its earliest days of settlement, as told to her by her Yankee stepfather and Norwegian grandfather; she typed manuscript for me, and listened to my endless laments about my inadequacies as a novelist, and discussed situations that could or could not happen on an island like Criehaven." Dot had never lived anywhere but on Maine islands (including Criehaven, Wooden Ball, Matinicus, and Gay's), so she had a plentiful store of island tales and a complete understanding of the islanders' way of thinking.

Dot was always good company, a witty storyteller with a long memory. She was instrumental in helping Elisabeth develop one of her greatest strengths as a writer—her ear for the lobsterman's dialogue. She helped Elisabeth capture the island voice, just as Guy helped her with the technical side of lobstering. In an interview with writer Estelle Watson Sanders, Dot revealed their secret: "When Elisabeth came to Maine, I knew she had led a sheltered life. . . . Yet I recognized that she was a writer who had a novel brewing.

So, I told her, 'If you want to hear some fishermen talk when no one is around, go upstairs over the kitchen [where a heating duct would allow her to eavesdrop]. From then on, she had no difficulty writing lively dialogue."

Elisabeth credits Dot with giving her the necessary push to move forward with her novel. Elisabeth told *Down East* magazine in 1994, "Dot was the one who encouraged me to write that first novel . . . I thought you had to apprentice as a short-story writer first. But Dot scoffed at that and told me to get on with it. So I did." And with that, the world of Bennett's Island was born. No one knew at that time, least of all Elisabeth, what the extent of that legacy would be.

Elisabeth wasn't the only writer at Tide's Way. Dot had been writing descriptive tales of island life for many years, though, like Elisabeth, she was hesitant to try writing a novel. While Guy fished, the two women quickly settled into a routine, both of them working at their writing projects and filling the rest of the day with outdoor activities. Their new life was begun.

Soon after they settled into Tide's Way, the three realized that the house wouldn't be suitable for a year-round dwelling. They purchased a small house on Pleasant Point, in Cushing, across from Gay's Island. This is where they spent their winters—all except for the winter of 1950–51, which they spent on Gay's Island. Their lives took on a pattern of moving back and forth between the island and the mainland with the seasons, living at Tide's Way during the warm months between May and October and heading back to Pleasant Point for the winter.

Guy lived with Dot and Elisabeth at Tide's Way throughout the 1940s, but eventually found the pull of Criehaven too strong to ignore. Lobstering off Criehaven was typically better than off the mainland, and even though for a while he had believed himself ready for life closer to the shore, it become obvious that Guy couldn't leave Criehaven for long. Eventually Guy established a pattern of going back and forth between Gay's Island and Criehaven, which continued until his death in 1957.

Dot and Elisabeth's friendship endured for several more decades. They would live together in the yellow house on Gay's Island (and at Pleasant Point during winters) from 1944 until December 1998, when Dot died at the age of ninety-five.

DOT SIMPSON

Aleda Dorothy Simpson was born June 28, 1903, to Agnes (Anderson) and Llewellyn Knowlton. Everyone knew her as Dot (or Aunt Dot to her many nieces, nephews, and other young people). She was taken to Criehaven, her mother's home, when two weeks old, and didn't return to the mainland again until she visited Rockland at age twelve. Criehaven was her home until she and her husband, Guy Simpson, moved to Gay's Island in 1944.

Her mother remarried when Dot was a child, and Dot grew to adore her stepfather, Herman Simpson. She portrayed him as "Papa" in the Janie series, books she wrote about a girl growing up on Criehaven. By this marriage, Dot became the older sister to nine brothers and sisters, two of whom survive her. They were portrayed as children in her books, and their shared adventures sparkle with life and affectionate memory. (After Herman Simpson's death, Agnes married Fred Wilson, who appears in *My World Is an Island*.)

Like Elisabeth, Dot was asked to submit some of her work for *Maine Speaks: An Anthology of Maine Literature*. In a brief biography included with her selection Dot wrote about her childhood: "My family lived on a small island—365 acres—twenty-five miles at sea, and all my grown-up male relatives were fishermen. I had the sea in my blood too, and as a youngster I felt sure I could earn my living from fishing when I grew up. When I realized such a thing could not be, I decided to write about the sea and islands and fishing people."

"As a child I never thought we were poor just because there was no way to get the extras that were not needed to hold body and soul together," Dot told writer Jack Barnes in a 1999 interview for the *Maine Sunday Telegram*. "We didn't have much . . . we had to learn to do without. I had a garden to weed; and when I was seven years old, I learned to handline." Dot was knowledgeable about boats and learned to row at a very young age. She also learned to knit bait bags and trapheads, a skill she kept up all her life. It was a no-nonsense life, filled with hard work, yet sparked by creativity and the love of literature that she shared with her friend Elisabeth.

When young Dot earned a nickel or a dime for running an errand, she bought notebooks and "eventually began filling pages with descriptions of the sea and sky, which were so tremendous and all-encompassing. I copied favorite chapters and verses from borrowed books into notebooks; meanwhile I was loving the island and its life, studying its people and trying to understand them completely." She was doing more than that: "I was learning how to write."

Dot attended the island school, where she read everything she could get her hands on. Reading was an important part of island living, and library and gift books continually made the rounds of the residents. She didn't begin high school until the age of nineteen, when her mother convinced her to go to the mainland and attend classes at Rockland High School. At twenty-one, when the state stopped paying her tuition, she was forced to regretfully drop out and return to Criehaven. She didn't stop writing, however; as Jack Barnes explained in his article, "Writing was an escape from the long days filled with domestic responsibilities, which included caring for her younger brothers and sisters. About eleven at night, she would sit at her typewriter and clatter away until two in the morning."

Two years after leaving Rockland High, when she was twenty-three, Dot married lobsterman and childhood friend, Guy Simpson. Her love of writing had not diminished; instead, it had grown to the point where she was writing stories, now filling her notebooks with not only her island world, but the people that inhabited it. Dot wrote in her *Maine Speaks* bio, "I thought I had to start out with short stories, so for twenty-five years I wrote them and sent them away, and they came back. I kept all this a secret; I didn't want to be laughed at."

In later years, Elisabeth returned a favor—just as Dot had encouraged her to release that novel she had within her, Elisabeth provided equal support to Dot, urging her to write her own novel. She did, and with great success. *Island in the Bay* was published by Lippincott in 1956 (reissued by Blackberry Books in 1993). This wonderful story was inspired by the experiences of one of her brothers as he learned the lobsterman's trade while living with their Norwegian grandfather.

When Dot was asked to choose a selection for *Maine Speaks*, she decided to include a portion of *Island in the Bay*. "Linn Goes Torching," chapter six of this first novel, tells of Linn's adventures while torching for herring, and is redolent with her family's love of fishing and the sea—the foundation of her life—and her affection for her grandfather, who inspired the character of Grampa:

> Fishing from any aspect was a joy to the old man. Linn marveled sometimes at the way Grampa would pick up a herring and turn it over lovingly in his gnarled stubby hands. And now Linn had a chance to bring in bushels of the silver fish; no wonder Grampa was happy, remembering the days of his boyhood when a herring was as much the staff of life as bread.

Once Dot began writing novels in earnest, the Janie series was born. Out of her desire for her nieces and nephews to know what it was like to grow up on a Maine island, grew four books about the young island girl named Janie Marshall: *The Honest Dollar* (1957), *A Lesson for Janie* (1958), *A Matter of Pride* (1959), and *New Horizons* (1961). In 1965, Dot published *Visitor from the Sea*, a story about Janie's sister, Becky, and her adventures on the island.

Dot was also the author of an acclaimed adult book, *The Maine Islands in Story and Legend*, written from material compiled by the Maine Writers Research Club. Originally published in 1960, it was praised in the *New York Times Book Review*. This book is still in print, and it serves as a valuable resource for all those who love the Maine islands. (Excerpts from *The Maine Islands*, specifically related to Criehaven and Matinicus, are included in Chapters 5 and 6.)

Dot's writing lives on in the work of playwright Jeffrey Watts, head of the Maine Educational Theater Company of Farmington. Watts adapted *A Matter of Pride* for the stage. His company travels to public schools, working with students of all ages in residency programs on theater education. Watts, who writes a great deal for children, says that he finds Dot Simpson's books timeless, universal, and wonderfully written, better than much of the young adult fiction available today—and ideal for stage adaptation.

A writer in love with the Maine landscape, much like her friend Elisabeth, Dot wrote movingly of her affection for her home in her biography for *Maine Speaks*: "I love the state of Maine, especially the coast, and wouldn't want to live anywhere else. It is more than the rocks, rivers, lakes, forests, fields and mountains, with the ocean rising and falling against its broken outside edge. We all have dreams, and one of mine is that Maine can be forever a place that puts a spark into the hearts of its people which can never be snuffed out, and will spring into flame whenever there is a need." Her legacy is a body of work filled with this dream. With people like Jeff Watts ensuring that her work lives on, Dot's stories will kindle that spark in a new generation of readers.

SETTLERS ON GAY'S ISLAND

In her 1960 book on Maine islands, Dot Simpson included Gay's Island in the Muscongus Bay section as one of the Georges Islands, so named "because they stream southward from the mouth of the St. George River."

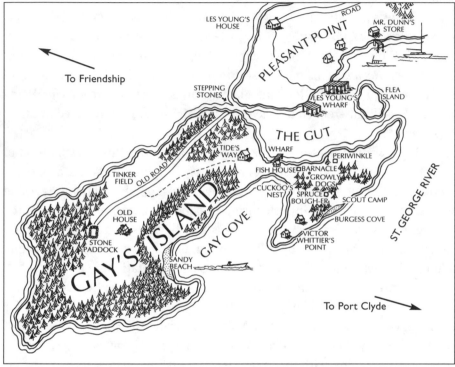

MAP BY DAWN PETERSON, FROM *MY WORLD IS AN ISLAND*

In her overview she noted: "If the imaginary boundaries of Muscongus Bay were to be squared, the compass points would be: Port Clyde to the east, Monhegan to the south, Pemaquid to the west, and Waldoboro to the north. In this square lie more than forty islands, large and small, inhabited and deserted. Some of the names have an odd charm: Hungry, Cranberry, Thief, Friendship, Haddock and Wreck. And let's not forget Jones Garden, and Otter Island. . . ."

This archipelago is rich in history. Garrison Island, for example, did have a garrison on it, to protect the people of Friendship. Dot wrote, "To the westward, Bremen attracts yachtsmen. There is a thriving weir at Cranberry, and on most of the islands lobstermen live, with only a small lacing of summer people among them." She seemed pleased to report that "Muscongus Bay is not a popular summer place, and in many ways it has kept incorruptible its essential character."

Charles B. McLane writes a bit more about the history and settling of Gay's Island in *Islands of the Mid-Maine Coast: Muscongus Bay and Monhegan Island*. He tells us that its earliest name was Burton's Island, although there is no written record that a Burton ever lived there. Benjamin Burton was an important personage in lower St. George (Cushing) and took part in the fall of Louisbourg (the French fortress on Cape Breton Island) in 1745. In a 1779 listing of islands, Eleazer Gay is mentioned in connection with the island, as well as a Mr. Elwell, both of them married to the daughters of prominent settlers in Meduncook (Friendship).

Eleazer Gay definitely settled on the island and may have been there before the American Revolution. McLane writes, "the British Admiralty atlas, *Atlantic Neptune*, surveyed before 1776, appears to show a residence near the middle of the western sector of the island where the Gays' farm is known to have been. . . . The 1790 federal census lists Eleazer with a household of eight. Eleazer was prominent in the affairs of Cushing following its incorporation in 1789; he was a selectman in 1789 and again in 1792; in other years he usually held some office. . . ."

Eleazer Gay hailed from Attleboro, Massachusetts. He served in the St. George coastal defense and gained title to his island piece by piece. His reign there seems to have been prosperous, with his property increasing in value each year. In 1819 Gay passed on the entire island to his sons, Eleazer Jr. and Mark, keeping for himself the buildings and one-third of profits during his natural life.

Another man to settle on Gay's Island was Oliver Chadwick, who in 1860 was the sole householder on the island. Oliver, his wife Sarah, and their son and daughter lived on the western portion, near the waist of the island, in the farmhouse that Elisabeth, Dot, and Guy would christen Tide's Way. "There is also a building on the waist itself," McLane writes, "which according to local residents was a barn Oliver Chadwick converted to a store catering to Pleasant Gut Harbor fishermen."

After Oliver Chadwick's death in 1875, Sarah remained on the farm into the 1880s. The Chadwick farm was rarely empty; locals have told Elisabeth that the farm was occupied at various times by Youngs, Lunts, and others, including loggers in the early twentieth century.

Jim Seavey, also mentioned quite a bit in *My World*, had spent many childhood years on the Chadwick farm. Jim visited regularly with Elisabeth and Dot during the one winter they spent on the island (1950–51). Elisabeth jokes that his wife would get him out of the house by saying, "Now, go and see what those girls are doing!" He obligingly visited them, and regaled them with stories of his childhood in the Chadwick house. He teased them by saying, "I've pulled more water out of that well than you'll ever do!"

Today Gay's Island is inhabited seasonally by about a dozen families, whose cottages are spaced around the shores of the island, mostly on the eastern end. One house is situated on the old cellar hole of Eleazer Gay's property. Elisabeth and Dot (before her death in 1998) had summered more than fifty years in the Oliver Chadwick farmhouse.

LIFE ON GAY'S ISLAND

Dot and Elisabeth developed their own individual working styles. An article written for the *Bangor Daily News* in 1961 tells more about the differences in their writing habits: "Elisabeth prefers working in the daytime and can do it even with considerable noise around her. Dot, on the other hand, does her best work at night and frequently toils past midnight. Each prefers not to look at or criticize the work of the other. They share the work, more or less, each cooking what she is best at. Dot, Matinicus bred, has a few lobster traps out but does not attempt any big operation. Both join in picking berries, of which there is a profusion, and making jams and jellies for the winter ahead."

Their days had a gentle rhythm. Elisabeth would wake early in the morning to write and handle correspondence. When that work was done, she would turn to physical activity—walking and beachcombing, doing necessary chores, and growing things in the garden.

In addition to their writing, household chores and errands, and outdoor pursuits, they engaged in various creative activities. Elisabeth's parents continued to visit until their deaths in the 1970s. Maude had encouraged Dot to begin painting, and both women would paint together during their summers on Gay's Island. Maude painted several scenes of Gay's Island, along with some portraits. Dot's paintings of the Bennett Homestead and the Sorensen House of Criehaven were on exhibit in Rockland for a time, one at a bookstore and another at the Rockland *Courier-Gazette* newspaper office.

Maude and Dot also applied their creative talents to whittling. One summer they made craft items for Fanny Davis's gift shop on Pleasant Point: small painted lobster buoys, miniature skiffs with oars, lighthouses, and perched gulls. This gave way to leather projects, and painting the interior of the farmhouse during subsequent summers. One year Maude even decorated the table and walls of the kitchen with wonderful designs.

Music was an essential ingredient of island life, and Dot and Elisabeth carried the musical traditions of Criehaven with them to Gay's Island. Dot was a self-taught fiddler, encouraged by her stepfather. She became very good at it over the years, playing often for the clubhouse dances on Criehaven. She also played tenor guitar and the baritone ukulele, and composed tunes to accompany her favorite poems. Elisabeth played the accordion, and together they entertained at many social gatherings on Gay's Island.

NIECES, NEPHEWS, AND FOSTER CHILDREN

Children were frequent visitors to Tide's Way. Nieces and nephews of both Dot and Elisabeth visited. Elisabeth's novel *Waters on a Starry Night* takes as its inspiration three small girls who stayed with them for a time on Gay's Island. "I wanted a way to [write about] the kids that had stayed with Dot and me," says Elisabeth. "I also wanted to write about a couple that got married so young and had these children, one right after the other. The kids stayed with us, the first three, when they were seven, eight, and nine; they were with us for about three months. And then they stayed with us again with their little sister, when they were older. Their parents were moving back to Criehaven, after living on the mainland for a while."

Their life with the children was full. Dot taught them how to sing and accompany themselves on the baritone ukulele. "They could all sing like anything!" says Elisabeth. "We had this record of one of my favorite singers, Calum Kennedy, and one of the songs is called 'Haste Ye Back, We Love You Dearly.' The kids learned how to play and sing that. . . [T]heir father came down to see them one day and they said, 'Well Daddy, we've got a surprise for you.' So they lined up with their baritone ukes and sang, and afterward, their father went out on the porch with his back to them—he was crying."

Elisabeth is fond of *Waters on a Starry Night*, as it brings to mind happy memories of the children's stay with them. In later years, the then-teenage girls would tell prospective dates that they could read all about them in the book. "I don't know how many boys read this book!" laughs Elisabeth.

Elisabeth remains in contact with the girls—now grown women. They all came to Dot's memorial service and sang some of the songs that Dot had taught them—a fitting tribute to the woman who had given them so much. One of the girls asked to keep Dot's guitar. A young man from the area inherited the baritone ukulele and shares this instrument with young people much as Dot did. Elisabeth feels that Dot would be thrilled to know her instruments are being put to good use.

These aren't the only children invoked in Elisabeth's writing, or indeed, the only ones to have spent time on Gay's Island. The old farmhouse was often filled with the sound of young voices as nieces and nephews and friends' children visited. It was a constant source of delight to Elisabeth that their island home was a perfect summer retreat for young people.

Elisabeth is particularly close to her niece Barbara, her brother Kent's daughter, who has spent a great deal of time with her through the years. As a child, Barbara accompanied the Ogilvies to Criehaven, and later joined Elisabeth on Gay's Island for the summer months, both as a girl and then as a mother with her own children. Elisabeth's love and support have played a big part in her life.

Elisabeth has always loved children, noting in an interview that they are the "wealth of the world." Her natural sensitivity and empathy toward children is reflected in her books for young people. Her friends have always been aware of this connection. "Elisabeth has a great love of, and interest in, children," says Elaine Fales. "I don't believe she will ever grow old, because her brain is so active and sharp. She is always up on what's important to children, and never looks down on them, which I think many adults do. She always shows an interest."

Her affection for children found wider expression when Elisabeth became a member of Foster Parents, Inc., more than fifty years ago. The program was initiated in Spain during its civil war, when two Englishmen found starving children and began to take care of them. It has since grown to include children from disadvantaged countries all over the world.

Elisabeth has sponsored a dozen foster children over the years, and describes her involvement as "engrossing and satisfying." She began in the early 1950s, as a foster parent to Bernardo, an eleven-year-old Italian boy. She still corresponds with Bernardo, who is now a married schoolteacher, and was pleased when he named his first daughter Elisabeth.

Her connection with the children includes sending gifts and some financial support along with frequent letters. Over the years, her foster children have come from Italy, Poland, Vietnam, Ecuador, the Philippines, Africa, and Chile.

The father of one Vietnamese child was a laborer who earned just thirteen cents a day and could not begin to pay for an education for his daughter. With Elisabeth's support, this girl decided on a nursing career and studied hard to achieve that goal. Elisabeth's foster child from Ecuador eventually became an engineering student.

Elisabeth still sponsors two foster children today, a little girl in the Philippines and another girl in Mali, Africa. Almost all of her foster children have been good letter writers and have corresponded with her for years.

VISITS WITH ELISABETH

Barbara Ogilvie Mosher, Elisabeth's niece and closest relative, lives near Elisabeth. Here she shares some of her fondest memories:

I can't remember life without Elisabeth. She is a part of my first memories, and continues to take part in my life. My father, Kent, was the middle of her three older brothers. My mother died when I was an infant, and after her death my father brought me home to his parents, Frank and Maude. Elisabeth was a teenager then. I called her Baba for years. As I grew, she read to me, sang with me, did dishes with me (she always got to wash, so I had to dry), danced with me—she took the role of big sister. One of my most treasured possessions is *A Child's Garden of Verses*, which Baba gave me for Christmas in 1937.

We went to Criehaven for the entire summer during my child-hood, from the age of two until I was eleven or twelve, when Elisabeth bought Gay's Island. We would leave Wollaston on an early Friday evening after my father got home from work. The car would be packed with all the necessities of a summer stay; there were times I would be up on the shelf behind the back seat. After a stop in Portsmouth, New Hampshire, for hamburgers and chocolate milk, we would continue on to Rockland, have breakfast at the Paramount Restaurant, and go down Tillson Avenue to catch the 7 A.M. mailboat to Criehaven. We stayed at Honeysuckle Cottage, next to what was Uncle Nate's farmhouse in the Bennett's Island books. My father and grandfather would "visit" us when they had their two weeks' vacation. My grandmother Maude, aunt Elisabeth, and I had the whole summer in "paradise." There were times when I would cry all the way back to Wollaston, missing Maine.

As I grew, Elisabeth continued to be a big part of my life, accompanying me to musicals and ballet programs in Boston—raising my cultural awareness! Obviously, she preceded me through North Quincy High School, and although I did well scholastically, I did not outperform my aunt, particularly in English class. Her mentor and supporter, Mr. Smoyer, a teacher of senior English, was the bane of my existence during my senior year. My talents lay elsewhere, not in English composition!

By the time I graduated from high school, Elisabeth was well on her way to being a published writer. Although I knew she made trips to New York, there was no noticeable difference in our relationship. She had her own place by then on Gay's Island. I spent summers there, and have many happy memories of get-togethers. There were always lots of people around, as I recall, including my father, grandparents, uncles, and aunts. We enjoyed lobster feeds, and singalongs with Dot on the guitar and Elisabeth on the accordion. There was always something exciting going on, like trips to Port Clyde for groceries on Guy's boat and—when Elisabeth bought a car—excursions to Rockland and other parts of Knox County.

After high school, of course, came college and eventually nursing school. My father was unable to provide much financial help. Elisabeth stepped forward and said she would sponsor me, which she did through one year of college and three years of nursing school. Eventually, I traveled south to Florida, but stayed in touch and returned home to Massachusetts and Maine as often as I could. Gay's Island was a welcome refuge from the everyday working world.

I married while living in Miami, and our daughter, Marilyn, was born there. When she was eighteen months old, in 1962, she and I came back to Maine for most of the summer. Marilyn basked in the attention of her great-grandparents and great-aunt Elisabeth. Later, my husband and I decided to return to New England to live, and settled in midcoast Maine in 1963. Our son, Douglas, was born here in 1966. Both children, now married and settled in Maine, continue with Elisabeth as part of their lives.

Of course, she also continues to be an important part of my life and the lives of my grandchildren, Rebeckah, Jacob, and Hannah. Beckah and Jacob have been lucky enough to enjoy times on Gay's Island, carrying on a family tradition of children and islands, thanks to Elisabeth.

MAINLAND ERRANDS

Part of Elisabeth's and Dot's routine was to make a weekly trip off island to run errands. This expedition involved quite a bit of logistical planning. After making sure that tide and weather were favorable, they'd row to the mainland (less than a quarter of a mile). They kept their royal blue car, a '68 or '69 Dodge, there at Pleasant Point. In the epilogue to *My World Is an Island*, Elisabeth described how much sheer exercise a shopping day involved:

> [It was] one long physical-fitness program. You may not jump up and down to music while wearing a fetching leotard, but you work out just the same—all the time. You go everywhere on foot, taking the rocky route around the shores for a change. Everything empty, such as water pails and wheelbarrows, goes down light and comes up heavy: lugged up the hill, pushed up the hill. The week's order of groceries is divided into manageable sections when we take it from the car over in the mainland driveway. This is the one time when a loaded wheelbarrow and tote bags go downhill, but once the stuff is into the skiff and taken across the moat, it is carried up over the rocks at the landing, and wheeled up the hill to the house. One reward for the work of bringing the food home: you burn up most of the calories from last week's order.

For islanders, the lowly wheelbarrow is a most important conveyance. In Elisabeth's juvenile book *Masquerade at Sea House*, the characters own a wheelbarrow named "The Sea Island Mercedes." In real life, Elisabeth has one called "The Gay's Island T-bird." When it was not in service trundling groceries, the "T-bird" often served as a makeshift desk for Elisabeth's typewriter when she wanted to work outdoors.

When they first moved to Gay's Island, they did their grocery shopping at Hap Wilson's General Store in Port Clyde, where Elisabeth first saw artist Andrew Wyeth ("Andy and I are the same age," she comments). They soon discovered Fales Store in Cushing, however, where they found almost all their needed supplies. "We came to know the Fales family, whose store has stood at the junction of the roads to Cushing and Friendship for generations. They serve the community in the true sense of the word."

Richard and Elaine Fales, owners of the store, fondly remember Dot's and Elisabeth's shopping trips. "They were very good customers, as well as friends," says Elaine Fales. "They had a tendency to do their shopping, and then Dot would walk around gathering up things and have almost as much again as the original lot. All of us got a big laugh about that, even though it was almost expected."

In addition to grocery shopping, Elisabeth and Dot would visit the post office, where Postmaster Lois Faulkingham also enjoyed visiting with them. Lois recalls that she first heard Elisabeth Ogilvie's name from her parents as they told of attending a special housewarming party on Gay's Island just after Elisabeth, Dot, and Guy had bought Tide's Way. For years Lois heard her father speak of the fun they had, and how he found Elisabeth to be such an attractive and interesting woman. Lois's curiosity was sparked.

Lois's grandmother had been in charge of the Pleasant Point Post Office, since renamed the Cushing Post Office, for thirty years. When she retired, Lois took over as postmaster for the next twenty years. Elisabeth and Dot always gave Lois and her grandmother signed copies of their books.

As a young girl, Lois was interested in writing, and her grandmother asked Elisabeth to read one of Lois's stories. Elisabeth wrote her a letter filled with encouraging feedback, telling Lois that despite her occasional use of too many adjectives, she had "a good sense of story."

Another mainland friend, ever since the first years on Gay's Island, was Jeannette Chapman, whose father delivered milk to Dot and Elisabeth. Jeannette is proud that her father is mentioned in Chapter 9 of *My World Is an Island*: "We took our milk from Clarence Wales, in Cushing—he left our every-other-day quart at the Youngs'."

Jeannette was a young girl when Elisabeth first moved to the area, and knew and loved her as a friend long before Elisabeth became well-known for her Bennett's Island series. Jeannette also appreciated seeing Elisabeth coming down the road in her "wonderful old blue Dodge"—they always knew it was her, driving by with her signature friendly wave. In later years, when she worked as a ballot clerk in Cushing, Jeannette came to know Elisabeth more. She appreciated Elisabeth's ever-present sense of humor. Jeannette still lives on the farm where she grew up, and where the milk route originated.

VISITORS TO GAY'S ISLAND

Their life on the island was by no means isolated. Elisabeth and Dot enjoyed visitors, and when the tide cooperated, they had plenty—so many that during the summer months it was often difficult to get much writing accomplished. Elisabeth's characteristic humility and sense of humor come through when she tells of an unexpected visit from lecturer Alton Hall Blackington.

Mr. Blackington was preparing a lecture about Maine authors, and Elisabeth had been chosen to join the likes of Kenneth Roberts and Ben Ames Williams. Mr. Blackington was coming to interview her and take some footage with his small movie camera. Elisabeth wrote in *My World*, "I've never known how those gentlemen felt about it, but I know that I was complimented to the point where I sat in a sort of smiling, imbecilic silence and did what I was told, wondering if he'd really use these movies he was so busily making, and if people would actually believe I was bright enough to write a book."

They weren't prepared for company when he arrived, and things in the farmhouse were in disarray. This didn't bother Mr. Blackington and his wife, who thoroughly enjoyed their visit. Elisabeth even agreed to milk their goat Patty for the camera, and soon their other sheep, Blackie, (also Mr. Blackington's nickname) got into the act. The two animals engaged in battle, cheered on by the squawking chickens, and Mr. Blackington caught all the action on film. Elisabeth notes that during all the excitement, she "stood by looking mutely distraught." Her expression, "entirely unrehearsed, is remarkably vivid on film."

In *My World*, Elisabeth also recounted their feverish anticipation of Mr. Blackington's second visit, and how they planned to be more prepared for this one. He'd sent a postcard in advance, so they had fair warning this time. As was typical on the island, however, their well-laid plans came to naught—he arrived in the midst of chaos, again with trusty camera in hand. Elisabeth's brother Allan was there, and he was the cameraman, capturing the further adventures of the group on Gay's Island. "Mr. Blackington (Alton Hall, that is) has plugged my books and shown movies of a distraught and disheveled E.M.O. all over the country. Patty is dead now, but she lives on film, and Blackie, who still kicks his heels over the lawn, has kicked them for many audiences. I must say Patty and Blackie were far more photogenic than I."

They had a delightful visit, despite Elisabeth's thoughts after they left: "We loved having the Blackingtons, but my sole regret is that I couldn't have met them at the wharf, looked poised and literary and *soignée*, in crisply tailored slacks and shirt from Vogue, waving a pair of dark glasses with jeweled frames. . . ."

Other intrepid visitors included an old friend from school, Hugh Boyd, and his partner, Dick Higginbotham. They had just purchased the *Boston Transcript* in 1946, and came calling to see whether Elisabeth would write an article for their first issue. "We had a wonderful time," Elisabeth recounted in *My World*, "and I must have been still under the spell of it a few weeks later when I wrote off an article about lobstering which still seems good to me whenever I read it. . . ." (This article appears on page 98.)

Elisabeth's dreams of presiding over a literary salon were often interrupted by the necessity of work—not just the labors of writing books, but the constant upkeep involved with their property. There was always something needing to be done.

One of the hardest workers in the family was Frank Ogilvie. He was definitely classified as a "working guest" when he visited. He painted the house, tightened up the windows, and built a doorstep (actually a long platform extending from the doorstep all the way to the corner of the house) and a new well curb. "Father is an indefatigable worker, and he takes the true craftsman's delight in his job," Elisabeth wrote in *My World*: "By profession he is in the insurance business, but his avocation is carpentry. Nobody gets any more tired than the rest of us when Father is working on a project, because we feel duty-bound to trot around behind him and admire."

In an article for the *Portland Press Herald* in 1978, writer Bill Caldwell recounted a typical visit with Dot and Elisabeth. Bill and his "first mate" Barbara came across the two women as they were crossing the Gut in a "scruffy working skiff." Reluctant to linger, citing their long list of chores, Elisabeth and Dot paused long enough for Elisabeth to sign a copy of *An Answer in the Tide* for Barbara, "half in ink, half in salt water; exactly the right mixture for the author of so many books set in the Maine islands," as Caldwell put it.

The Caldwells usually visited "these two wonderful ladies" each sum-

mer: "They are a grand pair, independent, sweetly gruff, and very hard working—at the typewriters, the garden, the fish house, the wharf and the skiff.
Our visits with them are highlights of every summer, but I go away feeling
like a lazy bum."

When he once asked if she'd finished her next book, Elisabeth answered
cheerily, "Yep. My new one is all done. Wrote it this winter. Finished now, ex
cept for the last four chapters. By the time Dot here gets finished typing the
rest, I'll have finished with the final four." This is a perfect illustration of the
partnership and easy cooperation the two shared during their decades of writing together. Caldwell found Elisabeth "slim, elegant, feminine and too darn
at home in the Gut to be a lady author turning out novels every year (sometimes oftener) which are snapped up by scores of thousands of ardent fans
across America."

Richard and Elaine Fales were also frequent visitors. Elaine fondly remembers their sojourns on the island:

> They either transported us across, or, if we went on our own, they
> always met us at the wharf. We would walk up through the tunnel of
> alders, where there were always all kinds of warblers in the summer
> months. Elisabeth taught me . . . about birds, and I was eventually
> able to identify many kinds, thanks to her.
>
> We always went on long walks on the island. No matter what path
> we took, Dot and Elisabeth had all these little picnic areas. You got
> the impression they had pretty good appetites! We always joked about
> it. If we lunched in the house, it was always in the sunporch. . . . In
> order for more people to be seated at the table, all kinds of things had
> to be moved aside—rocks, pieces of shells, broken glass, Indian arti-
> facts, books, partially written letters, anything. After that, we would
> eat—with a lot of tales told, mostly by Dot. The food was sort of an
> afterthought because we were enjoying ourselves so much.
>
> Elisabeth is a very kind, generous, interesting, friendly and sin-
> cere person. I stand in awe of her now more than I ever did when I
> was younger.

WALKS AND BEACHCOMBING

Just like her island heroines, Elisabeth enjoys taking long walks and exploring the shores, forests, and meadows of her lovely home. She and Dot
would often roam the island along their favorite trails, picking flowers and

birdwatching. The abundance of wildlife on Gay's Island was in sharp contrast to Criehaven, where not much animal life exists. (They always prayed that they would not stumble upon a moose, however.)

They would take beachcombing walks along the shore as well, examining their treasures and keeping some, including lobster buoys. Once Elisabeth found one that said "S. Bennett" on it.

> I stood staring at it for a long time with the hair prickling on the back of my neck. I hadn't known any Bennetts when I began the Bennett's Island trilogy. But here was a buoy that belonged to Steve Bennett, one of my own Bennetts from my Tide Trilogy.
>
> "Do you suppose it's big Stephen or Stevie?" Dot asked seriously, and then we looked at each other and laughed. But we carried the buoy home and have cherished it since. (*My World Is an Island*)

Elisabeth has also picked up artifacts made by the Native Americans who inhabited Gay's Island hundreds of years ago, including arrowheads, stone knives and scrapers. These items still wash ashore today, to be found by dedicated beachcombers.

Visitor Tim Moses wrote of Elisabeth, "She speaks of the Indians and their lives as though she knew them. She is connected to the past and to the present just as she is connected to the crags, valleys, and shores of this island. Just as she is connected to the lives of the characters she has created." It is this devotion to her island world, and her commitment to the preservation of her surroundings, that has led to Elisabeth's long involvement in the Nature Conservancy.

GARDENING

For years Dot and Elisabeth kept a vegetable garden. Elisabeth was not a born gardener, as she described entertainingly in *My World Is an Island*:

> I couldn't understand the unabashed candor with which Gardeners of either sex came right out and discussed things like manure. . . . Let a couple of these earthy souls get together, and the non-Gardener could jump from a tenth-story window without being noticed. To get any real attention from the Brotherhood you have to be a cutworm. . . .
>
> And then the Flower-Gardeners, who lead you to a dejected, leafless, dried-up stalk and say, with obvious pride, 'Mock orange! It's

doing beautifully, don't you think?' You smile feebly and make sounds of approval, but if you are an honest and uncompromising New Englander you can't come right out and be enthusiastic, can you? Not when you're entertaining doubts of your friend's I.Q.

During her first spring on Gay's Island, however, she cast doubt to the wind and jumped wholeheartedly into gardening:

> I say it without shame; I too became a Gardener. I became one of the mystic organization that spends so much of its time on its knees coaxing recalcitrant young cabbages and dealing with problem peonies. . . .We were Gardeners. Whether anything grew or not, we were addicted. We couldn't keep away from the place.

It soon became apparent that birdwatching accompanied the act of gardening. Soon after their garden was dug, they realized that much of their time was spent looking up in the trees, and identifying bird calls. "The two diseases seemed to go hand in hand," Elisabeth noticed:

> By late spring we were pointing out patted-down places in the soil and saying to visitors, "That's beets . . . that's Swiss chard . . . that's carrots," and the visitors were casting frantically around in their minds for something nice and encouraging to say. And then when they said it, we hardly ever heard it, because one of us was likely to shriek suddenly, "Oh, an olive-sided fly-catcher!"

ANIMAL COMPANIONS

My World Is an Island is filled with references to Elisabeth and Dot's many pets—cats, dogs, sheep, and goats—all well-loved members of the family. Elisabeth wrote of one trip with the goats and some other livestock:

> Guy took Patty, the little Toggenburg doe, and Blackie, the lamb. Patty was a sweet, gentle creature, and Blackie, rather big for a lamb, was a handsome and imposing animal, with eyes like sparkling brown jewels in his long black face, and sensitive ears like soft black felt. If possible, we presented a far more gypsyish appearance when we chugged up Pleasant Point Gut this time than we did the week before. I know the people on the Point must have been both intrigued and appalled. What is there about chickens in lobster traps, and a goat, that will give even the most respectable souls a raffish air?

"Blackie loved to beg cigarettes off the clammers," says Elisabeth in another anecdote. "They'd be down on the marsh digging clams when he'd come raring down on his hind legs, begging for cigarettes. That was probably one thing that made him sick." (Blackie eventually had to be put down due to ill health.) Elisabeth used Blackie as real-life inspiration for "A Weekend with Ebony," published in *Woman's Day* magazine in 1952. The fictitious Ebony has the same cigarette habit, and plays quite a role in this charming story. "There was a black sheep in Lacy's family—which turned out to be very lucky indeed," reads the lead-in on the magazine page.

Dot and Elisabeth had an endless capacity for loving animals. They owned two Australian terriers, their beloved companions Jill and Sherman; both lived to be more than twenty years old. Elisabeth incorporated these pets into her novel *Weep and Know Why*. In one short story, "Hubert and the Eternal Feminine," two cats are at the core of the narrative. Friend Elaine Fales comments, "Elisabeth loves cats and small dogs. No, that's not quite right, she loves all dogs, but has preferred small ones, probably because they were easier to handle. Some of her cats helped her do her typing, I understand."

Elisabeth has always enjoyed telling stories about her pets. In a 1999 letter to author Marilyn Westervelt, she described her most recent animal companion: "Joppy the lend-lease cat is with me—smiles when she catches my eye, and each night we have a silent battle about who's going to sleep in my bed—I win by pushing her from under the blankets (she can't bite me through them)."

Named for Janis Joplin, this big, lovable cat had belonged to Dot's nephew, but came to stay with Elisabeth when Dot was hospitalized toward the end of her life. With Joppy's companionship, "I never came home to an empty house; there was always a little face at the door."

GAY'S ISLAND AND PLEASANT POINT TODAY

The community of Gay's Island and Pleasant Point today, at the beginning of the twenty-first century, is still fairly similar to what Elisabeth depicted in *My World Is an Island*. Elisabeth still does her shopping at Fales's Store in Cushing and picks up her mail at the Cushing Post Office. The same people still come to the island, such as the Andrews and Robinson families. "I used to see Bill Robinson as a high-school boy going by with his dog, and now I see his grandchildren." Elisabeth observes.

She also speaks fondly of Roland Stimpson, described in the 1989 epilogue to *My World* as "the skinny kid with the beanie who rowed us over to the island the first time." He was the harbormaster in 1989, and remains a firm friend today. He and his wife, Barbara, live on Pleasant Point on the mainland. "Roland is just as quick and willing to help out now as when he was fifteen, and we have had to call upon him in some pretty drastic circumstances. Barbara is always ready to put the teakettle on to boil."

Elisabeth no longer spends every summer on Gay's Island, but lives on the mainland year round—except for seasonal visits to Tide's Way when her family is vacationing there. Gay's Island still remains a precious part of her life, however, bound by years of affection and shared memories.

5 ❧ CRIEHAVEN

THE ISLAND THAT LIES at the core of Elisabeth Ogilvie's writing not only fascinates Elisabeth, it is equally compelling for her readers, who easily lose themselves for hours on Bennett's Island and dream of one day visiting this magical place.

Judy Cushman, of Florida, says her husband does just that. Originally from Maine, Paul is easily transported back to his home state when he reads Elisabeth's novels. "When the days get too busy, Paul takes one of Elisabeth's books and some of the dried fish his brother sends him from Maine, and goes into his study. He shuts the door, begins to read, and is soon in another world. I peek in after a while and say, 'Are you still in Maine?' He smiles and says he can hear the seagulls, smell the salt water, and feel the chilly fog rolling in."

EARLY HISTORY AND SETTLEMENT

To understand Criehaven's hold on Elisabeth and its impact on the development of her characters, it is important to learn something of its history.

In 1985, a writer for the *Island Journal* talked with Elisabeth and Dot about Criehaven. "In Profile: Grand Dames of Criehaven, Dot Simpson and Elisabeth Ogilvie" contains their recollections of life on Maine's outermost island. Dot talked about the beginnings of the island community:

> DS: When Robert Crie went down to the island in 1850 or so, I guess it was a pretty rough place. There wasn't any sign of a breakwater, for one thing. But people built Criehaven up and it reached a peak. There was a year-round community. They had their own town meeting just like they have here in Cushing. They ran their own busi-

nesses and they hired their schoolteacher. They had a nice class of little kids, and they had a nice wooden steamship to go in there, the *Butman*. [The community] was going down when I was a kid—I saw the tail end of the best part of it.

Here is the history of "the best part of it," the Criehaven of the latter half of the nineteenth century and the beginning of the twentieth. Its story is well chronicled in Dot Simpson's book, *The Maine Islands in Story and Legend*. Dot grew up on Criehaven, and naturally her account is colored with affection. Having read Elisabeth's lyrical descriptions of the island, one can't help but support Dot when she disagrees with Horace Beck, who in *The Folklore of Maine* labels Criehaven "unattractive." Dot found it anything but, and described the island in glowing prose:

Criehaven, with its deep forests, its sunlit meadows, its old orchard blooming each year surrounded by tall dark spruces, its warm tawny stone that seems to shine almost rosily, and the exhilarating heights of Sou'west Point where one can smell the wild strawberries, growing so abundantly that one gathers them in ten-quart pails instead of a little quart dipper. . . . [The island] has an enchanting variety of coves, headlands, and cliffs.

Strictly speaking, Criehaven is the name of the settlement on Ragged Island, but in local usage "Criehaven" is used to refer to both the island and the village. The island is small by some standards, measuring approximately three hundred acres. Native Americans were no doubt the first occasional residents. They "sold" it to Henry Brookman, a Swede, who in turn sold it to Robert Crie, of Matinicus, in 1848. Crie was twenty-four years old when he purchased the island, and his young wife Harriet Hall, of Camden, was just nineteen when they moved to "South Matinicus." They set up housekeeping in a log cabin, and through the winter Robert cut wood and prepared planks for a house—the Crie homestead, built in 1849.

Elisabeth used this actual Crie history as a model for her Bennett family history in the Bennett's Island series. In *An Answer in the Tide*, Joanna reminisces about the early Bennetts who settled the island:

Young Jamie Bennett, who with his wife Pleasance had set up housekeeping in a cabin at Bull Cove in 1827. . . . They'd moved across from Brigport, and at first they'd been all alone on what was then known as South Brigport, or the South Island.

Charles B. McLane further chronicles the development of Criehaven in *Islands of the Mid-Maine Coast*, explaining that Robert Crie not only became a prosperous farmer, but also operated a booming fish-salting and packing company and sold supplies to fishermen. He made a good living selling salt cod to the Boston market. Captain Crie, as the largest landholder and "ruler of all he surveyed," was often referred to as "King Crie," according to McLane. He rarely sold his land, but preferred to rent it to tenants instead. He built homes for future islanders, to tempt them to move to his island.

Robert and Harriet Crie were married for more than fifty years, and raised five children on the island. In 1896, all of the Crie children, now married and some with children of their own, lived there as well, making the island's name ring true. Criehaven was growing, and its people wanted independence from Matinicus. The islanders decided to form a plantation. There was a problem, however. To be established as a plantation (a form of township), the islanders must have a post office—but to have a post office, they first needed a school. When Carl Anderson, Dot Simpson's grandfather, was persuaded to bring his large family to the island that year, Criehaven finally had enough children to warrant a school.

Once the school was in place, the post office was soon established. Horatio Crie was named the first postmaster, succeeded by his brother Eben. In 1896, Criehaven was incorporated as a separate plantation and became a self-governing community. In this same year, a steamer began making semiweekly trips to the island. Criehaven prospered, and existed as a successful plantation from 1900 until the 1920s, with the population ranging between forty-five and seventy people.

LEGENDS

Dot Simpson wrote that Criehaven was home to a variety of cultures and languages during its heyday. Norwegians, Swedes, and Danes shared the island with Scottish, Portuguese, and French Canadian neighbors. Some inhabitants became local legends. One favorite bit of local lore centers on a drifter named Harry Harbridge, who lived a rough-and-ready existence at the edge of the harbor. It was rumored that Harry had buried treasure in the woods, but it was never found. This wasn't for lack of trying by many of the island boys. Elisabeth included a whiff of this tale in *The Young Islanders*, where the young boys search endlessly for doubloons.

A colorful community, it boasted its share of mysteries, including men lost at sea. Although the majority of the island's inhabitants were fishermen, there were very few known deaths by drowning, except for the times when a lobsterman headed out to haul his traps and disappeared, never to be heard from again. (Even today, one hears news stories of lobstermen being killed when they become entangled in their lobster gear and are pulled overboard.)

One well-known story tells about a "good, honest man and respectable citizen," Criehaven's tax collector, Captain Hall. In October 1900, Captain Albert Hall started for the mainland in his sloop, the *Wild Rose*. After a short stay, he left Tenants Harbor to return to Criehaven. It was foggy and he had no compass, but he knew the coast well. When he was never seen or heard from again, people assumed it must have been due to illness and subsequent drowning, as he was far too competent a sailor to simply lose his way. Dot Simpson wrote about the aftermath of Captain Hall's disappearance: "A year later, Judson Young of Matinicus was tending his lobster traps about two miles southwest of Criehaven, and discovered that the difficulty he had in hauling one trap was due to its being entangled in the rigging of the *Wild Rose*. There she was in twenty fathoms of water, but still no one ever found the captain himself."

Dot wrote of another lobsterman named Ed Higgins who went out to haul one day, never to return. No clues were ever found as to the cause of his disappearance. Elisabeth's mother knew Ed Higgins and his daughter, who later worked in Boston, and was shocked when Ed was never heard from again.

THE CRIE FAMILY'S LEGACY

The Crie family dominated the early years of the island. In 1945 one descendant, Ethel Crie, wrote an article entitled "The 'Air Mail' of Yesterday and Today" that explained in detail what life was like on the island at the end of the nineteenth century. We draw heavily upon Ethel's fascinating account in the following paragraphs. She begins by describing the island itself:

> From east to west, stretching across the island, is a section of iron rock, seemingly giving to the area a strong backbone of resistance,—while along its southern section a touch of beauty is added by an admixture of marble and onyx rock. And over all lies a rich, black soil; laid down through the years by the thick forest of trees that covered the island.

The total population of the island at the turn of the twentieth century lived in a small village of about twenty-five people. Fishing was the primary industry. In addition, each of the seven families also farmed garden plots, mainly for their own use. The island had originally been covered with spruce, but by this time many clearings had been made, including enough pasture to feed four horses and about one hundred sheep. Most families kept chickens, and Ethel's family also had several cows and pigs to take care of the needs of all the fishermen and their families. Mail and supplies for the village store were delivered by the sailing packet *Mary B* once a week in the winter (weather permitting) and three times a week during June, July, and August.

> My mother started her married life in 1899 on this small island, situated twenty-five miles from the nearest mainland. The island was owned by my grandfather [Captain Crie], who had a wholesale fishing industry and . . . a small farm [and also ran] the general store and post office.

Ethel's article highlighted the amazing accomplishments of the islanders in those days—especially the women. Ethel's father traveled to the Grand Banks for cargoes of fish and was often gone for several weeks at a stretch. While he was away, Ethel's mother took over the post office and store, in addition to her duties as schoolteacher for the island and as mother of two small children. Also, she and Ethel's grandmother often stepped in during medical crises; when bad weather and winter storms stopped the boat from delivering supplies, they would use their own garden-grown herbs to treat the sick:

> Many a very sick patient had been brought through a bad illness with the aid of these two practical nurses, and the use of their simple, old-fashioned remedies. But almost every winter there were one or two cases that proved too serious to respond to the simple treatments and knowledge of these two women, and the more severe cases always seemed to occur when a real n'oth-easter was raging.

The islanders had an ingenious way of communicating with the mainland doctor when necessary—they used carrier pigeons. As Dot Simpson explained in *The Maine Islands*, "One of Robert Crie's sons [Horatio] took care of the pigeons on Criehaven, and in case of emergency a pigeon was sent off with a message. The bird could be depended upon to arrive in the doctor's loft, whereas in time of sail the mail packet was many times becalmed in the bay in summer, or held up by gales in winter."

"It was Dr. Edwin Gould who established the carrier pigeon service between the islands and his Rockland office," according to Robert Fillmore in his 1914 booklet, *Gems of the Ocean*. "This was the pioneer attempt to utilize carrier pigeons for the relief of the sick, and attracted worldwide attention as inquiries relating to this novel service were received by Dr. Gould from many different points, one from as far away as New Zealand."

When the doctor finally arrived on Criehaven, he would usually stay several days until the patient was out of danger. At the same time, he would hold a clinic in Ethel's grandmother's parlor, treating everyone with an ailment. The islanders were as grateful for the break in monotony as they were for the medical care.

Ethel noted the stark contrast between the relatively modern conditions of the 1940s, when she wrote her article, and those at the turn of the century:

> There is a telephone from the island to the mainland, and a phone call will bring the doctor over by airplane almost any time that he is needed, in about half an hour. If there should be a very bad storm, then he makes the trip in a large boat that brings him across the same day. So now the modern V-mail and the doctor always "get through" promptly, and the inhabitants on the islands benefit from the modern adaptation of the principle that originated from the flight of their earlier carrier birds.

These modern conveniences were still decades away in 1914, when the island boasted a winter population of about fifty, with a sharp rise in population during the summer months. "Criehaven is fast becoming a popular summer resort," Robert Fillmore wrote at the time in *Gems of the Ocean*. Dreams of an extensive summer colony were never fully realized, but Criehaven did attract dozens of summer visitors during these early years of the twentieth century, including Elisabeth's mother, Maude, and many artists and ministers.

One of the main attractions of the island at this time was Hillside Farm. Owned by Fred Rhodes (whose brother Edgar had married Elisabeth's Aunt May), this produce farm boasted beautiful grounds with walking paths, and accommodated summer boarders. In 1914, Fred Rhodes planned to retire and devote his time to making Criehaven a booming summer resort. He had already built several guest cottages, and drilled a well 216 feet deep. This well was guaranteed to hold ten thousand gallons of "never failing pure water," enough to service the whole island. Although this island never became the tourist attraction that others did, during these years it was a popular destination for many, who were drawn by Criehaven's myriad charms.

In these early years of the twentieth century, the island was proud of its "neat little school-house," wrote Fillmore, where church services were held each Sunday. Industries included farming, poultry, and sheep raising, with three hundred sheep belonging to Eben Crie alone. Eben was also proprietor of the general store at the time. The main industry, of course, was fishing. "The fishermen are prosperous and make a good living, most of them owning their own homes which are in attractive locations." Many of the fishermen also built their own boats, including the well-known boatbuilder of that era, Peter Mitchell.

During those years, the wooden steamer *W. G. Butman* made three round trips per week from Rockland to Matinicus and Criehaven between May 1 and November 1, and two trips per week during the winter. In the *Island Journal* interview, Dot reminisced fondly about the *Butman*: "She looked like one of these, you know, real business boats. She was a real steamship. Oh, how they would go in and out of that little harbor! You know how rocky it is now, but she did it, and she never went [aground]."

THE BREAKWATER

Criehaven's dangerous harbor was not only rocky, it offered scant shelter from winter storms. The island's fishermen needed a breakwater. A particularly bad storm in 1908 had destroyed the steamboat wharf and much of the lobstermen's gear. Dot Simpson described how the men risked life and limb to chip the accumulating ice from their boats during winter storms:

> They'd go out in the dory with two rowing as hard as they could.
> . . . They'd row from one boat to the next and drop somebody off. Then
> the first two fellows would go down to the next boat and get aboard
> and watch in case the other got in trouble. They didn't have fancy
> boats like they have now; they just had little 28- to 32-foot boats. In
> a northwest or northerly wind the boats would pound and pound and
> pound and pull hard on the moorings. The seas would come up
> higher than this room, so that their boats would be dipping down in
> it. It was a real job going out there in that wind to get the ice off, but
> if you didn't [the boats] wouldn't be there in the morning.

To address this dire need, in 1911 both Criehaven and Matinicus applied to the federal government for breakwaters in their respective harbors. Dot recalled that her husband Guy owned "maps and diagrams of where they measured the harbor. Some of the men from the government [were] down there looking at all the measuring." Apparently, this preparation was not sufficient.

Matinicus received its breakwater in 1912, but Criehaven did not. Residents were understandably furious, and thus began a long dispute with the government that did not end until 1938, when Criehaven harbor finally got its own breakwater.

Dot told *Island Journal*, "Nineteen thirty-eight was when it was built. I was down to the Ball [Wooden Ball Island]. My uncle and husband, they fished the Ball, so I didn't see any of the work going on, but I got snapshots of the scow there in various stages of it." Elisabeth added, "We always went for the summer, and I was just leaving. I had to go home to Quincy, but I always remember this young fellow and his wife and baby arrived, and he was going to be in charge. They rented a cottage to live in. Gee, I hated to go home when all this was going on!"

In his 1987 *Yankee* article, George Putz discussed his belief that the lack of a breakwater played a major role in ending the year-round community:

> Matinicus received its breakwater in 1912. Criehaven had to wait another 26 years. Only the hearts of men and women kept the community going. They built a community hall, kept the post office and school operational, and continued to farm and fish. But there was constant social erosion. The mainland, and even Matinicus, called many away.
>
> When finally in 1938, after decades of rancor and dispute with the federal government, the breakwater was built, it was altogether too late. There were only a handful of school-age children left on the island. By 1940 there were only three, and despairing of finding a teacher, their parents sent them to the mainland. In 1941 the jig was up. The mothers removed to the mainland with their kids, the fathers taking a last crack at autumn and winter fishing. The war took the men, and as of 1942, Criehaven as a year-round community died.

Even the breakwater didn't ensure total protection. In 1978, a rogue wave smashed its way through, demolishing half the gear and buildings surrounding the harbor. About a month later, the Groundhog Day Storm took care of what was left. "The day after the second storm an islander flew over Criehaven and radioed back, 'You've lost everything,'" reported Putz. In terms of damage to boats, gear, and docks, the island fishermen lost, on average, $20,000 each. One left, giving up his privilege (fishing territory), but the others rebuilt, knowing full well that it could happen again.

END OF THE YEAR-ROUND COMMUNITY

The demise of the year-round community on Criehaven began in 1940, with the loss of the school, and continued through World War II. By the late 1940s, the year-round community had pretty much disappeared. Elisabeth, Dot, and others have varying opinions about what caused the decline, but all seem to agree that the closing of the school signaled the true end of the island's heyday. In the 1940s, the Crie family sold their remaining island land to the Hogstroms, who lived on the island year-round until they retired in the 1960s. At that time, the Hogstroms sold the ninety percent of the land they had acquired to the Krementz family, who still own it today.

Dot's thoughts about what brought the end of the year-round community differed somewhat from the ones Elisabeth expressed in "Last Waltz on Criehaven" (included in its entirety later in this chapter). Like George Putz, Dot focused more on the importance of the school, but she also delved into the impact of the de-organization of the town.

I think Criehaven fell completely apart when they took the school away. If they could have just gotten a schoolteacher that year, 1940, it was, or 1941, I guess. But you see, they only had two or three kids and they couldn't afford to pay much for someone to come teach out there. Nobody wanted to come stay there all winter long and not go anywhere. You know, modern times. So they just folded up and sent the kids to the mainland and paid their tuitions. (*Island Journal*)

Dot recalled the time in the late 1920s when the island decided to "de-organize" as a town, declaring the island "wild lands" in order to lower their property taxes. Once Criehaven was no longer an official plantation, the island became part of Maine's "unorganized territory," with the state taking over many of the functions once served by the township. She saw this as another indicator that the Criehaven of years past was destined to change:

Back earlier the Cries and the Roses got together when they owned the biggest part of the property, the two ends of the island, and they talked the fishermen into de-organizing as a town for lower taxes. So then we got state schools. State this—state that. Everything was lovely, but nobody had time to have a town meeting any more and they really didn't care. Everything began drifting apart and that was when they took the kids off there in the wintertime. Without the wives and the kids, the men weren't going to stay there. So the fishermen would work like [the] dickens till Christmas and then take every-thing ashore.

Elisabeth saw the end of the year-round community as the result of all these factors, with perhaps the most telling fact being that newcomers to the island were of a "completely different mindset from the lifetime islanders." Times were different. People weren't willing to do without modern conveniences, as the old islanders had been. They were also unwilling to do battle with the ferocious, lonely winters twenty-five miles out to sea.

In the old days, Elisabeth said, the islanders had ways to endure those winters: playing cards, celebrating momentous events together, getting together for knitting bees and the sewing club—and especially, dances at the clubhouse. Putz described the fallen clubhouse in the 1980s as a victim of "senility, the walls and porch host to rot and moss" —clearly symbolic of the end of that golden era. Even so, the building still whispers of the many dances and celebrations, town meetings and lively debates, and holiday gatherings that once made it the very heart of island life.

Readers can picture the handsome Owen spinning his partner in a reel and Joanna tossing her black hair as she dances. One can also imagine the young Maude directing the island children in one of her skits and Elisabeth teaching the young boys a special dance. The clubhouse will live on forever in the pages of Ogilvie's books and in the hearts and minds of the islanders.

But memories weren't enough to sustain the islanders in the post–World War II era. They were unwilling to trade life on the mainland for this remote island existence. Dot and Elisabeth discussed Criehaven's future with *Island Journal,* and whether it would ever be anything but seasonal again:

> DS: It's not very practical. If it was just the breakwater that was needed . . . but it's these other things: a school and some kind of way for lugging mail and freight and stuff like that ashore. Now it's all done piecemeal—it's like carrying stuff in a teaspoon. . . . On Criehaven, where the summer people own so much, there will never be much of a chance now for men, for a town. 'Course their harbor is small, and there is not much room for any [mailboat] wharf.
>
> EO: And the fishermen themselves want to keep it limited.
>
> DS: It used to be when they were rigging those dories with a little sail and oars, and rowing away out past Matinicus Rock, and coming in after dark at night, and cutting the fish up and gutting them before they could sit down and eat their supper; them times was

hard. Hard? Lobsters were two cents apiece! Then things began to come up and up, and pretty soon, my goodness, they had a sailboat with a sail and you could sit there at a tiller and you didn't have to row and could take it a little easy.

My grandpa had a little sailboat called *Toothpick*. She was the cutest little old thing, and he went lobstering in her. He had a little farm there with a cow, pig, chickens and garden. He was well off and his cellar was full. What money he made, he'd buy some sugar and tea and coffee, and he lived to be 84 years old. He was busy every day of his life; that was his idea of living.

He used to tell us kids that we were soft, that we didn't know what it was to work, but I don't know how they could have it any softer than today. They have radios and depth finders, radar and color fishfinders. Then on top of that those fellows don't cut a bit of their own wood. You see, they never went through what my father or grandfather did. That's why Criehaven will never come back.

LAST WALTZ ON CRIEHAVEN, by Elisabeth Ogilvie

(Reprinted with permission from Island Journal, The Annual Publication of the Island Institute, *Vol. 13, 1996.)*

One day in 1900, a delegation from the island once known as the South Island or South Matinicus came to Matinicus and invited Carl Anderson, a Norwegian-born fisherman, to move his young family across to Criehaven, which was then the South Island's name. The Cries offered him a piece of land big enough for a house and garden, and a shore privilege; all would be deeded to him. For a man who had been living on rented premises ever since he gave up deep-sea fishing to stay at home and raise a family, this offer was not to be refused.

The reason for it was his family. The people of Criehaven wanted his children for their school. In the Anderson family history of the event, a school was necessary before there could be a post office. But the island seems to have been incorporated as Criehaven, with a post office, well before that date. And there must always have been a school on the island, because there had been children on it before Robert Crie acquired most of the island in 1850, and then began acquiring children of his own. We know the name of at least one person who taught there before 1900. He was Fred Rhodes, from Glen Cove, and he married the Cries' only daughter, Charlotte. They were given the eastern half of the island as a wedding gift. Later they sold the tip—the Eastern End—to one or more of the three Simpson brothers who had sailed down from Bucksport in a dory. These were not the first people to build and live at the Eastern End.

Fred Rhodes had become a farmer, and by 1900 Hillside Farm was doing a good business in produce for the Rhodes Brothers' markets in Boston, and [in accommodating] summer boarders, including ministers and artists.

However the dates run, the fact remains that Carl Anderson was invited to bring his children to the island for the sake of the school; he was promised land and a deed for it, and this was a gift not easily come by. There may have been a shortage of school-age children at that time, and perhaps the law required more children to keep the school going. The family, its goods, and livestock, including a cow, were moved across by a Criehaven crew, and Carl would live on Criehaven for the rest of his life. He would live to weep when the Germans invaded Norway in the second World War. Some time later he died in his sleep, which he would have wished; he hadn't had to be carried off his island to die on the mainland. Anna, his wife, had been taken ashore in her final illness, but she had made it clear she was to be buried on the island, and she was.

One of their daughters had grown up to marry the young man who had rowed her and her little brother from Matinicus. One of their grandsons, Carl's great-grandson, lobsters on Criehaven today, the last of a large clan. Though he has a house on the mainland, he spends only about two months in the winter there; the rest of the year he lives on Criehaven, though he is back and forth across the bay frequently, for reasons given below. His uncles have all retired, but they were Criehaven fishermen all their working lives, from the first peapods until the last hauls, except for the time they were away in the war. The youngest of the brothers, who wasn't old enough for the service, was one of the last four students in the school when the state closed it.

Constants

Like the seasonal fishermen who began lobstering at Criehaven when they could buy homes there after the war, Carl Anderson's descendants have had to live since that time without the things which were there in earlier times. Now it was a lobster buyer they lacked rather than a fish buyer for whatever they caught. There had always been a going store, a post office, and a regular boat service, even in the far-off days when mail, freight, and passengers came under sail.

For a long time now the post office and store have been gone, and the men have to sell their lobsters elsewhere, making weekly trips to the mainland in their boats to do business and get supplies, both for their work and [for] their pantries.

The school was another of the constants which everyone believed would always be there, world without end, while the pattern of life was gradually changing from that of the Crie fish business to that of a lobstering community. Around 1925, the islanders were convinced by some shrewd arguments that if they gave up their plantation status and became "unorganized territory," the state would support the school, their taxes would be much smaller; there'd be no need of electing a school committee and going through the teacher selection process each year. The state would provide the teachers. This was a relief, because nobody liked being on the school committee and having to listen to all the complaints.

Under the new regime one citizen was appointed school agent to collect an annual three-dollar poll tax from every adult male. This money went to the state, toward school expenses. The state employed a superintendent of schools for its unorganized territory, and the school agent was the link between him and the actual school.

When Lois Prior went to Criehaven to teach in 1935, she received a salary of ten dollars a week, and the family with whom she boarded received six dollars a week. Lois began with nineteen pupils, but on the second day of school whooping cough broke out and went right through the student body; it was spring before she had a full attendance.

Lois married one of Carl Anderson's grandsons, and there was a different teacher for the next year. Then Lois took the job again; she was a mother that time. Still another teacher took the school for the following year, but the state couldn't find a teacher after that, and Lois had more of a family at home. Some of her pupils had reached the eighth grade and begun high school, and one large family had moved away. There were four children left; the state was not obliged to keep a school going with less than seven pupils, and so the Criehaven school was closed. However, children could be boarded with some Matinicus families, so the community didn't shut down in any other respect. The schoolhouse was empty, which nobody had thought would ever happen, and the bell didn't ring, but Criehaven went on.

Until that last year, there had never been a time on the island when the school couldn't open because it lacked a teacher. True, a year was enough for most teachers, but there was always one for next year. In one way the building was the heart of the island, because it was where all the children were gathered. And before the clubhouse was built, it was the place where the big Christmas tree stood, and Santa Claus came, sleigh bells and all. Church services were held, with everyone squeezing into the seats, or standing, to listen to the visiting clergy from Hillside Farm, and local revivalists touring the islands to give some thumping good sermons. There was always singing. "Blat again!" one old man used to urge when they stopped for breath.

Mrs. Rhodes (Lottie Crie) taught Sunday School there. All the children always went appropriately dressed.

Some teachers didn't leave much of a mark, unless it was for bad temper, or being courted, a matter for much suspense and vivid conversation around the shore. But with truly gifted teachers a lot of good things happened. There was the one who could play the cottage organ and taught so many new songs, even part-singing. One teacher dramatized poems like "Barbara Frietchie"; the entire student body, except for Barbara, was the Confederate Army, carrying wooden rifles cut out by the oldest pupils.

They learned "pieces" to speak, funny poems, and the classics, benignly gazed upon by the framed row of the great New England poets. One teacher decorated the blackboard with colored chalks to celebrate the seasons and their holidays. Even if the teachers went away for Christmas, they would have the preparations for the school's special performance well underway, so it could be carried on without them.

If a teacher was young and willing, there were always enough young men on the island to make courting her both an active and a spectator sport. There weren't that many eligible girls for the occasional male teacher, after Fred Rhodes won Lottie Crie.

One teacher was pursued from the mainland by a suitor who came out on the mailboat one day and refused to leave without her. He won, she gave up her job that day, and they got someone to take them to Matinicus that night, in an open boat and bad weather. The next day they were off to the mainland. Let's hope they had a happy life.

There were teachers who gave their free time to coaching children in subjects that didn't go too far in the island curriculum, like math, hoping to see them make it to high school. There were those who took in some retarded children, teaching them as much as they could learn and protecting them in the schoolyard. There are persons alive who can tell you about every teacher they had for the full eight years at the Criehaven school, and it makes good telling.

Children going on to mainland schools were consistently on a par with the other students, and more often well ahead in basics like math and reading. In the island school they had learned at their own rate— slow or speedy—and received a great deal of individual tutoring in their weak subjects.

The Island Store

If a place can have two hearts, the store was the other one. On Criehaven it was combined with the post office and the wharf where fish and then lobsters were bought, and where the boat arrived with mail, passengers, and freight. The store was also the location of the telephone, which the Coast Guard installed.

First the Cries ran the store. Then as they thinned out, the Wilsons took it over; when Leslie Wilson had to give it up because of heavy family responsibilities, H. J. McLure stepped in. He was Herbert J., but was always known as "Mike." Like so many of the others, he had come to the island as a young man to fish for the Cries. When he bought out Leslie he was already buying lobsters, and then he became postmaster, and the quintessential island storekeeper. He stocked everything the men needed—rubber boots, oilclothes, work gloves, paint, caulking cotton, and so the long list went on. If a man asked him to order a certain brand of heading twine, he didn't argue that another brand was better. There were gasoline and kerosene supplies, and a store full of groceries. His wife and children could stand in for him when he was busy on the wharf, or behind the post office window sorting mail. He raised three batches of children on Criehaven, and they all became at some time in their lives active in helping to run the business.

Between Mike and Stuart Ames, the long-lasting successor to all those mailboat captains over the years, the store was like Polaris; it was always there, and no one seriously foresaw a day when Mike wouldn't be in it, and the *Mary A* not blowing her whistle outside Eastern Harbor

Point three times a week in summer, twice in winter. If Mike was as constant as the Northern Star, Stuart was also famous for his reliability. If it didn't look too good out in the bay but Stuart said he was leaving Rockland—imperturbable behind that cigar—you went, even if outside Monroe's Island you might wish you hadn't come. But he always made it. Sometimes it was too rough to get the boat up to the wharf in Criehaven's harbor, and he had to go around the island by way of the Eastern End and come into Seal Cove, where he would be met by a dory. Stuart and the mail went ashore first; his contract was to carry the mail. Everything else, including passengers, was extra.

After the school closed, not too much else changed, because Mike was still there, and Stuart still carried the mail. When Mike decided to retire, it was a shock, but understandable; it had been a long time since he was one of the Cries' young men. His contemporaries certainly could sympathize, but it was still a blow. However, he found an eager buyer from the mainland who had never run a store or a lobster business but saw a lot of charm in this island way of life. He seemed willing to learn, and stuck it out fairly well for a few years in this group of rugged individualists.

War, Retirement, and the "New Wave"

The war did not empty the island, though all the able young men enlisted, some before war was declared. Most of the remaining lobstermen had been in World War I. One of these got himself into the second war, and served on a mine sweeper.

Except for the restrictions and regulations imposed by the war, life went on much the same. There were Criehaven children going to school on Matinicus, and the store was still operating, though Mike was very much missed. Stuart still ran the mail. The lobstering became phenomenal; one theory was that the depth charges dropped not too far outside were driving the lobsters in. Whatever caused it, the great lobstering was still there for the returning soldiers and sailors.

When Stuart retired from running the boat, the new man decided he didn't like Criehaven harbor at all, so the Criehaven run stopped. The islanders had to go to Matinicus for their mail and freight. The store began to change hands rapidly. Nobody seemed to have the desire or the ability to make a go of it, as Mike had; but then, he'd been an insider who'd had a good island lifetime to do it in.

Now the groundkeepers, the men whose life had been the island for half a century or more (except when they were away in their war), began to retire. Their houses were bought by young mainlanders eager to get that good lobstering on uncrowded grounds (apart from occasional arguments with Matinicus about the lines). For such a radical population change, the "new wave" would be an appropriate name.

The closing of the school was not the reason for the demise of the year-round community. Neither was the war. It was the change from one era to another. The newcomers were of a completely different mindset from the lifetime islanders. These had either been born there, had come as small children, or as young people with the intent of making it their home. And they did so. Not that the women didn't love an occasional visit to the mainland, and they preferred to have their babies there; but old letters and postcards dating from the years before the breakwater was built record a mostly contented, busy community, with relatives coming to visit in the summers, parties and picnics, and the July Fourth celebrations written up in the Rockland newspaper.

Nobody loved the winters, but the islanders had ways to get through them; holidays and birthdays, card parties from house to house, with home-made ice cream and cake; the knitting bees when everyone would gather at one man's house. The fish houses where the men kept the fires going while they worked were their clubhouses—you could always find company there. The main place of assembly for everybody was the store, especially on boat day. After the clubhouse was built, there was space for two big Christmas trees, a wing with a pool table off the big room with the beautiful hardwood floor for dancing. The schoolhouse had been a tight squeeze for church, but there was plenty of room in the clubhouse for the Seacoast Mission services.

Everyone liked to read, and books were given as presents and passed around. Some people resented radio as an intrusion into the social customs, but sociability couldn't be killed that easily. As the men talked in the fish houses, telling yarns and arguing politics, the women enjoyed company while they knitted and darned and sewed on children's clothes or their own.

Though there were sometimes disagreements and grievances, they never festered into something serious. The population was too small; they knew how much they depended upon each other, both on land and water. They never had the long, wasteful feuds of some larger islands, where vendettas passed on from one generation to the next, and sometimes even today break out in vicious behavior.

Some "new wave" couples seemed to enjoy the winters they tried; they were all congenial. But they didn't want to make a life of it. Of the native sons, only three had school-age children, who were sent to school at Matinicus and brought home for the weekends. As adults they speak fondly of those winters but, after all, this had always been their "home" as it had been for their grandparents.

The new people weren't looking for "home." All of them already owned or rented places on the mainland. There were working wives among them—not a factor in the era that was passing. Those who came out in the summer with the children (who of course adored it) had worked before, and would work again when the children were old enough. They had talent and ambition, the desire to work, and the need. With the new technology, fitting out a lobster boat with everything a man thought he needed in order to compete became an exorbitant expense. Lobster traps and rope went along with it; everything to do with the business was costly, and everything depended upon how the lobsters behaved—and don't forget the insurance. Children's shoes cost the earth and so did everything else they wore (or wanted).

What If?

Supposing the island still had its constants: a good store and a post office, a regular boat schedule saving the men all the lugging they must now do for themselves. Supposing the school were open, with a good teacher. I think there'd be very few takers, even with the great television reception out there. A few might be willing to take a chance, but even with comforts undreamed of in the first half of this century they would soon be leaving. Twenty-five miles out, a speck of island surrounded by ocean, in winter? It couldn't possibly be home. Most people today aren't bred to it and they don't want to be. They'd be like the newcomers who flee from some larger islands closer to the mainland, and say they loved those places but they couldn't live there. The winters will do it, every time.

The Anderson-Simpson descendants have always hung on until they felt it was their time to quit. Jerry, one who still fishes there, loves it in the winter as much as in summer, but when he and his wife wintered there alone the one flaw was the sense of imminent danger; what would they do if the boat was in trouble out there in the harbor when one of those monstrous winter storms sent seas crashing over the breakwater? In the old days the big dories would be overboard and all the men taking care of the boats if it was humanly possible. But alone is alone, even with modern communications; Matinicus would be ready to help, but what if no boat could make it across? Now Jerry spends the worst winter months ashore, but in February he is wondering how soon he can begin getting ready to "set out" for spring fishing.

The loss of the clubhouse was the death of something which had once been as necessary to the islanders as their store and post office. It meant nothing to the "new wavers," except for a few who tried to help the most persistent islanders to save it. Their efforts weren't enough. The pool room and the dance floor are buried in rubble as if they had been bombed out of existence, destroyed through ignorance and indifference. The building could not possibly have meant anything to those who had not grown up with the excitement of the suppers and the dances, the boatloads coming from Matinicus, the summer people from the occasional yachts in the harbor. With or without them the dances went on to the music of the fiddle, guitars, and accordion playing for "The Lady of the Lake," "March and Circle," "The Boston Fancy," with the little ones jigging on the sides and babies sleeping in their baskets or carriages, and always a pool game going on in the next room. None of the new people had ever appeared in a children's performance here, and clapped wildly for the good sports among the adults who did the comedy sketches in the "shows."

The Criehaven survivors all have their favorite memories of life on their island, but every one of them says, "the dances . . ." in exactly the same tone. "Oh, for one of those hours of gladness," an old song goes about dancing in another place and time. "Gone, alas, like our youth too soon . . . oh, to think of it, oh to dream of it fills my heart with tears."

There is now a stable, if seasonal, population of lobstermen who work well together for the good of their community. It may not be completely Home, but it's part of it; no one can stay there spring after spring, summer after summer, autumn after autumn, and not love it. There are a few summer people of whose affection there's no doubt. There are no development schemes for the woods and bold shores; the Crie lands belong to a family who have preserved the homestead Robert Crie built and the buildings where his family kept the store and post office.

Mike's business premises have long since burned down, though his house still stands on its height and has always been cherished. The fires that happened quite often during the first years of radical change were symbolic of that change in all the previous years of island occupation; the fear of fire was built into every islander from early childhood, and it worked for a century and more.

The schoolhouse survives. The state sold it to a young woman whose father came as one of the new young fishermen. She has had a childhood and youth of Criehaven summers.

But on winter nights one likes to think that the island hasn't been simply left to the everlasting wind and the never-ceasing rote; it's not alone, but richly crowded with ghosts, and everything is happening again on three planes. The *Mary A* is coming into the harbor and Mike is striding down the wharf to meet Stuart and the mail. In school a first-grader is learning how to read, and someone else is working out fractions on the blackboard; or outside there's a game of Steal Eggs, swings squeaking, the older children practicing "Lady of the Lake" so they'll be ready for the next dance, where nobody who knows the steps ever has to sit for long on the bench.

At the clubhouse the eternal pool game goes on, and the dancers are sedately circling in a waltz, or romping down the hall while the fiddle bow dances "The Devil's Dream" and the guitars and accordion keep up with it. The musicians never get tired, and there's never a last waltz.

CRIEHAVEN TODAY

Criehaven today bears little resemblance to what it was one hundred years ago. During his visit to the island in the late 1980s, George Putz felt an air of melancholy: "Two centuries of occupation and the rigorous pursuit of maritime trade are these days reduced to the harbor and a few cottages within a ten-minute walk. The fishermen arrive, set up housekeeping, go out to haul, and haul again and again, and then, come fall, they leave. Life is not all of a piece, and the place is not everything in one's life any longer."

In a 1996 article, Edie Lau of the *Portland Press Herald* described an island greatly changed from its heyday in the early years of the twentieth century: "No one lives year-round on Criehaven, which makes the island one of 29 offshore summer colonies in Maine. But it really belongs in a category of its own, being the only island with a seasonal working community." In 1996, ten lobstermen were fishing the waters of Criehaven from spring through fall. An attractive feature of lobstering off Criehaven is that there's ample space for everyone—"It's not traps on top of traps," according to one lobsterman's wife quoted in the Lau article.

Despite its many differences, life on the island today still retains some of the old ways. "Criehaven houses have no electricity except by generators; few have running water," Lau wrote. "Residents rely on the sky to bring water for washing. They draw drinking water from a town well, toting it home in barrels. The hassles are the hard side of island living. 'Anything that's difficult, multiply it by a factor of two or three when you go offshore,' said Peter Ralston, executive vice president of the Island Institute in Rockland."

The arrival of Richard Krementz in the late 1960s and his ownership of ninety percent of the island carries on "the King Crie tradition of island hegemony," to use George Putz's words. "The infusion of Krementz money has done considerable good about the harbor and interior in the form of a massive new wharf and well-cared-for building and grounds, and no one need be idle if he's looking for paid chores." Approximately ten summer families now share the island with an equal number of lobstermen, and they have achieved a peaceful balance.

CRIEHAVEN REUNION

Criehaven residents from past days share a unique bond. Even though their island life ended years ago, they are still drawn together to share their memories. A group of former Criehaven residents met in April 2000 for their third annual reunion, and Georgeanne Davis of *The Free Press* in Rockland, Maine, was there to cover the event.

> Those who attended the reunion had grown up on the island and recalled the times when there still existed a strong community with regular mailboat and ferry service, a small school, and, eventually, regular flight service from Rockland. For most, it was a day to talk about a time that seems in many ways idyllic, when a small isolated community somehow managed to thrive 25 miles out in the Atlantic. [T]he memories of its heyday belong to the people who gathered to talk about the good—and not so good, say some—old days.

Virginia Wall organized the first such informal reunion for a handful of former islanders in 1997. The guest list has since grown to the thirty people that attended in 2000, ranging from those in their eighties to their grand-children and great-grandchildren. The guests enjoyed a table filled with treas-ured photographs and family scrapbooks, and welcomed island life chronicler Elisabeth Ogilvie.

Lois Anderson, the schoolteacher mentioned in "Last Waltz on Crie-haven," was there, and reminisced about her life spent on islands. Born on Loud's Island, she worked summers as a cook on Monhegan Island while in college, was a teacher on Criehaven during the 1930s, and spent forty-two years on Swans Island.

She arrived at the Criehaven schoolhouse to teach nineteen students in nine grades—sub-primary through eighth—and was paid ten dollars a week plus room and board. True to Elisabeth's depiction of island men courting the schoolteacher, Lois ended up marrying one of Carl Anderson's grandsons. In the *Free Press* article, Davis described daily life on the island during the 1930s:

> Lois Anderson and Virginia Wall were neighbors on Criehaven, their houses separated by only one other home. The two women laughingly recall when, as soon as their husbands had gone out to haul, they met on the sun porch and drank their coffee together. "We just wore out the Sears catalog," Wall says about the time when that was the only shopping available. But there were plenty of good times spent at the clubhouse, the island's community hall, where there were potlucks and dances for the whole family and over a dozen boats rode at anchor in the harbor.

The two friends recalled an elemental way of life, with just one main well for drinking water, shared by the whole island. Each family had to catch water for washing in their own individual cisterns. "There were no phones and no TV, and for a long time, no refrigeration," Anderson told Davis. Gas later became available for lights and refrigerators.

> They had gas-powered washing machines, and Anderson even had a gasoline iron, which operated under pressure, like today's Coleman camp stoves or lanterns. Ultimately the islanders purchased genera-tors and life became more like that on the mainland; but before that time, the women said, if you wanted to preserve something, it had to be canned, pickled or salted.

Lois Anderson often raised chickens for meat, which she canned, al-though lobster and fish were the best source of fresh meat. Many people at the reunion still remembered the profuse supply of berries that grew on the island—raspberries, blackberries, strawberries, and even cranberries—all of which were preserved or used for desserts throughout the summer. Virginia Wall could remember "sitting with a big dish of lobster and one of berries, just waiting for cream to come over on the boat."

The arrival of the mailboat three times a week, twice a week in winter, was a big event. 'Everything you had, you tugged onto that island,' Wall said. The two smiled at the memory of all the women taking their wheelbarrows down to the wharf to pick up the groceries and then trundling them home.

When Anderson went to Criehaven as a teacher in the fall of 1935, Elisabeth Ogilvie was then staying year-round with Dot and Guy Simpson. She recalled that Elisabeth and Dot always enjoyed themselves, including the time that Lois looked out her window and saw the two of them strolling along, all dressed up in funny outfits. When asked about this, Elisabeth remembers that they sometimes dressed up in clothes they found in the attic—"any old mix and match of stuff"—and go out calling. Dot's mother and younger sister would often join them on these outings. Lois also remembers Elisabeth's fondness for her pet goats. She let them roam free until the fateful day that they chewed up Mabel Crie's bathing suit, found on the clothesline. "They were kept penned up after that," Elisabeth recalls with a smile.

Lois spoke fondly of Elisabeth's writing, and noted, "Her descriptions of the island are out of this world. As you read her books, you can follow along the places you go on the island. Although she doesn't use the names, you know exactly where you are."

Anderson's daughter Sally also attended the reunion, as did Wall's son, Richard. The two have very different memories of their time on Criehaven. By the 1950s, the school and year-round community had disappeared, so families lived on the mainland during the year, returning to Criehaven for the summers. Sally Anderson went to school in Rockport, and remembers her regret when she had to leave her friends for the summer. She noticed the difference when she returned in the fall; new friendships had been formed, and they all shared memories and experiences that she had missed while on Criehaven. Sally also disliked doing her school shopping from the Sears catalog, no matter how much her mother enjoyed it.

By contrast, Richard Wall felt that the summers he spent on Criehaven, from ages five to ten, were the best times of his life. For him, school was just something to endure until he could return to the island. He knew from a young age that he wanted to be a fisherman like his father, but his dad urged him to try another way of life. Wall worked for the state for six years, building roads, but soon found it wasn't the life for him. He bought a boat, and his fishing life began. "That was thirty years ago, and his only regret was that he'd never match the sixty year fishing career of his father," wrote Davis.

Catherine Young Simaitis agreed with Richard Wall's estimation of life on Criehaven. She lived year-round on the island for thirteen years after her family moved there from Matinicus. Her grandfather was Peter Mitchell, the talented Danish boatbuilder. Peter Mitchell and his wife are buried in the Criehaven cemetery, where their stones can be seen today.

At the reunion, Ken Anderson proudly wore a T-shirt with the message, "Ask me about Criehaven." Ken has many ties to Criehaven and Dot Simpson, and has become the informal island historian. His great-grandfather was Carl Anderson (Dot's grandfather), and his grandfather, John Anderson, was a lobsterman. His father, Nick, continued the family tradition of lobstering and also built boats. A nephew of schoolteacher Lois Anderson, Nick was also a close friend of Guy Simpson. Dot Simpson's mother and Ken Anderson's grandfather were brother and sister, making Ken and Dot second cousins. Dot and Guy often babysat for Ken when his parents went ashore, strengthening the ties between the two families.

Ken Anderson and Richard Wall were childhood friends. They grew up having the run of the island, and spent hours rowing around in a skiff even though they didn't know how to swim. (Ken didn't learn until he moved to Florida at age ten.) Even though Ken has been away from Criehaven for much of his life, he always maintained his Criehaven ties, keeping in touch with his Aunt Lois. Ken's photographs from his early days on the island are prized, and he enjoys sharing his knowledge of Criehaven history.

A discussion of a return trip to the island took place at this reunion, even as all acknowledged it would be difficult for many of them now. Whether they next meet on the island or the mainland, all remain confident that their affection for Criehaven will bring them together again.

CRIEHAVEN CONNECTIONS

In addition to his ties to the Simpson family, Ken Anderson shares a connection with Elisabeth, having appeared in chapters 2 and 3 of *My World Is an Island*. As a child, Ken was on board his Uncle Rex's boat the day Elisabeth, Dot, and Guy moved to their new home on Gay's Island in August 1944:

> The *Racketash*, thirty-six feet, looked like a giant liner in comparison with Guy's twenty-eight footer, and she was loaded with

household gear and with people. She carried everything with ease.... On that morning, Rex's wife Lois and their little girl Sally were in the cockpit; Nick's wife Hattie and their small son Kenny were there; and sitting in one of our rocking chairs, holding her baby boy Brad in her lap, was Dot's sister, Madelyn Young. (*My World Is an Island*)

After many years away, Anderson returned to Maine in 1994, married a Maine woman, and is now the pastor of Harmony Bible Baptist Church in Spruce Head. While he was being interviewed for the position, one of the parishioners mentioned that she collected Elisabeth Ogilvie's books and loved them. When she discovered Ken's connection to the author, she said, "Well, I guess you'll be a pretty good pastor if you know Elisabeth!" He later arranged for this parishioner to meet Elisabeth, much to her delight.

Ken recalls attending a talk Elisabeth gave at the Jackson Memorial Library in Tenants Harbor in 1996. When someone asked her what drew her to Criehaven, she'd answered without hesitation, "The boys!" and laughed. Then she pointed to Ken and said merrily, "And his father was one of them!"

Lois Faulkingham is another local resident with a special connection to Elisabeth. Although Lois got to know Elisabeth well in later years when she was postmaster for the Cushing Post Office, the two women also share memories of Criehaven. Lois read Elisabeth's Tide Trilogy when she was in her early teens, and immediately fell in love with the Bennett family and their beautiful island. Lois's brother Bob worked as sternman for Dot's brother, Neil, and during her first visit to the island, in 1963, she stayed with Neil and his wife Winnie. Neil would play his guitar and sing in the evenings, and sometimes they would have dances in the clubhouse. Picnics and ball games were regular pastimes. Over the years, Lois stayed with several of the island families and had the chance to experience island life as depicted in Elisabeth's books. She treasures these memories.

Criehaven remains something of an enigma, and a magical place by its very remoteness. It's not an easy proposition to travel there, yet people still do. Some go because of personal family connections—they go to the cemetery, to look for family headstones, or to take a walk down to the Eastern End. Others travel to Criehaven because they love the Maine islands, and enjoy the adventure of traveling to one of the most remote islands of all. And still others come because of the Bennett's Island series, with the pure unadulterated desire to see this legend come to life.

REFLECTIONS ON A TRIP TO CRIEHAVEN

Coauthor Melissa Hayes had the opportunity to visit Criehaven in September 2000. It was the fulfillment of a longtime dream to explore "Bennett's Island."

My husband and I had the privilege of going to Criehaven with *Mug-up* newsletter subscriber Sari Bunker. Wife of Matinicus (Brigport) lobsterman Vance Bunker, Sari intended to visit the island and take photographs to share with other subscribers. Once Sari and I decided to make the trip together, plans firmed up quickly, and Labor Day weekend found us heading over to "Bennett's Island" in a lobster boat.

Sunday morning dawned—the day of our journey to Bennett's. My mind was filled with a tumult of thoughts and emotions. As we walked down to the wharf, my feet barely touched the ground. Sari met us there, along with Vance, who had obligingly decided not to haul his lobster traps that day. We climbed down the slippery metal ladder into Vance's skiff, precariously balancing our camera equipment, and motored to his beautiful boat, the *Sari Ann*. The day was calm, warm, and slightly overcast. As the boat slipped out of the harbor, Sari and I grinned.

As Criehaven came into view, I felt like Philippa, Vanessa, or Rosa, bravely facing my new home. The welcoming arms of the harbor greeted us as we disembarked at the Krementz wharf. The sight of the old store and post office buildings, freshly painted and just as I had imagined them, felt warmly familiar.

Carmen Norton met us almost immediately at the wharf. The caretaker of the Krementzes' rental cottages, Carmen cheerfully greeted us in front of a map she had painted to welcome visitors to Elisabeth Ogilvie's Bennett's Island. The map depicts all the houses (that are still standing) found in the series, and points out where various landmarks are to be found. The cemetery, the Bennett (now Krementz) Homestead, the ice pond, the Eastern End—all were there within our reach.

We were filled with all the expected emotions, and found Elisabeth's words of caution—"Don't be expecting Bennett's Island"—to be unnecessary. It was still Bennett's Island to us.

We saw the Bennett Homestead, the house Robert Crie built, set regally on the hill, and headed in that direction after meandering a bit in

Schoolhouse Cove, finding some "lucky rocks" (the ones with stripes, according to Sari). The schoolhouse is still there—minus the belfry and now converted to a cottage—overlooking Schoolhouse Cove.

Dick and Peggy Krementz were expecting us, and welcomed us into their home. The views from their back deck, overlooking Camp Cove (called Goose Cove in the Bennett's series) and Matinicus Rock, were breathtaking. We were thrilled to see the view from the tower they have added to the house, and the original timbers in the cellar, placed there by Captain Crie's own hands back in the 1840s.

After sharing a mug-up in the main sitting room (a section of the original Crie home), they joined us on our walk around the island. We first visited the cemetery, following a trail through the hushed, solemn woods. Arriving in the cemetery was a powerful experience; one could not help but look for Joanna sitting on the stile, munching an apple—or hand-in-hand with Alec—or mourning his death.

We passed the graves of Peter Mitchell, boatbuilder during the early days of the island, and Carl Anderson, Dot Simpson's grandfather. We also saw the grave of Herman "Papa" Simpson, Dot's beloved stepfather. The Crie graves—set apart from the rest and bordered by a fence—include an impressive monument to Captain Robert and Harriet Crie and the graves of their sons Eben and Horatio. We even found remnants of the original black wrought-iron fence that must have surrounded the cemetery in its early days. A small garden is located in the corner of the Crie family plot. Surrounding the cemetery are lovely tall spruces, though there is no sign of the apple trees that figure so prominently in the Tide Trilogy.

Having paid our respects in the cemetery, we walked back toward the harbor. On the way, we visited Joanna and Alec's house, a Victorian built from plans purchased at the Columbia Exposition, Chicago World's Fair. A grand home, it boasts its own lane leading down to the harbor. This was originally the home of Horatio Crie. The current owner invited us in, and Sari commented that it was easy to imagine Joanna and Alec there. We could see Joanna cooking supper, and looking out the window down the lane, waiting for Alec's return.

On the way to the harbor, we stopped at the village well, still in use today. I couldn't resist drawing up a bucket of cold, clear water, imagining all the Bennetts who had carried water to the house, placing the bucket carefully on the dresser in the kitchen. All Criehaven residents still use the well for their drinking water, and gather rainwater in their own cisterns for washing and bathing. Each house has its own generator for electric power.

All around the harbor are other homes so vividly described by Elisabeth—The Binnacle, Rosa's house, Jamie's house, Mark's and Philip's houses—and the foundation and fireplace that are all that remains of Joanna and Nils Sorensen's place. The anchor, mentioned so often in the series, is all but covered over by beach rocks, the result of years of wave action. Sari and I easily imagined the Bennett boys coming in from a day of hauling, and the mailboat coming around Eastern Harbor Point.

One of the most stirring moments was when we first saw the clubhouse, scene of so many pivotal moments in the Bennett's books. We were surprised to find it still standing, as accounts we had read seemed to indicate there was nothing left but a pile of rubble. On the contrary, the building is still there; leaning, shaky, with the roof falling in, but with hardwood dance floor still intact.

The separate room for the pool table has now caved in, and the kitchen is in similar disrepair, but the fallen state of affairs did not prevent us from imagining what it must have been like in the glory days. We could almost hear the sound of jubilant feet stepping in rhythm to the strains of "The White Cockade," the fiddle and accordion competing with laughter and shouts. One of the Krementz friends who had joined us on our walk vividly remembered attending dances there in the early 1970s, his face alight with the memories.

We next entered the old store and post office, which is filled with beautiful woodwork. Today, it serves as an informal lending library and island museum. The old glassed-in post office is found at the back, with mailboxes still in place. Some still proudly bear the names of the old islanders, including a Simpson or two.

Next we took a stroll down to the Eastern End, passing through the gate and following a path that became well worn with use in the Bennett books. A ruin of Charles and Mateel Bennett's house is perched on a hill, overlooking the water. It is a lonely spot, but filled with the rugged splendor Elisabeth describes.

Off this path to the Eastern End, we found a spot to eat our lunch on some of the tall golden rocks. Facing south toward Matinicus Rock and the open ocean, it was an ideal location to enjoy the burst of sun that appeared, bathing the island in a warm glow. We met some of the other islanders that day, and found everyone to be friendly and warm. Even though the old days are gone and there is no longer a year-round community, we still sensed a spirit about the place—a feeling of camaraderie, shared joy in the island's beauty, and a feeling of deep contentment.

Yes, the island has changed since we met Joanna Bennett here in the 1940s, but such is the power of Elisabeth's writing that, having traveled to the real place, we were not disappointed. The legacy of Criehaven is only strengthened in our hearts. We understand the lasting effect this island has had on Elisabeth, even though we were there for but a single day.

Photographs

All photos from Elisabeth Ogilvie collection unless otherwise noted.

Elisabeth Ogilvie in front of Tide's Way, Gay's Island, in 1990. PHOTO BY DEBBY SMITH

Left: Frank Everett Ogilvie at age twenty-one, in 1905.

Below: Maude Elizabeth Coates on Criehaven in 1906, age twenty-two. Demonstrating her love of theater, Maude dressed as a "Salvation Army Lassie" and posed with Captain Robert Crie.

Above: (Left to right) Allan, Kent, and Gordon with baby sister Elisabeth and kittens in 1917, Dorchester, Massachusetts.

Left: Frank and Maude Ogilvie in about 1939.

Left: Elisabeth, age five, ready for a swim on Criehaven.

Below: Six-year-old Elisabeth dressed for her "Firefly Dance" on December 17, 1923. Written on the back of the photo: "Miss Elizabeth Ogilvie, who will take art in the entertainment under the direction of Miss F. Marie Pentz, for the benefit of the Post Santa Claus party."

Right: The Ogilvie children in 1926, at Quincy, Massachusetts.

Elizabeth, about age seven, dressed in her Scottish Highland dance outfit, Quincy, Massachusetts.

Above: Criehaven in the early 1900s.

Right: Elisabeth on Criehaven in the 1930s. COURTESY OF ERIC ANDERSON

Above: Elisabeth and Guy Simpson on
Criehaven during World War II.

Below: Enjoying a fish fry at Burgess
cove, Criehaven, during the early 1940s.

Dot (with oar), Frank and Maude (in boat), Elisabeth, and brother Kent pushing off from Gay's Island, late 1940s.

Top photos: Dot and Elisabeth making music at Tide's Way, in the late 1940s. Canine friends Smokey and Susan posed with Dot.

Dot, Guy, and Elisabeth alongside Guy's boat, the *Dot 'n' Liz*, on the shore of Gay's Island, late 1940s.

Gay's Island in the 1950s.

Elisabeth's "glamour shot," taken for the *High Tide at Noon* book jacket in 1944, when she was 27 years old.

Right: Elisabeth snowshoeing on Gay's Island in March 1951, during the one winter they lived on the island. This was the most snow they'd had all winter.

Below: Working outdoors on Gay's Island. The barn and Blackie's shed show in the background. Photo taken by Alton Hall Blackington during his first visit to the island, late 1940s.

Dot and Elisabeth on the porch at Tide's Way in 1990. PHOTO BY DAVID BUCKMAN, COURTESY OF MARTHA REED

CRIEHAVEN TODAY

Above: Standing on Dick and Peggy Krementzes' new wharf, looking toward the old store and post office, with the binnacle off to the far right. PHOTO BY SARI RYDER BUNKER

Below: The Homestead, now owned by the Krementzes, was the model for the Bennett family homestead. PHOTO BY SARI RYDER BUNKER

Above: Elisabeth spent her Criehaven summers in this house adjacent to the village well. It was the model for Jamie Sorensen's house. PHOTO BY SARI RYDER BUNKER

Below: The stunning coastline of Criehaven, with the "golden rocks" featured so often in Elisabeth's Bennett's Island books. PHOTO BY SARI RYDER BUNKER

Above: The old schoolhouse, now a cottage, with an outhouse to the right.
PHOTO BY SARI RYDER BUNKER

Below: Schoolhouse Cove. PHOTO BY SARI RYDER BUNKER

Now in ruins, the clubhouse was the scene of countless dances in the Bennett's Island series. PHOTO BY SARI RYDER BUNKER

The path to the Eastern End. PHOTO BY SARI RYDER BUNKER

6 ✖ MATINICUS

KNOWN TO OGILVIE READERS as Brigport, Matinicus is the island most closely neighboring Criehaven, and the largest in a cluster of islands that also includes Wooden Ball, Matinicus Rock, Seal Island, Ten Pound, and No Mans Land. Of these, only Matinicus and Criehaven are inhabited, with Matinicus now having the only year-round population. Twenty miles south of Rockland, the island is nearly two-and-a half miles long and about a mile wide.

Matinicus and Criehaven have always been closely linked. Over the years, islanders from both places have visited the other, coming to dances and social events. Elisabeth talks of going to Matinicus for ice cream, or just to drive around the island, and Matinicus folk came over in droves for the Criehaven dances.

There is some rivalry between the two islands. Monhegan and Criehaven are the only two Maine islands that have a recorded boundary line for fishing, so some touchy situations can develop when traps are set inside the Criehaven lines by Matinicus fishermen. Elisabeth incorporates this history into her novels, making Brigport a key "character" in the Bennett's Island series. As the closest neighboring island, it is a frequent destination of Bennett's Islanders. Likewise, Brigport folk often come over to the Bennett's Island dances, and trap wars between the two islands often cast a shadow over the Bennetts.

A description of Brigport in *Storm Tide* depicts the island in typical Ogilvie fashion:

> Beyond the harbor and its two high points of red-brown rock,
> Brigport stretched its long lean length upon the sea; in the early

morning sunlight, pasture and dark spruce forest and white houses, with great barns, looked across the sound at Bennett's.

In *Gems of the Ocean*, Robert Fillmore describes the island this way:

On the western side the land is low with beautiful, sloping green fields and would remind one somewhat, on approaching, of the outlying islands which are called 'keys' along the West India coast. The eastern shore is rugged and bold, with a picturesque little harbor. The shore is lined with cottages, fish houses and wharves. The breakwater is on the northern side. This part of the island is well wooded with evergreen trees.

Matinicus has white sand beaches that are not only lovely, but are also home to a variety of seabirds. Over the past two centuries the outstanding bird populations have drawn first Native American hunter/gatherers, and later ornithologists to Matinicus and its surrounding islands (see "Matinicus Rock").

EARLY HISTORY AND SETTLERS

Dot Simpson notes in *The Maine Islands in Story and Legend* that Matinicus is translated as "place of many turkeys." *The Dictionary of Maine Place Names* says it's Wabenaki for "far-out island." Another source says it was originally called Manasquesicook, meaning "a collection of grassy islands." Whatever the translation, Matinicus has quite a dramatic history. Dot writes that, among other visitors, "the Vikings may have landed there looking for fresh water; [and] French fishermen were there in the sixteenth century, leaving behind them remains of stone huts."

The first recorded mention of the island is in the 1671 journal of the English traveler John Josselyn, where he wrote that the island was "well supplied with homes, cattle, arable land, and marshes." Others besides Josselyn came to Matinicus, including William Vaughan of Damariscotta, who set up a fishing station there during the years 1725 through 1728. All through the mid-1700s Native Americans came out to the Matinicus archipelago to fish, hunt birds, and collect eggs, in a peaceful manner. By 1757, however, Vaughan's fishing station was gone, and only one family remained on the island—that of Ebenezer Hall. His story is at the core of the intriguing, and somewhat grisly, history of the island.

Ebenezer Hall, of Falmouth (later Portland), had settled on Matinicus in 1750, building a stone house for his second family, which included his new wife, the former Widow Green, and her three children, Daniel, age fourteen, and two girls ages nine and seven. During the time of the French and Indian War, the French paid Indians a bounty for the scalp of every white man they killed. This was a fearful time to be living alone on an island, which the Hall family was soon to discover.

In *Tales of Matinicus Island: History, Lore and Legend*, Donna Rogers reports that Hall added to the tension in 1751, when he and his son killed two Indians who came to the island, burying them in the garden. In 1753 the Penobscot tribe made a formal complaint to Governor Spencer Philips that Hall had twice burned the grass on neighboring Green Island, disrupting their fishing, and warned that if Hall were not removed in two months, they would handle the problem themselves. "He didn't, and they did," Rogers writes, "laying siege to the house one day in June of 1757, killing him and capturing his wife and [daughters]."

The descendants of Ebenezer Hall formed a reunion association in 1906, and purchased a bronze tablet that was set in a boulder near the spot where Mr. Hall was killed. The tablet reads: "Ebenezer Hall. The first white settler on Matinicus Isle, Maine, killed by the Indians, June 6, 1757." That boulder with its tablet can still be seen today, and is featured in Elisabeth Ogilvie's *Call Home the Heart*. This novel is set on fictional Teague's Island, modeled on Matinicus, and captures the proud spirit of its clanlike families.

Ebenezer's son from his first marriage, young Ebenezer, eventually returned to Matinicus, and with his wife raised fifteen children. His wife was from the Young family, and Ebenezer's stepbrother (and fellow survivor) Daniel married her sister. Other members of the Young family also moved to the island, and, Dot wrote, "soon there were so many of them it was said that if you went out and shouted the name 'Young!' from the top of Mt. Ararat, overlooking the harbor, practically everyone on the island would answer."

TRADE AND TRANSPORTATION

Matinicus was originally part of Vinalhaven township, but in 1840 Matinicus Plantation was formed, including Criehaven (then called South Matinicus, or South Island) and Matinicus Rock. There were many successful farms at the time to supply the families with food, but the main industry was cod fishing. Today there are no farms on the island—the islanders are all fishermen, with fast boats and the latest in technology.

In the mid-1800s Matinicus was involved in the West Indies trade, sending ships with lumber, salt fish, and other profitable materials. Rum was a popular drink at the time, and was often brought back among the other goods. These early days of trade and travel bred a population known for its courage. Simpson noted in her history of the island that Matinicus men have always been a brave lot, usually volunteering to fight in the country's wars and not waiting to be drafted.

For one hundred years after Matinicus was settled, there was no regular mail or transportation service of any sort. The self-sufficient islanders made infrequent trips to the mainland when someone was going ashore, and took care of delivering mail and freight then. It wasn't until 1852 that Lewis Ames attempted regular service. A short-lived enterprise, it only lasted one year. Another twenty-two years went by with no organized system.

In 1874 Captain Henry Philbrook began a lifetime of service to the islanders. He made 552 trips with his small schooner *Everett* before exchanging it for the larger *Julia Fairbanks* in 1879. Between 1879 and 1908, Philbrook made another 2,850 trips, not including those that were unscheduled. In 1888, Captain Henry ceased carrying the mail but he and his brother still made trips for another twenty years, using at least three more vessels before retiring.

Captain William Butman and his steamer ship of the same name took over the service in 1897. The *Butman*, as described in Chapter 5, carried the mail for a quarter century until she sank on May 27, 1915, seven miles out of Matinicus on a return trip. The passengers and crew escaped safely in small lifeboats. According to Donna Rogers, in *Tales of Matinicus Island*, "In 1921, the Rockland, Matinicus and Criehaven Transportation Company was formed, and the sixty-foot *Calista D. Morrill* was purchased to make the run. . . . Captain Stuart Ames operated this boat until 1938 when his new boat, the *Mary A*, was commissioned." This ship continued service to the island for several decades, until she was declared not seaworthy in 1978.

Today, the U.S. mail is flown in five times a week to a small airstrip at the north end of Matinicus. (A weathered sign there reads, "Welcome to Matinicus International Airport.") The trip that used to take a day, then several hours, can now be accomplished in just minutes. While there is no longer regular service, the state of Maine provides Matinicus with a state ferry once or twice a month to bring cars and larger freight. And of course, islanders make their own way to the mainland whenever the need arises, either by boat or their own planes.

THE ISLAND COMMUNITY

In *Matinicus Isle: Its Story and Its People*, Charles Long writes, "It is not known for a certainty just when the first school-house was built. The first of which there is any definite record was probably erected not far from the year 1800. It was situated nearly opposite where the church now stands."

Donna Rogers describes how, during the winter term, "sixty or seventy students, some as old as twenty, tended to make life miserable for that one unfortunate teacher." The old schoolhouse could not accommodate the expanding population, so after much debate, the plantation approved funding for a new building, constructed in 1859–60. The school building was then completely renovated in 1900 and equipped for grades one through eight. Older students went to the mainland.

In the 1960s, new state requirements made the schoolhouse obsolete, so a new one was built. "Today [1990], the new school sits by the old one, brightly lit, well heated, with the best of equipment, including three computers, TV, and a talented, enthusiastic teacher." (*Tales of Matinicus Island*). The school population is drastically different from that of the 1860s—with just six students at the beginning of the 2000–2001 school year—but the commitment to the island school is still strong.

The old school building is still used for various functions, including the twice-weekly Emporium held during the summer, which features books, crafts, and baked goods for sale. The building is also home to elections, town business meetings, pet clinics, a periodic medical clinic for school physicals, and other "town father–approved" activities.

The town fathers referred to here are the three assessors elected to run Matinicus Plantation. Also elected at the annual town meeting in April are a three-member school board, a tax collector, treasurer, and town clerk. A Power Advisory committee takes care of the island's power source—three large generators with computerized switch gear—which makes Matinicus the smallest self-generating public power utility in the world.

The Baptists started a church on the island in 1808, and the current Congregational Church of Matinicus was built in 1905, with the Reverend W. H. McBride serving as its first pastor. Ministers from the Maine Seacoast Mission conduct services there now, and usually a minister resides on the island for the entire summer. The church serves as a place for community suppers and social events, in addition to the services, which begin at seven P.M. every Sunday night through July and August, and are open to people of all faiths. The Matinicus cemetery is a picturesque spot surrounded by tall trees;

its headstones proudly bear the venerable old names of the island: Philbrook, Ames, and Young, to name a few.

When asked by an *Island Journal* interviewer why Matinicus is still going today as a year-round community, and Criehaven is not, Dot Simpson had the following reply:

> Matinicus ancestors go way back to the Revolution and before that, even to the Indian wars. There's something grown into them, I think. They are a different breed. You see at the end, Criehaven went and hired all these people to come there and work and then they settled. They were foreigners, actually—Swedes and Irishmen, and so forth. There were French Canadians. When I grew up I listened to more different accents like my grandfather's and grandmother's. I could hardly understand them when I was a little kid because they had such strong accents. But over on Matinicus, they all talked Yankee. I'm talking about what I knew when I was younger.
>
> But on Matinicus the people fish there and work there and their kids keep coming along in the steps of their fathers. They've got all that [common] undivided land on the island. Maybe some of it's been sold here and there but everybody has a little interest in it where it's been undivided property all these years, even if they are one of 95 kids. They say, "My grandfather fished over there and my father and my uncle and I got a right." So even if they don't have a place to build a house or camp, a fisherman like that can come out on a boat and live in the harbor. If they live aboard a boat in the harbor, they go off lobstering their traps and they get to Matinicus that way, you see. Their blood is in there from the beginning.

According to Donna Rogers, the poet Edna St. Vincent Millay visited Matinicus often, and wrote one of her more famous poems about the island. It captures in a few lines the essence of island life and the steadfastness of its people:

The Gut

Having your words and not a word among them
Tuned to my liking, on a salty day
When inland woods were pushed by winds that flung them

Hissing to leeward like a ton of spray,
I thought how off Matinicus the tide
Came pounding in, came running through the Gut,
While from the Rock the warning whistle cried,
And Children whimpered, and doors blew shut;
There in the autumn when the men go forth,
With flapping skirts the Island women stand
In gardens stripped and scattered, peering north,
With dahlia tubers dripping from the hand
The wind of their endurance, driving south,
Flattened your words against your speaking mouth.

—Edna St. Vincent Millay

MATINICUS ROCK

"The Rock: two syllables to stop you in your tracks, hard, uncompromising, final." Dot Simpson captured the mood of Matinicus Rock effectively when she wrote those words. "Thirty-two acres of granite ledge drop off in sheer cliffs on the southerly side, and on the north side is what is euphemistically called The Landing. Boats, which can come in for a landing only when the seas permit, must be hauled up a slip."

Matinicus Rock, located five miles south of Matinicus, is the outermost marker not only for Penobscot Bay, but also for the coast of Maine. A rugged, windswept place, the Rock is home to gulls, arctic terns, and puffins. Ornithologists from all over the country travel to Matinicus Rock in the summer months to observe the puffins—usually from sea, since vessels are seldom able to land in the swells and surf that constantly break over the island.

Around the turn of the twentieth century, Matinicus Island's notable bird population attracted the attention of William Dutcher, who founded the National Audubon Society in 1905. In an earlier post he had "hired lighthouse keepers and islanders to protect the bird population from egg hunters, and from being killed off for the millinery market." (*Tales of Matinicus Island*). Dutcher—and his successor, Carl Buchheister—grew to love Matinicus, and visited often to observe the bird migrations. Today, the surrounding islands of Ten Pound, Matinicus Rock, Seal Island, and No Mans Land all come under direct Audubon supervision.

In *High Tide at Noon*, Elisabeth describes "the foghorn at Matinicus Rock mooing like a disconsolate cow." In 1827 the first lighthouse was built at Matinicus Rock. Made of cobblestones, the building had a wooden tower at each end. These towers were dismantled in 1847, and a granite structure with semicircular towers took their place. Until 1923 there were twin lights that had to be tended by hand; now, only one automated beacon remains. The ground on which the light stands rises fifty feet out of the sea, which makes the tower at its peak an impressive ninety-five feet. Its light is visible for fifteen miles.

The lighthouse station at the Rock used to be tended by families with children. These children grew up in the white houses, surrounded by constant spray from the ocean. They were a stout-hearted lot, running nimbly along the cliffs—as Dot Simpson describes, enjoying their "dangerous but thrilling playground." The annals of the Lighthouse Service are full of heroic deeds, and Matinicus Rock has its proper share.

Abby Burgess is one of those heroines. Dorothy Simpson recounts her brave tale in *The Maine Islands in Story and Legend*. One day in 1856 Abby's father, the keeper at Matinicus Rock, sailed across to Matinicus Island. A sudden fierce storm stranded him there, leaving seventeen-year-old Abby to tend the light. During the next four weeks of roaring wind and crashing waves, Abby kept the lamps trimmed and burning, saved the family's chickens from certain drowning (thereby feeding the family) and took care of her invalid mother and four sisters. Her dauntless courage inspired many, including a fellow lighthouse keeper's son in later years, who married Abby. (A newly commissioned Coast Guard cutter out of Rockland, Maine pays homage to this brave heroine today, proudly bearing the name *Abby Burgess*.)

"With the beginning of World War II, the Lighthouse Service as such ceased to exist." (*The Maine Islands*). The Coast Guard took over, and Coast Guardsmen soon lived on Matinicus Rock where families used to roam. This isolated post was referred to as Alcatraz by some of the Midwestern boys who served there. Dot described a forbidding place: "The wind always blows . . . and with nothing to break the force of the Atlantic, spray can drench the whole ledge like a savage and blinding rain. In really wild storms surf tumbles over it in a flood." The picture makes Abby's dedication seem even more valiant.

7 ❧ LOBSTERING

E‌LISABETH'S FASCINATION WITH lobstermen and their families has led her to explore this way of life in many of her novels, most intensively in her Bennett's Island saga.

Lobstering has been a core industry in the state of Maine ever since the early 1800s. In the early days, lobsters were so plentiful that they were often caught by hand or with a gaff. In the 1820s, a special type of boat called the swell smack evolved, equipped with a tank of seawater for keeping lobsters alive and fresh. The lobster pots at this time were semi-rigid nets, open at the top and shaped like baskets. These were dropped into the water and raised quickly after a lobster crawled in. The lobsters entered a "parlor" on one side and moved back through the interior entryway leading to the other end, called the "kitchen."

Lobster canning became a big business from 1840 through 1880, increasing the demand. Around the turn of the twentieth century, fishermen began converting their dories, skiffs, and sloops to power. By 1930 the typical lobster fishing boat had taken on a classic form and was powered by a gasoline engine. Today, most are diesel-powered.

Around 1830, lobster fishermen began to use rectangular or half-cylinder lath traps. These wooden traps were the quintessential symbol of the Maine coast for the next 150 years. Elisabeth often mentions lath traps in her Bennett's Island series. In a typical passage from *The Seasons Hereafter*, Philip and Barry work on building new gear at Philip's fish house, "listening to the familiar rhythm of trap nails being driven. From Nils Sorensen's fish house came the spasmodic whine of a circular saw as Rob Dinsmore split laths. Nils, Owen, and the island's best mechanic, Matt Fennell, were working on the engine."

During the 1980s, rectangular traps of steel and plastic-coated wire mesh took over. These traps last longer, and do not require as much manual labor for repair and upkeep. Although they are certainly more practical, some would argue that these new traps take away from some of the picturesque aspects of lobstering in Maine.

Trap heads, the mesh inserts, have always been a vital part of the lobster trap, wire or wooden. These heads are laced tautly into the traps, held open with a hoop called a funny-eye. The lobster crawls through this mesh funnel, seeking the bait, enters the trap, and cannot crawl back out to escape. Trap heads are "knit" (netted) by hand from a ball of twine, starting with a loop hooked over a nail. Each lobsterman has his own pattern for trapheads. Dot Simpson was known for her ability to knit both bait bags and trapheads, a skill she kept up all through her life.

Often the women in a family knit trapheads for their men. Vanessa knits for Owen in *The Seasons Hereafter*, and Joanna knits for her brothers and father:

> Her hands were quick and strong, and her knots held. She didn't mind the oiled green twine that was harsh to her fingers. It didn't take long to knit up a ball; she sat by the sitting room window and worked at odd moments, while she was waiting for the men to come down to breakfast or in the few minutes before the dinner potatoes were done. Or she might spend an hour or so in the afternoon while Donna mended, and they would talk. (*High Tide at Noon*).

The independence of the lobstering life appeals to those who prefer to decide for themselves whether they work or not on a given day. They spend long stretches of time on the water, usually working alone. Sometimes they take along a helper, known as a sternman. Lobster fishermen are often stereotyped as independent men-at-sea, but in fact they are part of a very complicated society.

Not only men work their traps and enjoy this independent lifestyle in Elisabeth's books. Rosa joins the ranks of the lobstermen on Bennett's Island, and Elisabeth describes a typical day of hauling for Rosa in *The Summer of the Osprey*:

> Beginning work, she loose-ballasted each dry trap with flat rocks

from the two crates in the stern, to hold it down until it had soaked up and the built in ballast would be enough. She fastened in the stuffed and juicy bait bag and slid the trap overboard, . . . letting the new warp run out and tossing the blue and yellow buoy after it."

Rosa thoroughly enjoys her lobstering life, and more than keeps up with her male counterparts.

Because lobstering is a dangerous job, it demands an individual's full attention. To be successful, a lobsterman has to possess certain technical skills and a willingness to work hard. There are great dangers inherent in this endeavor, and Elisabeth includes in her books terrifying episodes of boats being lost in a storm, or of lobstermen getting a foot caught in a rope and being pulled overboard, leaving their boats to spin endlessly in circles.

Maine lobstermen are prohibited from harvesting lobsters below a certain minimum size or above a maximum legal size. They also cannot take any "berried" (egg-bearing) females. Licensing of lobster fishermen became a law in 1917. Many of the state's lobstering laws were instigated by the fishermen themselves when they formed the MLA (Maine Lobstermen's Association), enabling them to bargain collectively with wholesalers and to protect their resource from uncontrolled harvesting.

Apart from the MLA organization, the most important people in a lobster fisherman's life are the men who fish with him from the same harbor. Often referred to as "the men I fish with," they are much more than that; they are his life and soul. Without them, he would have no mutually recognized fishing territory and no support system in times of trouble. These groups are not recognized by the law of the state, but are supported by an unwritten law of the sea.

Rosa finds this to be true when she moves to Bennett's Island. In *The Summer of the Osprey*, she is told by Mark, "I don't know who'd object to your fishing that handful of traps. We try to keep down to a dozen fishermen here, and we've only got ten now. . . . We've got another rule amongst ourselves, and that is, when everybody starts fishing short warps around the island in the summer, nobody fishes more than two hundred pots." In *High Tide at Noon*, Elisabeth explains that, with the closed season, the men were busier than ever. Their traps had to be brought in, dried out, repaired, and stacked in trim rows around the shore. They brought their boats up on the beach to be painted and overhauled.

As readers have learned in many Ogilvie novels, if a lobsterman places a trap in another group's territory, he can expect swift consequences, such as destruction of gear. Charles enlists the aid of his brothers in *The Dawning of the Day*, when he finds somebody's been fooling around with his traps. Some had been hauled and dumped with the doors left open; some were gone "clip and clean" and couldn't be found at all. Typically, in this instance, the family bands together to help resolve the problem.

George Putz addressed the topic of fishing territory, or privileges, in a 1987 article for *Yankee* magazine, explaining the system observed by the island men of Criehaven:

> One's right to fish within the informal but rigorously maintained Criehaven boundaries is owned, like property. Except for two of the men with old family fishing rights, all of Criehaven's current 11 lobstermen purchased their fishing privileges. [Some privileges come with a cottage, or at least land on which to build, and access to a wharf.] As for fishing territory, it is just as if painted lines existed on the surface of the ocean, even though they exist only in the minds of men. Ends of points, hilltops, lighthouses, and buoys—even particular trees along the shore are lined up one to another to create these extraordinary properties. The system works, and when need be it is enforced by the destruction of invading fishing gear.

Lobster fishermen support each other in emergencies at sea or on land. If one fisherman should have engine problems or run out of gas, other members of the group are there to help. They keep in contact at all times by citizen's band radios tuned to the same channel. This strong sense of community within the lobstering fraternity is part of the spirit of Ogilvie's novels. This is certainly true in *Waters on a Starry Night*, where the men don't think twice about going out to find Lyle Ritchie when he doesn't come in from hauling.

Supporters of the lobstermen often organize benefit dinners, called "mug-ups," when one of their own needs help. Other lobster fishermen may take over when one of their own becomes ill, usually tending his traps and giving the proceeds to the family until he is able to fish again. Within each group, cliques of friends and relatives form. They help one another with jobs that require group effort, such as launching or hauling up a boat or a float, or replacing an engine.

A man is either a good fisherman or a bad one, but only in comparison to others in the local lobster fishing group of that harbor. A hierarchy ranks the fishermen from "highliners"—those who catch a lot of fish and have high incomes—to "dubs," those at the low end of the scale. Lyle Ritchie (*Waters on a Starry Night*) refers to himself as a dub when he is at the lowest ebb of failure. Being known as a highliner can naturally affect the way a person is treated throughout life. Given time, these men can become folk heroes in their coastal fishing communities, and their stories are told for generations. Those men enhance their reputations by having nice homes, new trucks, large and well-equipped boats, and many other objects that are valued in the community. Most of these possessions have symbolic as well as practical value.

Occasionally during the day, lobster fishermen stop their boats to talk on the radio with members of their group; rarely do they chat with men from the neighboring harbor groups. When fishermen meet on the water and want to take a break, they tie their boats together. In *Strawberries in the Sea*, Jamie pulls up alongside Rosa's boat to share a mug-up and a chat, foreshadowing their future relationship.

Lobstering has had its ups and downs over the years, with prices fluctuating depending on supply. As Elisabeth writes in "The Lobsterman's Wife" (printed later in this chapter), no price is really high enough for what the lobsterman does. According to Bob Morrill, of the National Marine Fisheries Service in Portland, 2000 was a banner year for lobster landings. Maine provided nearly seventy percent of the nation's lobster supply that year—more than fifty-seven million pounds, the highest landings ever recorded for the state. The value to the lobstermen was an impressive $187 million—a sharp contrast to the figures discussed in Elisabeth's 1946 essay.

Elisabeth talked about lobstering today in "The Scriveners," (*Down East*, 1994):

> Not much has changed, really. . . . Of course, everything's all wrapped up in technology now— radars, lorans, color machines to watch the bottom with, and VHF radios. All of this makes it so much harder for these men today to keep ahead of their expenses than it used to be. And of course there are many more traps in the water than we'd ever seen in the old days, so the competition is much more intense.
>
> But the basics are still the same. They still go out at dawn with their dinner boxes and thermoses of coffee. They still fill their bait bags, worrying if the seiners caught enough herring for a good supply of bait for tomorrow. They still break their traps over the washrail and hope there are a few counters in them and plenty of snappers for

later in the season. And they still wrestle with the problems that were born with the business: they still get warp caught in their wheels; they still struggle to get untangled if another hurried and perhaps careless lobsterman has set on top of them. And they still get into the occasional trap war.

THE LOBSTERMAN'S WIFE, by Elisabeth Ogilvie

(Originally published in the Boston Transcript, *June 1946)*

She stands at the window, the shadows of the room thick behind her, and looks out into the dusk that grows steadily deeper across the sea. It's a March night, and almost as cold as any mid-winter evening could be. Out on the harbor points the surf gleams and thunders; with her concentrated listening, the thunder seems to grow, the wind is rising, coming in puffs, each puff stronger than the last. Already there's a run in the harbor. The harbor's always bad in a westerly; a man coming in, bone-chilled and tired, has a hard time getting up to his mooring when the buoy keeps bobbing, and the boat keeps rolling in the crisp top-chop.

She turns away from the window, knowing it won't bring him home any quicker to keep watching like this. She strikes a match and the light leaps up, driving the shadows back until they are dancing shapes in the corners of the big kitchen. Then the light settles down to the steady yellow glow in the lamp chimney.

Or if it is from some mainland shore she watches, in a square white house set on some spruce-spangled point, she might snap on a light. But either way, kerosene or electricity, the waiting is the same. So is the constant nibble of anxiety in spite of the fact that he has always come home before. She is the lobsterman's wife.

To us, to all city-dwellers, to the inland people, the lobster is a luxury food. We can either take him or leave him alone. He lies on a bed of cracked ice, waving his claws feebly, and at the moment his price is very large indeed. Most of us walk by without a backward glance. Maybe we snort a little. No need of charging such a price for something that's mostly shell, anyway. . . . But to some of us, even if the cost is prohibitive, the sight of those lobsters lying there calls up a whole chain of associations, a sequence of pictures flashing by, of sights and sounds and smells.

They might have been caught by a fifteen-year-old boy rowing a peapod, running a string of thirty traps; about all his young strength can handle, when it comes to hauling a heavy, water-soaked trap by hand up to the gunnels of his little rowboat. Before the war, if he's got into his teens and gone to lobstering, because he had to stop school and start looking out for himself, he wouldn't be making much. With a great deal of saving, of patching up second-hand gear, he might have enough to buy himself some fairly decent clothes to go to the movies in, or to church, and he'd be able to throw a little into the family exchequer. But if, by luck, he's started his lobstering in war time, he's banking good money out of his thirty pots; he's bought War Bonds, he's filing an Income Tax return. He looks as slick on Saturday night as any prep school lad; and maybe he's planning on getting himself a power boat pretty soon.

This boy was born into a lobsterman's family, he's cut out for lobstering. If he were taken away from the sea he'd be forever half-starved and thirsty, because the sea is in his blood and bones. But he has a glint in his eye, and a cocky tilt to his head, because he's making money. He's conquered the sea. The hard times that his father tells about are over. Impossible to believe that the old man ever had to grub along, catching harbor pollock for bait because he couldn't buy herring, hauling fifty traps before he made as little as seven or eight dollars to feed ten kids that never had quite enough to eat. This boy is the youngest. He doesn't remember those times. He lives like a prince. His bait is rich and juicy herring, the lobsters love it. And the lobsters are crawling as they haven't crawled in years. He has merely to go out on the sea, and he can haul up riches from the bottom. Because he is fifteen, he knows it will always be the same.

The family man—the man whose wife waits in the March dusk, trying not to think of the dozen things that could happen, the fouled wheel, the stopped engine, the riding turn around a man's leg to pull him overboard—the family man knows the hard times. When he is getting seventy-nine cents a pound for the lobsters he brings to the lobster car at the end of the long day on the water, he remembers silently the days that were equally as long and cold, but which seemed longer and colder because his oilclothes were so tattered, and he was burdened with the knowledge that there was only a handful of lobsters to catch, and twelve cents a pound to receive for them. It was a thankless job, enough to make the best of men turn bitter; getting up before daybreak, starting off with his scanty dinnerbox, getting home at dusk, with his handful of lobsters and then his handful of change. And there was no other work for him to do. Even if there were jobs, lobstering was all he knew; to put him indoors was to cage a gull, and he would turn sick and be no good whatsoever.

Sometimes his wife picked cranberries and sold them, made preserves from field strawberries, braided rugs; his children dug clams—and clams weren't the five dollars a bushel they are now. They lived on salt fish, biscuits, turnips, pork gravy; they let their chickens run, because grain was so expensive. They usually managed to keep a pig, and it was the pork that warmed their blood in winter time and kept the children active. His wife knit trapheads for other men who had bigger, better boats and could run longer strings of traps and make more money, so that their wives didn't have to ruin their hands with the coarse, oily, splintery green marline.

He is making money now. He has a better boat, and he doesn't have to worry about how much his engine will stand, because he has a decent engine for a change. His oilclothes aren't cracked and tattered, a new pair of boots isn't a major item. His youngsters don't have to leave high school and go lobstering; they do it because they see the money being made, and there aren't many sons of fishermen who wouldn't swap school for a pea-pod any time. The wife who waits—with as much quiet anxiety as she waited in the old, heartsick, back-breaking times—has new things in her house, the pretty wallpapers and curtains she used to look at in the cat-alog without any hope of having. She has a permanent wave, and she has probably paid as much for her "good" coat as the doctor's wife, or the lawyer's wife, or anyone you can mention. When she isn't worried about the wind rising suddenly, or some other unforeseen thing happening, she can look at the sea and not be ashamed of loving it. The sea is giving something back now. It is looking after its own, royally. Back in the hard days it was a bitter thing to belong to the sea and hate it at the same time. You could not get away from it; your family became a hopeless, vagabond crew with neither pride nor dignity if you took them away from it to try something else. You always came back, but in return for your bondage you were cruelly battered and abused.

Little by little the state of the lobsterman changed. They say there are all sorts of reasons. Here in Maine they say it's the double-gauge law, against which some of the lobstermen argued so bitterly when it was passed. The law said that no lobsters over a certain size, or under a certain size, should be sold. Now, a few years later, the law is bearing fruit. Its fiercest opponents are beginning to admit it.

Others say it's the hand of God, paying the men back for all those barren years. Whatever it is, it has kept up all through the war; and with a true, and almost Godlike, justice, it has kept up since the boys came home. They were called away just as the rich times began; on foreign soil they read the letters from home telling them that their cousin or uncle or neighbor made ten thousand dollars last year. . . . When at last they crawled out of their foxholes, or crossed the frontier of Germany on their way home, they expected with the inbred fatalism of the sea's own that there'd be an immediate slump both in prices and lobsters. But they found out what was really waiting for them.

Along the coast of Maine this winter the hammers have been busy, the new traps, all clean yellow spruce lathes, are rising in stacks beside the fish house doors, the new boats slide off the ways. Weekends the lobstermen come to town, if they're mainlanders; if they're island men they come in their own boats when they think they can afford not to go hauling for a day or so. But it isn't often that they take a day off. There's too much to do before the prices go down and the hauls slack off. The older man who has grown weathered and resigned in his years of thankless toil, the young man home from the war, the boy whose eyes are bright with the sense of his own power and invincibility—you see them on the streets of the coast towns, well-dressed, well-groomed, buying the best from billfolds richly lined.

They deserve it. They know they do. Their work is as hard as it ever was. There's the salting of the bait, there's the baiting-up; the continual lifting and lugging of heavy traps, soaked with water and ballasted with rock; there are the cold and windy days, so many more of them than the warm bright ones; there's the occasional thievery, when traps are robbed, or even cut off, and a man feels as if he is walking a tightrope in the dark because he doesn't know who's persecuting him or why. And there is the future ahead. Except for the boy, they don't expect this Golden Age to last. The bottom will fall out again some day, the price will plummet to twelve cents—or even less. Maybe they'll have something saved this time, though. A better boat, some warm clothes that will wear because they weren't cheap to begin with, War Bonds to cash in, insurance on the children.

The boy will have the hardest time adjusting himself. He will be as helpless as the older ones have been in the past. He will leave his gear on the beach, sell his boat to buy a motorcycle, and strike out to see the country and make his fortune. He will come home again, as surely and certainly as the swallows come across the sea from Africa in the spring. He will curse the ocean, but he won't be able to get away from it. He will marry, and his wife will try to make both ends meet; she will watch and worry from the kitchen windows just before she lights the lamp. There will be children, and he'll think of the fine clothes he bought for himself when he was in his gaudy, triumphant teens, the thirty-dollar jackets, the seven-dollar shirts, the six-dollar gloves. . . .

The cycle will keep repeating itself. There will be a time of plenty again, and he will see his own sons setting a fence around the world and claiming it for their own, and he will know the lesson that they must learn as he did.

The lobsters lie on their bed of cracked ice, and if a lobster can dream, they remember the dark, cold, green depths where they lived, the waving kelp forests where they hid, the rocks under which the male found and claimed his female, helpless in her new soft shell. The people walk by the glass cases, shudder at the prices or at the spiny armor of the creatures themselves. And behind the lobster, in a world so far removed from this glistening city store with its rush of human traffic that it is actually an alien world, like another planet, there lies the richness and the poverty, the tragedy and the gaiety, the triumph and the bitterness, to which we are all heir. In one little-known fragment of the American scene you have all of Life; or rather the essence of it.

And its keynote—its motif—is the shadow of the woman who, through meager times or bountiful ones, is forever watching, straining her eyes through the dusk or the fog or the unexpected snow squall.

I wonder who was the first man who dared to eat a lobster. Doubtless many a woman, when her man is overdue and she can imagine almost anything happening to him, wishes that someone had strangled that daring soul in his infancy. Ask her about the price of lobsters. She will tell you that no matter how high it may go, it will never be really enough.

8 ❧ SCOTLAND AND THE ISLE OF LEWIS

SCOTLAND, THE LAND OF Elisabeth's ancestry, has exerted a powerful attraction for many members of her family. The rich history of this place, filled with conflict and bravery, has inspired much of her writing. Her love for Scotland is second only to her love for Maine; in fact, Scotland's climate, rugged landscape, intricate coastline, and islands remind her a great deal of Maine.

Scotland covers about thirty thousand square miles, including 787 islands, many of which are inhabited only by seabirds. One-third of the people live in the four major cities of Dundee, Edinburgh, Glasgow, and Aberdeen. The Western Isles include the Inner Hebrides, the most familiar of which is Skye; and the Outer Hebrides, including Harris and Elisabeth's favorite, the Isle of Lewis. Glasgow, another city frequented by Elisabeth during her visits, is Scotland's oldest city, dating as far back as 500 A.D.

Visitors sense the special aura of the country as soon as they arrive. It is evident in the granite walls, buildings, and bridges; in the abundance of public golf courses; in high teas and drams of whisky; and in the music of the bagpipes and equally melodious speech patterns. The people of Scotland created their own unique identity over the course of many centuries, made more valuable by the fact that it was so hard won.

FIGHTERS FOR FREEDOM

The Scots have been forced to fight for their independence repeatedly during the past nine centuries. King Edward I of England and his army invaded Scotland in 1286, bringing death and destruction. Leaving a ravaged country behind them in 1297, they also left with Scotland's most treasured possession, the Stone of Scone, on which the Scottish kings traditionally were crowned. (Elisabeth refers to this relic in one of her "Scotland novels," *The Silent Ones*, which teems with the history and geography of this fascinating place. Characters Alison and Ewen are discussing Scottish history when Alison says, "I know about the Stone of Scone. It's under the throne in Westminster Abbey when British royalty is crowned, and it was once kidnapped by Scottish nationalists.") To this day the Stone has never been permanently returned to Scotland.

Despite this failure to retain the Stone of Scone, the Scots have a history of winning against enormous odds. In 1314, Robert the Bruce and his Scots militiamen fought against the English at Bannockburn. Although they were outnumbered, the Scots won, earning them the right to decide their own destiny without interference from England.

Scots fought alongside Joan of Arc in 1429, when she led the French to break the English siege of Orleans. Some of Elisabeth Ogilvie's ancestors joined this courageous battle. The Hundred Years War (1338–1453) brought an even wider division between the English and Scots, which to this day has not entirely disappeared.

Following Robert the Bruce was the brief reign of David II, and then Bruce's grandson, Robert the Steward, became king. This was the beginning of the royal line of the Stuarts. Disagreements with England faded under the rule of James IV; and when he married Margaret Tudor, sister of Henry VIII, the relationship seemingly was secured. However, James then quarreled with Henry and invaded England, only to be defeated at Flodden in 1513. Everything that had been gained at Bannockburn two centuries before was now lost.

Charles Edward Stuart, the son of James Francis Edward Stuart and grandson of James II of England, was born December 31, 1720, in Rome. In 1745, he arrived in Scotland (landing on the Outer Hebridean island of Eriskay), determined to restore the Stuart dynasty to the British throne. A number of Highland clans came to Bonnie Prince Charlie's assistance, helping him take Edinburgh, defeat a British force at Prestonpans, and advance as far south as Derby, England, before being forced to retreat.

In April 1746, however, his forces were utterly routed at Culloden, where Bonnie Prince Charlie and his Highland army of Jacobites fought bitterly against the British. In this famous bloody battle lasting less than an hour, the Highland clansmen, greatly outnumbered by government troops, were slaughtered in a fierce round of musketry gunfire.

Bonnie Prince Charlie was a fugitive for more than five months, but the Highlanders never betrayed him, and he escaped to France in September 1746. For a number of years, Charles Edward wandered about Europe. Secretly visiting London in 1750 and in 1754, he attempted without success on both occasions to win support for his cause. In 1766, on his father's death, Charles Edward returned to Italy, where he spent his last years. He died in Rome on January 31, 1788.

Since 1745, Scottish history has been intertwined with English history, and even now many Scots still painfully recall the unnecessary cruelties and vindictiveness inflicted by the English. There have been several movements for Scottish nationalism, and a temporary parliamentary success in the 1960s. Today Scotland has its own Parliament, and support for the monarchy is said to be declining.

THE OUTER HEBRIDES AND LEWIS

Before ever visiting it in person, Elisabeth explored Scotland through detailed research, in an effort to understand its history and its claim on the hearts of her family. She has always felt it unnecessary to physically visit a location in order to write about it, believing that one can gain an understanding of a place by careful reading and intensive research. In "Speaking of Magic Carpets" (*The Writer*, September 1981), she advised fellow writers about how to write about that magical "Other Place," confiding that she spent years accumulating information about Scotland:

> Scotland was the Other Place for me, and I was a long time getting ready for a trip I wasn't positive I'd ever be able to make... I had gathered so much material over the years that, when I did get there, my chief surprise was that Scotland looked just like its pictures. From all my collecting I knew a good deal about the Isle of Lewis before I ever set foot on this rugged island off the western coast of Scotland. I'd begun reading up on it when I found that my great-grandmother came from there.

Elisabeth's first actual visit to Scotland in 1979 was the fulfillment of a longtime dream, and Dot was pleased to accompany her. They made the journey on the *Queen Elizabeth 2*, a passage of several days, as Elisabeth has never had any desire to travel by airplane. They enjoyed the trip immensely.

Traveling with an affable driver and guide (with whom they became good friends), Elisabeth and Dot spent five months touring the country, including an extended stay on the Isle of Lewis, home of Elisabeth's great-grandmother Peigi MacLeod.

The islands of Lewis and Harris are connected, although they are usually described as separate; perhaps this is due to their stark differences. Their combined size is 825 square miles. Harris is mountainous and rocky, and Lewis, just thirty feet away across a small connecting bridge, is larger, flatter, and sometimes described as less scenic. This certainly is not Elisabeth's opinion; she loves its rugged, dramatic compositions of sea, sky, and land, with long stretches of sand along the Atlantic—so reminiscent of her beloved Maine.

Stornoway, the capital city, is the commercial center of the islands. Weaving, farming, and fishing are the major occupations of its population of twenty thousand. Fishing estates on Lewis include complete river systems and chains of lochs. The world-famous Harris Tweed is manufactured on both islands, but more is made on Lewis due to the greater percentage of the population employed in its production. Tourism is a significant part of the island's economy today.

The islands of Harris and Lewis are just a part of the Outer Hebrides, which also include the islands of Eriskay, South and North Uist, Benbecula, and Barra. The Outer Hebrides are a Gaelic stronghold, and have captured Elisabeth's imagination like no other part of Scotland. The three-mile-long island of Eriskay is where Bonnie Prince Charlie landed in 1745. It was on twenty-mile-long South Uist that he sought refuge after the Battle of Culloden. From this island he was rescued by Flora MacDonald. (This area is vividly portrayed in Elisabeth's novel *The Silent Ones*.) Some lobstering is done on North Uist (seventeen miles long), and a lighthouse stands on the head of ten-mile-long Barra. Benbecula, the smallest island at seven square miles, means "Mountain of the Fords" in Gaelic.

Fifteen miles from Stornoway, Callanish is home to the dramatic Standing Stones, another source of inspiration for *The Silent Ones*. The stones stand as high as twelve feet and are arranged in a circle around a taller central menhir. The Callanish stones stand higher than they did before encroaching peat was dug away in the 1850s, as it was from several other stone circles nearby, all clustered around Loch Roag. Speculation about their likely astronomical purpose continues. While they are no longer considered "false men" turned to stone by some magic spell, they are still enveloped in a mystery that stretches back more than four thousand years. This mystery clearly intrigued Elisabeth, and she set out to explore it in her novel.

In a profile for *Maine Life*, Anne Tirrell-McLaughlin asked Elisabeth about her thoughts after visiting Lewis. "The Standing Stones of Lewis just shout for a Hebridean suspense novel," Elisabeth told her. "When I first saw pictures of the Standing Stones, I knew that I wanted to use them and their mythology. And of course I gathered more material on the spot." Sure enough, from those six weeks in the Outer Hebrides, a suspense novel emerged.

JENNIE COUNTRY

After their stay on Lewis, Elisabeth and Dot crossed Scotland to visit Ogilvie country in Angus, on the North Sea, and found it was also the land of Dot's family, the Simpsons. They then returned to the West Coast and spent a month in the seaport hub of Oban, exploring every corner possible, by car, train, and ferry. "*Jennie About to Be* was another flower of that spring and summer in Scotland," says Elisabeth.

The Jennie books (described in Chapter 15) represent some of Elisabeth's most well-loved work. This series explores the life of a young woman who marries, moves to Scotland with her husband, and ends up emigrating to America in the early 1800s. Elisabeth's exhaustive research on Scotland, its people, and its history greatly enriched the series.

She included many real Scottish locations in the Jennie books. The vista of Ben Lomond, a mountain with spectacular views from its 3,200-foot summit, is part of *Jennie About to Be*. Another setting is the Strath Naver, located across the northern tip of Scotland toward the West Coast. This lovely area had a stormy history during the Highland Clearances—when small farmers and their families were forcibly evicted from the land—evoked so powerfully in *Jennie About to Be*. To the south is the port of Ullapool, where many Scots embarked for North America during those Clearances.

Farther south on the mainland is the Forest of Glenmoriston, where the Redcoats searched in vain for Bonnie Prince Charlie after the battle of Culloden. Fort William is another important setting in the first Jennie book. It was from this town that Jennie and Alick sailed on the *Paul Revere* to America. Nestled at the base of Britain's highest peak, Ben Nevis, Fort William was established as a line of garrisons to control the Highlands in the seventeenth century. It is now a town of Victorian-era buildings, with the old forts demolished and new accommodations built for the railroad in 1864.

Jennie and Alick do more than just explore the Scottish terrain during their journey to the New World. Elisabeth also used these characters to bring to life many essential aspects of the Scottish identity, including the tartan.

The tartan—the first recorded mention of which dates to the thirteenth century—is thought to have originally denoted where the wearer lived, rather than the family name or clan. The clan system derived from the Gaelic definition of family, and at last count there were eighty recognized clans. The kilt did not become popular until the reign of George IV during the 1820s. Before that time, the tartan was worn wrapped around the body in lengths of up to sixteen feet; in the early days, it had to be removed before battle.

Elisabeth dramatically conveys the importance of "the plaid" during her account of Jennie and Alick's trek across Scotland. It affords them protection throughout their journey, serving as both clothing and blanket: "The warmth was delicious; even her feet, tucked in under the plaid, were warm . . . the way she felt now she could have lived as cozily in the plaid as a snail in its shell; but they would have to use it as a blanket tonight."

THE PULL OF SCOTLAND

Scotland didn't only inspire *The Silent Ones* and the Jennie series. It also served as muse for a suspense novel, *The Devil in Tartan*, and a young adult book, *Too Young to Know*.

During Elisabeth's second trip to Scotland, in 1986, she first visited the moors of Culloden, site of the famous battle. Elisabeth and her brother Gordon had both long been intrigued by this place and its history, knowing that Ogilvie ancestors had fought here. Their research into this period of history found its way into *The Devil in Tartan* and Gordon's historical romance novel, *Jamie Reid*.

She also traveled to Castle Urquhart, on the shore of Loch Ness. Now a dramatically picturesque ruin overlooking the bay, the castle was destroyed after the early Jacobite Rising of 1689. This is the spot famous for sightings of the Loch Ness Monster, and Elisabeth took her turn searching for the creature. She was ultimately disappointed in her quest for Nessie, but still ponders the idea of having a future heroine actually see the Loch Ness Monster.

In the spring of 2000, Elisabeth made her third trip to Scotland. Before her departure, when asked if she could believe she was going to Scotland again, she answered, "I won't believe it till I'm aboard the ship. My father would always say, 'If all goes well and nothing breaks water by the shingle'— the shingle meaning the beach in Nova Scotia. I realize now what that meant: it might look clear going in, but something could still happen later on."

Elisabeth didn't realize the hidden portent in her words. She traveled alone to Scotland via the *QE2* in May 2000, but her trip was cut short by a fall in Glasgow. After just two days in that city, she tripped and fell, breaking both legs. She ended up on the eighth floor of the Glasgow Infirmary for two weeks, then endured a flight in an airplane, something she had never intended to do. Accompanied by attendants, she was flown home to Maine and taken to a care facility in Rockland, where she received intensive physical therapy. With her resolute Scottish spirit, she undoubtedly dreams of returning to Scotland again someday.

PART III

Her Writing Life

"I would rather write than do anything else"

9 ❧ HER CAREER

SIXTY-FIVE YEARS HAVE PASSED since Elisabeth Ogilvie published her first short story about Bennett's Island. Her readers fell in love with the island and its people from the very first page, and have followed these characters through years of adventure, triumph, and tragedy. From the opening lines of *High Tide at Noon*, the reader has no doubt what the central presence in the story will be:

> The Island lay very still under the clear golden light of a mid-summer noon. The whole world was bathed in a windless silence, steeped in warmth. Yet the air, alive with a peculiar clarity, had a sparkling edge.

From the first novel, Elisabeth's powerful descriptive abilities were evident. Her understanding of background was implicit in every passage she wrote. In these early books she conjures her setting out of tall spruce trees and sea spray, strengthened with the cry of the gulls and the sound of boats in the harbor. Before long, the island stands in front of the reader as a fully formed character, whether limned in sunlight or wrapped in fog.

With her debut at age twenty-seven with *High Tide at Noon*, Elisabeth was on her way, with no idea of what was to come. The Bennett's Island series has since extended over five decades and eight more novels, bringing both critical acclaim and the devotion of thousands of readers.

Critics and readers alike had much praise for *High Tide at Noon*. David Tilden of the *Weekly Book Review*, wrote, "The book has a vigor and substance which would do credit to an author with a long string of titles to her credit." The *Christian Science Monitor* concurred, praising "the staunchness of

Joanna . . . the quality of the style, the beauty of the description of island scenery, and the gusto of the life [portrayed]. . . . " Margaret Wallace of the *New York Times Book Review* wrote, "Miss Ogilvie's writing . . . has a warm and homespun quality which suits her story well. There is an honest smell of salt and seaweed in it."

It didn't take long for Elisabeth to write the second installment of the Bennett's series, *Storm Tide*, which was published just one year later, in 1945. This novel received critical praise and won two awards: the New England Press Association Award for Best Novel in 1945, and the Northeast Woman's Press Association Award in 1946. Her agent Donald MacCampbell was correct in his prediction that people would want to know more about this family. Elisabeth herself was eager to discover what they would do next. The adventures of the Bennett's Islanders continued in *The Ebbing Tide*, the third book in the series, published in 1947.

From the beginning, Elisabeth remained true to her ideals: to capture the essence of island life, creating a setting completely interwoven with the spirit of its people; and to write about families experiencing real life. Elisabeth put it simply when she said, "The island has made its people what they are."

When asked recently to describe her feelings about her first novel, Elisabeth responded, "I think I did a pretty good job of putting a family together that would last. Of course I can see my youth in it—mine and Joanna's." Elisabeth would continue to grow with Joanna over the course of nine Bennett's books in the next half century, their shared initial innocence turning to wise-eyed, knowing smiles.

IN LOVE WITH LANGUAGE

Elisabeth has always been in love with the English language. Even as a child of six, she felt a fascination for words—a line of poetry, a verse from a hymn—and the responses they evoked in her:

> I had such an infatuation with words, the looks and sounds of them. . . . Certain lines of poetry retain for me the original glory with which they burst upon a child. "What was he doing, the Great God Pan, down in the reeds by the river?," and there's "October's bright blue weather. . . ." I was absolutely enraptured with lines from the Psalms: "And he shall be like a tree planted by the rivers of water, that bringeth forth his fruit in his season." What did it mean? At six I didn't really know, but I did know that it was rich and beautiful. You

know what it's like. Our memory banks are stuffed with ravishing treasures collected by our five senses.

Certain hymns she loved as a child provided an endless source of delight. Her intense imagination heightened her joy while listening to favorites, such as "Holy, holy, holy; / All the saints adore thee; / Casting down their golden crowns / Around the glassy sea."

I remembered how, when I was little and we sang that hymn on Sunday mornings as the choir came in, I used to have a picture of all the saints, dressed in beautiful robes like the figures on icons, sitting around a glittering sea in high-backed chairs, like the ones on the church platform for the minister and the deacons; and at a given moment they all took off their tall golden crowns and cast them into the sea.

Inspired by the sound and texture of words and the images they awakened, Elisabeth was compelled to write at a very young age. From her earliest years, she was an avid reader, ever expanding her knowledge of literature, characterizations, and writing styles. Reading was a natural bridge to writing her own stories.

She loved stories of all kinds, and reveled in the act of describing and setting a scene. As told in Chapter 3, she began to hone her craft while a student at North Quincy High School. Her experiences on Criehaven provided her with her muse, one that inspires her work to this day. By the time she was fifteen, Elisabeth knew she was destined to spend her life as a verbal alchemist, turning simple syllables into pure gold.

Her innate talent molded by years of diligent study and practice, she stands capable of creating a setting so vivid that the reader is transported there. And having experienced this world, the reader craves a return visit— once is simply not enough.

HER BODY OF WORK

Elisabeth has written forty-six books to date. Of these, nine make up the Bennett's Island series, with the final installment, *The Day Before Winter*, published in 1997. She wrote five general fiction books during the early years of her career, including one novel set on Matinicus ("Brigport" from the Bennett's series) entitled *Call Home the Heart* (1962), and another, *Waters on a Starry Night* (1968), set on Gay's Island.

So strong was her affection for her home on Gay's Island that she agreed to write a book about her early years there. *My World Is an Island* (1950) is a loving memoir of her life with Dot and Guy Simpson in the 1940s. The book glows with affection and humor, and is filled with people and animals that were dear to her.

Elisabeth indulged her delight in the mystery genre when, beginning in 1956, she left the Bennett's Island setting sporadically to create a collection of suspense novels, beginning with *No Evil Angel* (1956) and ending (for now) with her most recent, and one of her favorites, *When the Music Stopped* (1989).

Fifteen Ogilvie books are juvenile novels, including four set on Bennett's Island. Consisting of *Whistle for a Wind, How Wide the Heart, The Young Islanders*, and *Ceiling of Amber*, the Young Bennetts series is peopled with many of the characters from the adult series. Another four of her juvenile books were published by Scholastic Books as part of a popular Young Love series in the 1980s.

Elisabeth explored the world of historical fiction and celebrated her love for her family's ancestral homeland when she began her Jennie series in 1984. *Jennie About to Be, The World of Jennie G.,* and *Jennie Glenroy* follow Jennie from the Scotland of the early 1800s to a shipbuilding town on the coast of Maine. *Readers Digest* has produced a condensed version of *Jennie About to Be*, increasing the book's readership tremendously. Down East Books will publish the eagerly anticipated fourth book in the Jennie series, as yet untitled, when that manuscript is complete. Many of Elisabeth's books have also been published in England, and some in France.

Her writing hasn't been limited to just novel-length work. During her years at North Quincy High School, she wrote many short stories for *The Manet*, and early in her career she wrote short stories for national magazines. This was the training ground for her work as a novelist. Although she hasn't written as many short stories as she'd like, the ones she has produced have been well received.

Elisabeth also wrote five articles on the process of writing for *The Writer*, the oldest magazine for literary workers, founded in Boston in 1887. Here she shared her wisdom on such topics as the importance of exercising your imagination, putting yourself in your protagonist's skin, creating a believable atmosphere, and perhaps most meaningful to her, the incredible significance of "background," which she calls "the most important character."

FICTION INTO FILM

In her long career, Elisabeth has had two brushes with the world of film. One of these was the novelization of a movie script, *Honeymoon*. An RKO movie released in 1947 starring Shirley Temple and Franchot Tone, *Honeymoon* was created from a story by Vicki Baum and a screenplay by Michael Kanin. Elisabeth was asked to write the novelization of this funny, romantic story, set in Mexico City, about a love-struck teen and a military man. Elisabeth's agent MacCampbell signed her for this job—a "quick and easy" source of income, says Elisabeth, and the only assignment of this type that she ever took on. MacCampbell was involved in the romance paperback field as well, but that was a genre that did not interest her.

In 1957, the British film company J. Arthur Rank made an eighty-minute black-and-white film version of *High Tide at Noon*. The movie starred British actors, including Flora Robeson and John Haywood, and was filmed at North West Cove, Queensland, Nova Scotia. The screenplay by Neil Paterson retained much of the original story, although it did change some key components, including the Bennett name (Mackenzie in the film).

High Tide at Noon was shown at the Cannes Film Festival and received very good reviews. A showing was once arranged at the Beacon Hill Theater in Boston, and Elisabeth planned to see it there, but at the last minute it was canceled and replaced by another film. Elisabeth didn't see it until years later, and although she was not overly impressed, she did remark that, "It was fun to see my characters walking around. They hired English actors who attempted Maine accents—very amusing." Elisabeth feels that it would be difficult for her to see her work translated into film by any director and actors, as the characters are so real to her. She has envisioned them to be a certain way, and they have inhabited her imagination for a lifetime. It would be impossible for any film company to re-create this world to her satisfaction.

ELISABETH AND HER PUBLISHERS

Elisabeth enjoyed a warm relationship with her first publisher, Thomas Y. Crowell of New York, which published the Tide Trilogy. In the early days of her career, many publishing firms were still small, informal, and family owned. Elisabeth's relationship with Thomas Y. Crowell Company was so casual that the publisher, Bob Crowell, invited her to Connecticut to meet his family, and personally escorted her to the photographer for the dust jacket photo. Elisabeth remembers, "Bob took me to the place to have the photo done—the same place where all the movie stars had theirs' done—and guess what? I turned out looking like a movie star!" This photo, which graced the dust jackets of her earlier books, is shown in the photo section following p. 84.

After her first three books were published, MacCampbell moved her to the McGraw-Hill Company. For the next forty years, McGraw-Hill published all of Elisabeth's books, beginning with *Rowan Head* in 1949, and ending in 1989 with *When the Music Stopped*, the last Ogilvie book released before McGraw-Hill decided to stop publishing general fiction. Elisabeth was always happy with the services McGraw-Hill provided.

During the 1940s, publishing was quite different from what it is today. "I was lucky to be starting out then," Elisabeth says. "There were still a lot of publishing houses and a good market for fiction. Many of them were willing to take a chance on a new author, on a book that would probably only sell a few thousand copies at best. They'd invest a lot of time in you, a lot of personal attention in trying to help you develop. One of my editors was Edward Aswell, who had worked with Thomas Wolfe. He took me to lunch at the Harvard Club. I was very young, and hugely impressed.

"All that has changed. Most of the old publishing houses have been eaten up by big conglomerates. It's much harder for a young writer now." Elisabeth recognizes the advantages of having an agent these days. Now represented by Watkins Loomis Agency, Elisabeth appreciates having her agent handle contract negotiations, copyright renewals, and myriad other details related to getting her books successfully published.

After McGraw-Hill ceased to publish general fiction, Elisabeth was left still holding her manuscript for the third Jennie book, *Jennie Glenroy*. After some searching, she signed with Down East Books of Camden, Maine. Down East published *Jennie Glenroy* in 1993, and *The Day Before Winter*, the ninth Bennett's Island book, in 1997. Down East Books has also published paperback reprints of many of her formerly out-of-print books, such as the Lovers Trilogy (*The Dawning of the Day, The Seasons Hereafter,* and *Strawberries in the Sea*), *The Summer of the Osprey*, an updated edition of *My World Is an Island*, and the first two Jennie books. In addition to publishing the fourth Jennie book, Down East Books is looking into reissuing the Young Bennetts series.

HER ROUTINE

After many years of writing for publication on a daily basis, Elisabeth has her morning routine well established. She has always been an early riser, unable to sleep past four or five o'clock in the morning, and she says that she does her best writing in these early hours of the day, "before the world gets at me." She writes for several hours, usually finishing her work by noontime. This leaves her afternoon free for exercise, gardening, taking a walk, or visiting with friends. "I'm not a recluse. People drop in, and—I'd just as soon be sociable, up to a point. I don't really know how to say this— lots of times I've seen someone coming and I'll think, oh gosh! But afterward, I've enjoyed it. The only thing is, when I'm working on a book I want to really concentrate on it; I don't want to do anything else."

When she is at her mainland home during the winter months, she gets up early, has a cup of coffee, and sits at her table by a big picture window. She watches the lobster boats go out to haul, knowing each fisherman by name. She writes at this table each morning, often listening to classical music on the radio. When the music doesn't suit her, she puts on a tape. If she decides to write more in the evening hours, which happens occasionally, she props herself up with pillows on the couch and writes there.

"I set aside a certain time period each day to write," she says. "You have to schedule it; otherwise, the daily routine will eat up all your energies. For young authors just starting out, that's particularly important," she adds. "A lot of times you won't feel like writing, won't have any ideas. You have to make yourself do it. You can always revise what you've written, or even throw it out. The important thing is to keep writing."

In addition to writing for about five or six hours each morning, Elisabeth may find time during the day when she will write down thoughts that have come to mind. She has several yellow legal pads scattered all over the house, on which she writes in longhand—and often the one she's carrying around with her contains scenes from three different books. Of course, when necessary, she'll scribble notes on any paper that she has at hand. "Sometimes the notes are pretty cryptic. If I don't get back to them quickly, I can have difficulty trying to figure out what I meant," she admits.

While working on her latest book, the fourth in the Jennie series, Elisabeth has compared her writing process to "quilt blocks, being put together very carefully by hand, on pieces of yellow paper." She always starts with a rough outline and knows how she wants it to end—lessons learned early from her first agent, MacCampbell. After that initial phase is completed, "It's just a matter of fitting things in, as they should go together."

After writing the first draft by hand, Elisabeth types her manuscript using an old Royal manual typewriter—no computer for this writer. She tried using an electric typewriter once, but it wasn't a good fit: "I sit and look out the window a lot—I think, I wait and meditate—and I could hear the darn thing running, so it made me nervous to use up all that current and not do anything with it. So with the old Royal—why, it's just a couple of old friends together, I guess."

One typewriter isn't enough, however. On one of their trips to Scotland, Elisabeth and Dot rented a studio apartment in London for a month. Elisabeth had a deadline on a juvenile book at the time, so she bought a little Japanese typewriter for thirty-six pounds in a stationery shop. In an article for *Maine Life* in 1980, she referred to it as "inscrutably Japanese with a Cockney accent." That typewriter now lives on Gay's Island.

When writing on the island, Elisabeth keeps to a similar routine. She gets up early, usually before five o'clock, and writes at the porch table, or outside with the typewriter perched on the wheelbarrow:

> In the years when there was always somebody else in the house at summertime, [Dot and I] wrote all over the place. I had a couple of favorite sites in the woods to which I'd lug my typewriter and paper, escorted by a cat or two. . . . We built a twelve-by-fifteen-foot office on the shores of the Gut for an indoor workplace where everything could be left spread out. Now it's a favored spot for certain guests to sleep.

Patricia Morgan described Elisabeth's outdoor writing routine in a 1985 article for *Down East*. She strolled with Elisabeth on the well-trodden Gay's Island paths:

> Soon we're in a grove of pines, with red-brown needles cushioning our steps, and the silence seems even deeper, yet comfortable; familiar. In a fern-filled clearing Elisabeth pauses. "This is one of my writing places," she says. "There should be—yes." From under a moist clump of ferns she drags forth a lichened board, places it atop two rocks, and indicates a tree-stump bench. "All the comforts!" she smiles.

HER PROCESS

Elisabeth discussed her writing process in detail in "Speaking of Magic Carpets" (*The Writer*, Sept. 1981).

> I always work out my story in outline, but I don't use up my impetus by making it too elaborate. My outline is bare-bones to begin with, and the details can be rearranged later on. I always have a few

big scenes in mind when I start the work. More will develop as momentum builds up, and one good idea leads to another.

So I have a beginning, some high points, and an ending, and the challenge is to get from start to finish with the most entertainment possible along the way. I have absorbed enough from my reading to fit my story roughly into its frame of reference, but I don't get hung up on the details that are not already in my mind. (There's always something you'll have to hunt for, no matter how thoroughly you think you've prepared.)

I skip over the gap, but I make a note of it in big letters in the margin: FIX. I'll get back to it. Meantime, my characters must move on, even if at that point we ignore the way they travel into the next scene. Anyway, I'll have plenty of time later to hunt up the missing facts and work out the details.

I tend to write in clusters of related scenes, rather than in chapters, and as I begin each new chapter, I outline the action in detail so that the people, events, and places will all mesh into the hoped-for result—a smooth lead into the next part. I leave off for the day while the work is going well, often in the middle of a paragraph or even of a sentence. Then I can go right on with it the next morning and be into a scene with my first swallow of hot coffee.

Elisabeth has a specific strategy for handling the next phase of the process. She doesn't read her first draft right away when it is finished. That would lead to immediate rewriting, which she considers "fatal to the momentum." Even though her first draft is often a "miracle of incoherence," covered with notes in the margin and red ink everywhere, she puts it away and leaves it for several days while she goes on to non-writing tasks such as gardening, cleaning out closets, beachcombing, or just taking walks. These physical tasks refresh and prepare her for the next stage of her writing process, when she edits and revises.

Soon she can't wait to get started on writing the second draft. At this point, she breaks it into chapters, considering each one as a separate entity.

I'll write the missing parts and revise some of the already-written work. I'll check for the overuse of certain words and replace them from my thesaurus. Most of all I'll be incorporating the missing research material, fleshing the bare bones into vivid and vigorous life. The people of the book are going to see, smell, hear, and feel everything that I would be seeing, smelling, hearing, and feeling if I were there.

This all takes time, and when I reach the end, I'm so tired of words, I can't even bear to write a letter. But usually, within a week or so, I can't leave the manuscript alone. For the third reading I'm equipped, I hope, with coldly professional vision. Now I can see where the action is impeded by the weight of too much detail, too much local color, or where I sound like a guidebook or a character is spouting away like a reference book. There is a more natural way to get those facts across. . . . I also see where scenes can be enhanced by more atmosphere rather than less, and I still change words, checking with the dictionary and the thesaurus.

Elisabeth so loves her craft that she cannot limit herself to just one story at a time. She always has two or three stories in her head at any given moment, and at least one "on the back burner," ready to dive into when she has finished her current project. She joyfully anticipates working on each of these story ideas.

Working on several projects simultaneously means she had to devise a system to organize them effectively. Her solution: one storage box for each book to hold all her notes and reference material. She finds it no more difficult to keep track of each story line, with its multiple characters and plots, than to keep straight all of the families she knows in real life—although to imply that her characters aren't real is perhaps a disservice.

Dot helped Elisabeth develop her ear for authentic regional dialogue, and was always ready to confer with Elisabeth on the authenticity of background or island culture. During their many years together on Gay's Island, Dot would type Elisabeth's manuscripts and offer relevant feedback during the editing process. She would even run interference when it came to visitors, ensuring that Elisabeth would not be disturbed when she was immersed in her writing.

Elisabeth does indeed become thoroughly involved with the people she's writing about. When asked the obvious question of whether her characters come alive for her and become friends, she answers with a resounding "Yes." It is not surprising that the creator of these characters feels this way, when countless letters from readers echo the same sentiments—they feel that they intimately know these people and become involved in their lives.

Unlike some authors, who have a freer rein with their characters and often let the story develop as it goes along, Elisabeth is usually pretty sure of where each of her characters is headed; however, "sometimes they take unexpected twists in the road to get there. Minor characters might have some surprises, too." Elisabeth becomes fascinated with all of her characters: "The Bennetts weren't the only ones. Some books were more difficult to write, and I'm very proud of them because they had more ticklish places in them, and needed more imagination. The Bennett's books seemed to write themselves, as many of the characters and events were based on real-life ones."

GROWTH OF HER WRITING

While the essence of Elisabeth's work has remained the same—books about good people and their struggles in life—her scope has broadened since her first work. Although she'll always be best known for the Bennett family and their island, Elisabeth Ogilvie has proven herself equally skilled in other settings and genres, such as her historical Jennie series set in Scotland, and her mystery/suspense novels set in various locations, including suburban towns. Whether Elisabeth sets her novels on the rugged coast or the busy streets of a city, whether her characters are in a lobster boat or a chaise-and-four driving in a park—before long, she transports the reader to that locale.

Readers regularly approach Elisabeth and ask, "When are you going to write some more about Bennett's Island?" Such is the power of that family and that place—it gets under the reader's skin. Elisabeth admits that of all the settings she has created, Bennett's Island is probably her favorite. Despite this personal feeling and her awareness of readers' desire for another book on the Bennett family, she nonetheless came to the conclusion that she had done all she was going to do with that island world. *The Day Before Winter* will remain the last in the series.

When asked recently about the first Bennett's Island novels, Elisabeth chuckled and said, "I've read some of my early books this year, and I thought while reading them, I haven't improved any since then—because this is darn good!" This doesn't mean that Elisabeth's writing hasn't developed: "I hope my writing has matured over the years. The Bennetts and Sorensens of my earliest books are still very much alive to me . . . Many things have changed with the times on Bennett's Island, and the six young Bennetts of *High Tide at Noon* have gray in their hair and grown-up kids [in the later books]. But they're still islanders in their own kingdom."

When asked which heroine stirs her most, Joanna Bennett or Jennie Glenroy, Elisabeth responds, "I like them both. I think they would have liked each other. Neither is afraid to get involved in life, and they are strongly loving women, too." There is no doubt about the similarity between these two resilient, courageous women, and their passionate devotion to their families and homes. In fact, they share these traits with all Ogilvie heroines.

Elisabeth has said that she loves all nine of the Bennett's Island books equally, and the same is true of the Jennie series—she can't choose just one favorite among them. "That's like asking anybody who their favorite child is! I can't say which is my favorite, because the characters are all so real to me."

"THE IMPORTANT THING IS TO BEGIN"

"I've always written," Elisabeth says. "I've always had the desire to write. I don't really know where it comes from. Writing is a compulsion—you don't really have a choice about it. You have to do it."

From the beginning, Elisabeth combined her fascination with words and her love of reading with an innate ability to express herself and to create her own stories. As a child, she would talk out loud to herself at bedtime, spinning long, complicated tales in an effort to fall asleep. She also made up stories each day walking to and from school.

Even as an adult, Elisabeth can't resist writing stories in her head, no matter where she is or what she is doing. In "Suspense in Fiction" (*The Writer*, January 1970) she described "the writer's compulsion to make descriptive sentences out of everything":

> At two in the morning, out with the dog, I forget my annoyance as composition automatically takes over: "As she stood shivering on the lawn waiting for Jill to stop eating grass, clouds blew across the face of the moon, and in the sudden dark she heard—" or saw—what? Bolting for the house, dragging the dog, I knew afterwards it was probably a deer out there, but for story purposes, it's someone on a surreptitious errand. Looking over old books in a deserted house is a natural stimulant; I came right home that day and started a story.

Writing has become an almost instinctive process for her, as natural as breathing. Her theories about writing, and how to be successful at it, are equally unpretentious: Immerse yourself in reading and writing, and don't ever stop. A college education is not required, according to Elisabeth. She didn't have one, and has managed quite nicely.

To encourage anyone who thinks college is necessary, my background is comprised of a reading family, a solid high school education, with very good English teachers from the seventh grade up, a couple of University extension courses in writing for publication, and a lot of reading and a lot of writing; being encouraged in school and at home to write.

When I think of the enormous amount of writing we did in the public schools of Boston and of Quincy when I attended them, I think I must have written a million words before I graduated. It all paid off, because developing a gift for writing easily and fluently is absolutely necessary: without it, the best ideas in the world are wasted. So many people are appalled at the thought of writing even a short letter. I think if I had a child, I'd have him write a letter to someone once a week, beginning with a short paragraph when he could first print. . . . My advice to all struggling writers is the same as I give in this article: BEGIN. PLUNGE. The more you do, the easier it becomes. ("Suspense in Fiction")

Elisabeth must have poured some of her own deep feelings about writing into the following passage from *When the Music Stopped*, voiced by the character Eden Winter: "As I began to write, I knew this was how the alcoholic or drug addict feels when he finally gets his drink or his fix. Who'd want to give up that marvelous moment when your life shudders back into your own hands? The difference was that my addiction earned my living. . . . " It's certainly not financial gain that drives Elisabeth, however. She once announced that even if she won the lottery, she would continue writing because she loves it so much.

"I would rather write than do anything else," says Elisabeth. "In fact, I can't imagine a day going by without my having put something down, if it's only notes or a paragraph of description." Not even while traveling in Scotland on vacation: As Anne Tirrell-McLaughlin wrote in her 1980 *Maine Life* profile, "Vacation or not, she proves her claim that she just doesn't feel natural when she isn't writing, and accepts even the drudgery of the profession without complaint." The little girl who once resented ballet rehearsal grew up to recognize that practice and routine has its place, especially in writing. She has found joy even in the less glamorous phases of the process.

She does much research for her novels with the help of the Bangor Public Library, which sends her books through the mail, including many hard-to-find volumes. For example, while researching her fourth Jennie book, Elisabeth needed to know what kind of novel Jennie would be reading in the 1820s. The Bangor library obliged by sending her some examples of popular literature during Jennie's time. (She notes that Jennie enjoyed reading Jane Austen and Sir Walter Scott.)

Elisabeth offered some practical advice for would-be writers in a letter to one of her fans:

> My brothers and I, Depression kids, all educated ourselves; we were all single-minded, each had a strong ambition in one particular field before we left high school, and went for it. We all got there and then some. I don't think there's any better training for a writer than writing (reading too). But [write] something every day. It's the everyday routine that counts.

She also talks about the different stages one goes through with a project, urging new writers to avoid perfectionism:

> Don't think it has to be perfect in the first draft. Don't stop to correct anything. You can do that later. If you're going to polish every sentence along the way, you ought to stop trying to be a writer and be a jeweler instead. And always stop [at a point where] you're writing well. You can always pick it up tomorrow.

But it's important to finish the story:

> Finish everything you begin. I keep notebooks of phrases—figures of speech, names for characters, possible situations in a few sentences—but I have an end in view. When I can't sleep, or I'm at the blank stage in a book, it's a tonic to take out [some] of these ideas-person-settings-gimmicks and try to put them together. Some good books have resulted from this practice. To help finish what you've begun, have an outline. I write three drafts and [even] then may not be satisfied with the final one, and write in changes before the publisher can read it.

Her advice, in summary:

> Write. Stick to it. Read, and I don't mean what's popular. You can educate yourself in literature. I read mysteries and good straight novelists. I take the classics in small but regular doses, so I'll know what the erudite people are talking about. I don't get hung up on a word.

Put in anything, and keep on going. You can find the right word later.
The same with characters' names and looks.

FAVORITE AUTHORS TODAY

Elisabeth reads as much as ever, and her homes are filled with books. She has a wide range of favorite authors, which crosses centuries and genres. She has enjoyed the novels of Rumer Godden and Angela Thirkell, Charles Dickens and Hugh Walpole, and she also likes the work of Iris Murdoch, Paul Theroux, and Herman Wouk. She enjoys classic authors like Henry James, noting that his books are "very relaxing to read in bed . . . relaxing in the way doing physical fitness exercises is—you exercise your brain, and then you're ready to sleep." She equally admires the work of Jane Austen, and Charlotte and Emily Brontë.

Mystery is one of her favorite genres to both read and write, and she was once described by journalist Bill Caldwell as a "detective story addict, devouring a book a day." Some of her favorite mystery writers are Tony Hillerman, P. D. James, Ruth Rendell, Anne Perry, Ngaio Marsh, Dot Sayers, and Elizabeth Peters.

In a 1985 interview in *Down East* magazine she expressed her appreciation of fellow Maine author Stephen King: "I think he's got a great imagination. I read *Salem's Lot* . . . I got a big kick out of that, and I've read *The Shining* a couple of times. That's my favorite. But I guess my reading of him is limited because about the only time I read is when I go to bed, and that isn't the sort of stuff you want to read and then try to go to sleep!" Other Maine authors she enjoys include Sarah Orne Jewett, Mary Ellen Chase, Carolyn Chute, and Ruth Moore, with whom she corresponded. She also enjoys a friendship with famed Maine author John Gould, and they both shared books with Bill Caldwell.

Elisabeth enjoys writers such as Miriam Spark, Gail Godwin and Anne Tyler, who write about women's issues. Another genre she enjoys is fantasy, especially Tolkien. She has read *The Lord of the Rings* several times, and even mentioned it in *The Road to Nowhere*.

A BELIEF IN READING

Elisabeth is enthusiastic about the renewed zeal for reading in recent years, thanks in part to Oprah's Book Club and other reading groups. She supports the idea of anything that gets people reading.

Ever one to keep up with the times and the literary landscape, she has read all of J. K. Rowling's Harry Potter books, and found them to be very imaginative, good stories, appealing to both children and adults. She is upset by the fact that some communities in the South and elsewhere have banned them.

Elisabeth does not believe any book should be banned, and feels that if students really want to read controversial books, they will find them eventually, at the public library or elsewhere. "Imagine—one place down south, they banned *The Diary of Anne Frank*. I couldn't believe it—it was for one sentence, 'It doesn't matter what you believe in, as long as you believe in something.' Anne Frank did not say, 'It doesn't matter if you don't believe in God'— she said you should believe in something."

As for language, Elisabeth says, "You know, there are some people who never read a book, and then they pick out one that the kids get at school, and they hit a dirty word the first thing." She reflects on a conversation she had with a friend, who asked her once if she'd ever read J. D. Salinger's *The Catcher in the Rye*. She answered that she had and thought it was a good story; she really sympathized with the main character. Her friend said that some parents didn't want their children reading that kind of language. I said, 'I didn't think this one had a lot of dirty words; he was very moderate.' But he said 'Well, the teacher probably didn't use good judgment in the way he tried to present it.' I said, 'If the kids want to read the story, they'll read it.'"

Elisabeth remembers a time when some parents raised concerns about their children being asked to read the poem "Richard Corey," by Edwin Arlington Robinson. It appears in many literature anthologies, and Elisabeth read it in high school. "The poem is about [a man] who shoots himself," she says. "Someone in the education department said that with all these teenage suicides nowadays, they didn't think it was a good idea. But I think more people stood up for it, saying they all read it, and that their children should be able to read it, too." She believes in the freedom of speech, and that all types of literature should be available to students today.

ELISABETH'S FANS

Elisabeth's formula has been successful, and her books enjoy an enduring popularity. Her fictional creations have enriched countless lives, and her reader base continues to grow. Elisabeth always replies to new fans, when they write to her, "I'm delighted to be 'discovered' after all these years!" and confesses to a sort of "Gee whiz!" feeling upon reading some of their letters. Undoubtedly, this support from her readers keeps her working.

Some fans have been reading her books since the beginning of her career, eagerly awaiting each new release. Joan Muchowski writes: "I've been reading Elisabeth Ogilvie's books since the late 1950s when I was a young bride, and when I visited the Maine coast in 1988, it was everything I thought it would be. . . ." Many are reading Ogilvie books that have been passed down to them by their own mothers, faithful readers for years. Others have just discovered her in recent years, to their total delight.

Although Elisabeth says that she writes first for herself, for the pure pleasure of writing, an unanticipated result of her work is the vast following she now enjoys. Always considerate and warmly appreciative of her fans, and true to her philosophy of the importance of letter writing, Elisabeth has answered almost every fan letter she has ever received, taking pains to answer questions and provide whatever specific information is requested—such as a list of the Bennett's Island series in order, or even a recipe for a treat mentioned in one of her books.

In 1997, when Down East Books published *The Day Before Winter*, her readers greeted this long-awaited continuation of the Bennett's Island series with much celebration. At one book signing event, when a newsletter for her readers was proposed, Elisabeth's response was typically humble: "Why sure, though I don't know what you'll find to write about!"

The quarterly newsletter began with a mailing to about sixty-five potential subscribers, some of whom had attended the book signing. The response was overwhelming. By February 2001, circulation of *A Mug-up With Elisabeth* numbered well over four hundred, with subscribers in forty-one states (including Alaska), Canada, and the Dominican Republic. Now entering its fourth year, the newsletter continues to expand in size and topics covered. (For subscription information, see p. 316.)

Elisabeth's initial concern that there wouldn't be enough material has proven to be unfounded. Readers enjoy having a resource that lists Elisabeth's books in chronological order and contains reader mail, reviews and synopses of her novels, questions answered by Elisabeth, and articles written by readers about their favorite Ogilvie books or Maine memories. The newsletter has expanded to include maps, recipes, informative articles about the life of a lobsterman and other facets of Maine life, a Swap & Sell column for Ogilvie books, and a special glossary of Maine terms (see Appendix 2), written by Luthera Dawson, of Thomaston.

The interest is such that during the summer of 1999 the first subscriber luncheon event was held. Elisabeth Ogilvie was the guest of honor, and those present were able to have her sign newly reissued copies of books from the Lovers Trilogy. Fifty-four newsletter subscribers from all over the United States attended, thoroughly enjoying the chance to spend time with Elisabeth and other Ogilvie fans.

In the fall of 2000, sixty-four people attended the second luncheon. Some came from as far away as California, including relatives and old friends of Elisabeth's, as well as many new subscribers. All were thrilled to hear Elisabeth speak about her work, to get their books autographed, and to share their passion with other Ogilvie readers. An added attraction was the opportunity to view photographs and a film of Criehaven. More gatherings are planned for the future.

During the course of her career, Elisabeth has been involved with professional writers' organizations such as the Authors Guild and the Mystery Writers of America. She has often been invited to speak to audiences at schools, libraries, and professional organizations such as Maine Media Women, and one of her short stories was included in *Maine Speaks: An Anthology of Maine Literature* (Maine Writers and Publishers Alliance, 1989)

Her popularity extends well beyond the New England area. The Minnesota Women's Press Book Group on the Road has included her in two of their literary road trips. This book group reads the work of authors from a certain geographical region, and then travels to the region to explore it, in both a literal and literary way. For the Maine trips, they read *High Tide at Noon* along with books by Sarah Orne Jewett, Ruth Moore, Anita Shreve, and Susan Kenney. They actually visited with Elisabeth and Dot on their first trip, and with Elisabeth on their second.

READER COMMENT

Over the years, numerous Mug-up *newsletter subscribers have written to express their gratitude for Elisabeth's books. One such reader, Carolyn Benedict, eloquently captured the sentiments of many:*

The down-east area of Maine is my favorite spot in the United States. The rocky coastline, the islands in the bays, the green mountains, the turbulent Atlantic Ocean, all are as familiar to me as is the state of Indiana, where I have spent my seventy-six years.

I have never been to Maine and I will probably never get there, except in my reading. Elisabeth Ogilvie has given me all the experiences that have made me love it so much. And along with the setting she has peopled my mind with her characters, known to me as well as I know those with whom I brush shoulders every day.

I no longer have the urge to travel to Maine—I know what it feels like, how it smells, how the different seasons change the landscape, and I know the people, especially the inhabitants of Bennett's Island. If I were to go to Maine, I would be looking for Joanna, Nils, Jamie, Rosa, and all the others whose faces I visualize as I say their names. I have difficulty believing that they really do not exist. They are all my friends.

10 ❧ THEMES IN HER WORK

CRITICS HAVE FOUND IT DIFFICULT to assign a single label to Elisabeth Ogilvie's work. Called by turn historical, romantic, or regional fiction, it simply can't be pigeonholed into merely one category. This is fitting, as her work crosses genres as surely as it transcends time and place.

Elisabeth is a self-proclaimed writer of "background," so the regional description is an apt one. Most of her books do contain a love story—whether it be a passionate relationship, an ill-fated one, or even a calm, sedate love developed over many years of marriage. Her Jennie series and *Whistle for a Wind* are examples of historical fiction of the highest caliber. All of the labels are appropriate to a degree, because Elisabeth's books are multidimensional, with several strands of plot and character development. Each contains some sort of message, even if it is just the fact that strength of character *matters* in our world. And a pervading sense of wonder infuses all her work—awe in the face of the natural world, and a fresh, eager willingness to take on life in all its glory and all its pain.

Her books seem to be united by several common threads: the power of the natural world, the passions of her characters, and the strength of the family to overcome obstacles and do the right thing. Ultimately her characters face the shared struggles of all humanity with dignity and courage.

Elisabeth weaves these themes into plots that move steadily and surely to their conclusion. Skillful storytelling demands confidence in the value of the story's message. Elisabeth possesses this confidence, and even while she claims no specific agenda and says she does not intentionally structure her books around a societal truth, they deliver one all the same. Her stories communicate the idea that goodness counts for something, even when we are surrounded by life's darkest struggles. Elisabeth allows her characters to prevail over evil and sadness, and her plots consistently bear out her theme that character matters.

Writer Margot McWilliams agrees, noting that Elisabeth "has a sunny take on life in her novels."

> While she doesn't idealize her characters exactly—they get peevish and petty, even downright surly—they do share a deeply rooted common core of values and human decency. They love their families, their place in the universe, and their way of life. They interact with the outside world as leaders and role models.
>
> They walk tall and proud, bearing their young on their shoulders, and they're sufficiently sensitive to be consistently mindful of the needs of others. To play against the virtues of the Bennetts, Ogilvie brings in the world's evils. Drug-dealers, embittered state wards, adulterers, murderers, and lobster-trap thieves can be found skulking around in her books. They are, however, invariably either defeated or won over. ("The Scriveners," *Down East*, October 1994)

HER STYLE

Another reason for Elisabeth's success in portraying life in coastal Maine is her writing style, which is every bit equal to her content. Her emphasis on solid, respectable people providing for their families and taking responsibility for their actions is echoed in her substantial prose. Her writing is solid—lyrical and evocative when describing the landscape she loves so well—but also unadorned when it comes to telling the facts as they are.

Elisabeth draws the reader into her fictional world in a simple fashion. She begins by describing a few moments of a character's day—the way a fisherman packs a lunch before going out to haul, or how a mother gets her children ready for school. She then builds on this foundation with such realistic descriptions that the reader is soon immersed in the environment and the culture of their daily life.

Pamela Thompson, an Ogilvie reader who left Maine for Wyoming as an Air Force wife, writes: "What a gift Miss Ogilvie has of re-creating the sensual aspect of the coast of Maine. I can read a chapter in *The Day Before Winter* and feel the crisp breeze, smell the salt air, hear the gulls overhead, and taste those molasses cookies. I found the other books in the Bennett's Island series just as comforting for one who longs to be by the sea. I am so glad to have found this wonderful piece of Maine to savor in the lonely plains of Wyoming."

Some readers love the vivid depictions of family life, the frequent mug-ups, and details of lobstering. Others appreciate the ability to vicariously walk the island shores, and still others fall in love with her characters. It is a combination of these elements—overlaid with the pervasive mood and setting—that makes Elisabeth's novels so compelling.

In addition to weaving a spell with her background, Elisabeth has also been called a philosopher, for her ability to provide subtle insight into the human condition. Her writing is so satisfying because it is firmly rooted in storytelling. She begins with a plot-driven narrative that has no need of histrionics or huge explosions—just a series of powerful, life-changing events. The characters react to these events in a believable, honest way. Along the way, Elisabeth carefully constructs a web of words that lifts the reader and holds him up while the story develops.

RESPITE FOR A WEARY WORLD

Once readers enter her world, they find it often stands in stark contrast to today's society. In Elisabeth's books, simple pleasures are enough, and families stick together through calm and travail. In an era where shock value is often paramount and writers specialize in exploring multiple layers of dysfunction, Elisabeth portrays what is good in the world, and her readers wholeheartedly embrace this vision.

In setting as well as plot, her work provides a welcome respite for a weary world. She captures a way of life long gone—a simple time before the explosion of the Information Age, where microwaves and cable television, cell phones and fax machines, e-mail and the microchip have forced an acceleration of life that is hard to maintain.

Even in 1944, when times were arguably much simpler, Margaret Wallace wrote in the *New York Times Book Review*, "*High Tide at Noon* is a kind of novel we rarely see in these days, perhaps because most novelists are too harassed and battered by the claims of the present to remember the past in tranquility. There is room and to spare for this sort of evocative writing. It is a fair guess that Elisabeth Ogilvie is going to make a lot of her readers—and not only those who love the New England coast—homesick for some world of their own vanished now beyond recall."

Elisabeth Ogilvie's gift is that she shares with us the real experience of island life distilled to its purest essence—a struggle to live, with dignity, by the strength of your own physical labor and moral beliefs. She sets her stories in an environment that can be both magnificently beautiful and harshly unforgiving. The ever-changing sea provides a dramatic background for the brave men who fish its waters. No less impressive are their wives, who must be cut from equally substantial cloth in order to survive the many demands on their reserves of strength.

Elisabeth portrays a society markedly different from today's cutthroat world. In a seemingly gentle way, she tells the story of a group of characters who have to work together and help each other in order to survive. Although feuds and personal disagreements exist, in times of crisis those are set aside. In the end, cooperation and basic goodness carry the day.

In *Waters on a Starry Night*, all the men go out in a storm to look for Lyle Ritchie, including Lyle's sworn enemy—ironically the one who ends up rescuing him. A fellow lobsterman's wife states matter-of-factly to Thora, "You know how it is when one man stays out longer. They figger they might's well go back out and see if he's got engine trouble, instead of going home and taking their boots off and then wondering. It's just routine."

This matter-of-fact solidarity is another attractive element for today's readers, who may be isolated by distance and technology, and for whom life without an extended family or a strong community network is often the norm. Elisabeth's books re-create for our jaded world an era where the bonds of family loyalty and neighborhood did not succumb to a selfish focus.

Elisabeth understands that her readers want some form of escape when they read her books. She wants to provide this, but she does not do it lightly. She doesn't minimize the ugly realities of life or ignore them; they are present, but can be overcome with human integrity. It would be a disservice to suggest that her books, "gentle and episodic" though they may be, are simply an opportunity to shut out the world for a time. They provide an escape with a lesson—a fuller awareness of one's own responsibility and integrity.

A paragraph from *Ceiling of Amber* embodies the very essence of Elisabeth's style and the mood she creates:

> The warm kitchen, the smell of food, the loud purring of the cat
> in the rocker, the storm kept at bay—it was all bliss. Doubts and anx-
> ieties had been left outside. Over beans and coleslaw and hot biscuits
> they told their mother about their day, and she told them of hers.

REALISM VS. IDEALISM

Some critics argue that Elisabeth's work is part of idealistic, rather than realistic, Maine literature, claiming her picture of island life in Maine is

Utopian and therefore not representative of true life. "Perhaps it was actually because of her persistent commercial success, but the 'real Maine' advocates included her among those they insisted were not writing realistically about Maine life," Jeannette Cakouros wrote in a 1991 article for *Maine in Print*.

Elisabeth does not waste much time responding to such criticism. She is comfortable with the fact that she writes about what she knows of the Maine island culture—how it truly was. Sanford Phippen, considered by some the originator of the "real Maine" movement, is a good friend of Elisabeth's and values her work. As one of the editors of *Maine Speaks,* Phippen included Elisabeth's short story "Scobie" in this anthology of the best Maine literature.

Elisabeth appreciates the work of Carolyn Chute, the writer perhaps most acceptable to the "real Mainers" school. "I read [Chute's] *The Beans of Egypt, Maine* twice," says Elisabeth. "I read it just to see what everyone's talking about, and then I began reading all the reviews, so I read it again thinking of what the reviewers were getting at. I think she's good, a good writer. She took something that hasn't been publicized in Maine, so she's got something new there, and she's made the most of it. She certainly has created people . . . that you don't forget in a hurry. Not likable, certainly, but vivid, very vivid. It's sort of come into the language now; you say, 'Oh, I know a family up the road, just like the Beans,' and everyone knows what you mean."

Chute feels the same about Elisabeth's work. The two authors have corresponded, and upon meeting Elisabeth for the first time several years ago, Chute told her that she had loved Elisabeth's books since childhood, and she was one of the authors who had most influenced Chute's own writing.

When discussing the differences between the Maine worlds created by Chute and Ogilvie, Elisabeth says that her setting presents a different, yet still authentic, view of Maine. When asked if she felt that Bennett's Island was too idyllic, Elisabeth answered firmly, "No, and for this reason: I'm writing about the village life as it used to be. The people have become so real to me that they act just as those people would have acted. It's a clannish sort of life, with the school and the post office and the mailboat coming—self-contained. In my books it's a little different in that I have one large family that seems to be about two-thirds of the population out there, while actually . . . on Criehaven as I knew it, there were three or four large families—not inbred, by any means, but there would have been marriages, so there were a lot of cousins."

Elisabeth perhaps unknowingly answers her critics in this excerpt from *The Dawning of the Day*. During a dance at the clubhouse, Joanna and Philippa discuss the island celebrations:

"Sometimes we've had dances up here that have been wicked disappointments," Joanna said to Philippa. . . . "But when there's a good dance, it's like this. Everyone wants it to be good, and they've got it in them to make it a fine thing. It's another sort of feeling, an outgiving. For a little while, all the grievances are stowed out of sight."

"I shouldn't think there were too many grievances on a place like this," said Philippa.

Joanna gave her a dark, subtly mocking glance. "It's not Utopia."

With this simple exchange Elisabeth is quietly underscoring the fact that although at times the island may seem too good to be true, human frailties are ever present to leaven the atmosphere with a dose of reality.

Her knowledge of life in a lobstering village is based on her own real experiences there. She lived that life, just as much as Chute lived her experience, and Elisabeth has modeled her characters on their real-life people. Their personalities and actions are rooted in reality, and Elisabeth feels comfortable with the paths they take. She has responded to inquiries about this issue in several published interviews over the years:

It's my family and I can do whatever I want with them. ("Elisabeth Ogilvie: True-Life Romance with a Shake of Pain," *Maine Times*, November 1991).

I know that what I'm writing about is the truth as far as the lobstering life goes. ("Elisabeth Ogilvie: Tides of Change," *Maine in Print*, 1991)

I've actually been accused of glamorizing island life, usually by people who know little or nothing about it. Lobstermen aren't illiterates, and they aren't poor. At least they haven't been since the Depression, when lobster was selling for 12 cents a pound. Fishing is a capital-intensive industry. There's a lot of money tied up in boats and equipment. If someone is in trouble financially, it's usually because they're overextended. I write about life on the islands as it really is, not as someone who's never been there imagines it. ("Author Finds Inspiration on Maine Coast," *Lewiston Sunday*, 1989)

It is also her choice not to allow the modern world to invade her books too thoroughly. Elisabeth readily admits that real-life islanders today enjoy modern conveniences as much as the rest of us. "Criehaven has cellular phones now, and village community life is gone, but the way of life I wrote about in the 1940s is still possible. It all depends on how you want to live," Elisabeth told Betta Stothart in the 1991 *Maine Times* interview.

Perhaps the person who has most ably answered the "real Maine" advocates is Dot Simpson, the true "child of Criehaven." When asked for her comments on the Bennett's Island series, Dot answered thoughtfully,

> Well, I'll tell you this much: if Elisabeth'd never written the three Tide books, nobody would ever know how it was out there. The Criehaven that I knew growing up is gone. But as long as those three books are in print, people'll know what it was like to live on that little island, the atmosphere, the relationships of people with each other—and the descriptions, people, places—everything. It's almost like a photograph. It's all changed there now, all the people I knew have died or moved away, but I can read those books and remember it just the way it was. She really captured it. ("Returning to Elisabeth Ogilvie's Bennett's Island," *Down East*, 1985)

Betta Stothart reflected about Elisabeth's lifetime literary contribution in her *Maine Times* article:

> Islands, salt water, wet breeze, romance, community struggles and relationships—these are the keys to her stories, as they are clearly the keys to her heart. Her leading characters are independent, self-determined people, with pride that in Greek tragedy would certainly lead to downfall. A good deal of attention is given to romance, mischief and intrigue, and there is usually a generous shake of pain. Ogilvie's characters are driven by hard work and long days; their lives are bare and frugal, their values shaped by basic needs. Consistently, her books recount a forgotten way of life where water was carried, wood cut, vegetables grown, where today's bombardment of convenience items doesn't exist."

THE MOST IMPORTANT "CHARACTER"

> *The island has made its people what they are. It imposes a peculiar discipline on them, and they must obey if they are to survive and prosper.* —Elisabeth Ogilvie

Elisabeth is often called a novelist of background, and for good reason. Her compelling settings form the backbone of her work, and she doesn't hesitate to explain why: "The story should spring up from the background. Though human passions are the same everywhere, there should be essential elements peculiar to this setting alone. There must be happenings that can occur only in this place."

"Elisabeth Ogilvie is a writer in love with landscape," wrote Susan Quinn Berneis in *Twentieth Century Romance and Historical Writers.* "Her descriptions of the physical surroundings of her novels are so detailed and portrait-like that the setting almost becomes another character. By the final chapter of each of her books, one is so minutely acquainted with every mood and view of the environment that one could be transported to that place and never feel lost. This sensitivity to scene gives these novels an immediacy and reality not often found in romantic novels today."

In her review of *When the Music Stopped,* Carol Kontos made a similar point, noting that "her characters are believable because they fit so comfortably in their setting. . . . For Ogilvie the background is always an inescapable and alive part of the story. Without it the other elements have no existence. . . . And perhaps it is this strong sense of place—the weather, the seasons, the tides—that explains much of her popularity. Readers understand the attitude that has guided Ogilvie's writing for over fifty years, [when they read Elisabeth's own words]: 'When all the loves are gone and the wars won or lost, it is the place that remains.'"

Elisabeth gave practical advice to fellow writers who wish to develop their skills of description in "The Practice and the Passion" (*The Writer,* April 1985). Her suggestion: Practice every day.

> Wherever you are, town or country, you're surrounded by wealth. Take a bit of it each day and describe it in detail. People, place. Sounds, smells. Search out the tiniest particulars; don't dismiss anything as trivia. Try to make the vignette come alive for someone who hasn't the slightest conception of the reality.
>
> Spending at least a half-hour a day on this—faithfully—will show you great results in a week, assuming that you have the passion to commit yourself to it. Minute observation will become second nature to you in time, like any other skill which, as you become expert, doesn't require a conscious, labored effort. Without false emphasis but with a sure knowledge of your background and a meticulous attention to detail—from the games of children to the adults' tragedies, whether on a city block or a Maine island—you can make your reader

see, smell, hear, and feel its presence below, above, and behind everything else.

Your gift for observation will make you instinctively add those
seemingly insignificant touches that add up to authenticity. Your
imagination will put you on the scene in your protagonist's skin; *your*
senses will be taking in everything, *your* heart will be thudding in
suspense, because *your* passion has taken charge.

Elisabeth has always had a deep emotional attachment to the settings
she creates. The setting most fundamental in her work is Bennett's, her quintessential Maine offshore island modeled on her beloved Criehaven, with its
heartbreakingly beautiful setting and the excitement of the lobstering life. No
less important to her are the people. "I fell in love with the island boys," she
says frankly. "They were all lobstermen, of course, and they seemed so much
more mature and independent than the boys back home."

She is also fascinated by the idea that island communities are "micro-
societies with their own set of rules, social mores, and sometimes even laws,
all of which are peculiar to the place but not necessarily the times." She explores this theme in each of her island books. One of the island "laws" she
noted as a young girl was that island women never went down to the docks
when their husbands returned from their lobster fishing. "I have no idea why,
but no self-respecting woman could go down there. You just didn't do it." This
was all part of the island mystique she sought to capture in her books.

Elisabeth skillfully uses her descriptive powers to help push forward the
narrative's action. In her 1966 article for *The Writer*, she used *The Seasons
Hereafter* to illustrate why background is the most important character.
Quoting the following example, Elisabeth notes how she "kept the strong
rhythms of life beating like a counterpoint to a woman's private experience by
the use of a few simple devices." In this scene she sets her character's fierce
emotions against the calm start of another day for the fishermen:

> She got frantically out of bed and saw Western Harbor Point and
> the breakwater washed bronze and rose with the sunrise. A boat was
> going out by the breakwater, and the man was putting on his oil-
> clothes, now and then touching the wheel.

"Vanessa is frantic with her own confusion, yet life goes on, there is a clear
sunrise and the boats are going out," Elisabeth explained. Whether or not
Vanessa is distraught, the boats will go out and the tide will ebb and flow. "The

harbor is the heart of the place, it dominates her. She keeps coming back to it."

The course of action in the story can only happen because it takes place where it does—on an island. Owen and Vanessa first meet because Owen has come to ask Vanessa's husband Barry to help him seine herring. Fishing, living by the ocean, and the isolation of the island give the lovers permission to seek each other out under false pretenses, as when Owen "invites" Vanessa to join him by mentioning he'll be seeking his lost traps in Ship Cove. "As simply as this, the appointment is made," Elisabeth explained. "They can meet in a lonely cove because the island has so many such coves, and because he has a legitimate excuse to be out there at midday. She of course can take long walks without question." And Van does—she so often seeks the refuge of being outdoors when faced with the passions of her own life that she appears almost gull-like in her determination to "fly." Like Thora in *Waters on a Starry Night*, the restless Vanessa is drawn outside to cool her fevered emotions and seek answers.

Elisabeth sees Vanessa as "a victim of the most important character in the novel—the island." Then Elisabeth asks a final question in her article: "At the end, who is to say whether his wife holds Owen or Bennett's Island does? Vanessa doesn't know."

Elisabeth uses her masterful powers of description to make other settings besides Bennett Island come alive. She set several novels on her own Gay's Island, including *Waters on a Starry Night, There May Be Heaven, The Witch Door, The Dreaming Swimmer,* and *Weep and Know Why*. This island provides all sorts of unique opportunities for plot and character development.

Although these islanders live closer to the mainland, they still fall victim to the caprice of ocean and weather. Thora Ritchie's daily routine in *Waters on a Starry Night* is often dictated by whether her trip across the Gut will be a smooth one. Getting the children ready to meet the bus on the other side entails bringing old newspapers to sit on in the dory and battling a cranky outboard motor on cold winter mornings.

Elisabeth describes the life of Thora, and all lobstermen's wives, in this passage: "Here is a world of stunning beauty and often of stunning brutality. Here are men making their living in an intensely physical way, on terms of truce with the elements. The women live accordingly. . . . The very nature of a lobsterman's wife is to be strong and stoic." They know their husbands could be lost at sea at any moment, so they are trained to be calm. Thora shares these traits with Joanna and the other lobstermen's wives in Elisabeth's novels and in her short story "The Lobsterman's Wife" (see page 141).

In the Jennie series, Elisabeth was faced with the challenge of re-creating a landscape apart from her beloved Maine. Only after doing exhaustive research and traveling to Scotland was she prepared to write. "When I sat down to flesh out the bones of the story, I was there. To make this background come alive and show how Jennie was emotionally involved with it, I had to be passionate about its creation from the start until it was in its final version on the printed page." The Highland Clearances provide an example of plot driven by environment in *Jennie About to Be*.

No less powerful is Elisabeth's use of the Standing Stones at Callanish, true-life inspiration for *The Silent Ones*, which naturally evoke a sense of drama and atmosphere:

> The morning was overcast, East Loch Roag was choppy green and gray, with glints of cold light when the sun almost broke through the shifting layers of cloud. Peat smoke blew down on the wind. . . . She felt lonely this morning, it had grown on her since she passed Callanish, and she'd have appreciated a visit beside Charlie's fire.

Readers of her work can attest that Elisabeth always fulfills the directive she gives fellow writers: "The *feel* of the place must be so strong that readers are captured and imprisoned in its scents and sounds and the special atmosphere peculiar and private to it."

HER CHARACTERS

Elisabeth may be an architect of background, but she is equally skillful in building her human characters. She is able to see inside the human psyche to create rich and diverse characters. Readers feel deep affection for many of the characters, and long to know more about their lives.

When asked if any of her characters are based on real people, Elisabeth answers that once or twice she's "made a real portrait of someone, out of affection." Usually, however, she takes certain attributes from real people and combines them to create unique individuals. Whether it is the stoicism of a lobsterman's wife, or a child's view of tragedy, Elisabeth sees into each character's heart and determines with perfect sensitivity what they would do next. She doesn't resort to character types, and rejects outright the weak, vulnerable heroine. Similarly, she doesn't shrink from portraying evil and conflict.

Critics also praise Elisabeth's characters. Susan Quinn Berneis said in *Twentieth-Century Romance and Historical Writers* that they are "as vivid as the settings":

One feels that these people have lives apart from the span of time covered in the book, that the novel is merely a fascinating slice of a larger life. This feeling is reinforced by the author's ability to use the same characters in a later work, as is the case with *Weep and Know Why* and *The Dreaming Swimmer*. She repeats this success with her historical novels [the Jennie series]. The successive works might be called sequels, but they are stronger than mere sequels with none of the flavor of afterthought.

Ogilvie is an author who observes and notices; her eye for detail is unerring. For this reason, she is skilled at evoking sudden menace in everyday situations. In such works as *The Summer of the Osprey* and *The Road to Nowhere*, the secrets that people try to keep and the failure of communication between even the closest people show how life can suddenly change for worse as well as for better.

Elisabeth is equally skillful at handling relationships in her books. As a keen observer of nuance, she writes insightfully of the difficulties of maintaining romance. Berneis writes, "There is no emphasis here on happy endings, nor does culmination automatically bring happiness. Her characters must work hard to make their relationships work. . . ." And work they do, from the earliest sparks of attraction, through the toughest struggles of a decades-old marriage. Elisabeth handles each stage with understanding and empathy, and her characters remain believable throughout.

Although she never married, Elisabeth beautifully renders the essence of marriage and its many innate difficulties. When asked how she was able to write about it so effectively, never having been married herself, Elisabeth answers, with a twinkle in her eye, "Well, you have to have an imagination!"

Elisabeth is able to draw from her own rich life experience when creating many of her male characters. She grew up with three brothers, and a father who was one of six boys himself—all strong and vibrant personalities. A passage from *High Tide at Noon* seems to describe Elisabeth and her own family: "Joanna, watching them with their big, whole-hearted mirth, father and sons alike, felt love and pride run through her like a warming fire. She met her mother's smiling eyes and a little current of understanding passed between woman and girl. *Men*, it said in loving amusement. *Our men*." In addition to the Ogilvies, many Simpson men and boys surrounded Elisabeth, along with the lobstermen of Criehaven and Gay's Island. "What with all this masculine stuff around, they sort of all appeared," Elisabeth has said of her heroes.

She was wise to model her male characters on the real men in her life. The men in her books are some of the most quietly charismatic in modern literature—most notably Owen Bennett, Nils Sorensen, and Alick Gilchrist. Elisabeth confides that in her first Bennett's books, she always envisioned Owen to be a sort of Cary Grant figure. She described Owen early on in *High Tide at Noon*: "The Bennett smile was a little different in Owen. It held at once a sweetness and a reckless charm that was known to work wonders." Many of her readers agree—he is one of her most popular male characters.

One key to Elisabeth's male characters is their common core of values. It would almost appear that they are too good to be true, except that Elisabeth allows them their share of human weakness. They react to circumstances with a thoroughly believable sense of realism. They make mistakes and fall down— it's just that they aren't afraid to pick themselves up and try again. Many of Elisabeth's heroes are faced with harrowing predicaments, which give these down-to-earth men a chance to show their tough moral fiber and basic sense of decency.

Nils Sorensen exemplifies these qualities throughout the Bennett's Island series. Whether Joanna's friend, lover, or husband, he is always at her side when she needs him. In *The Ebbing Tide*, unbeknownst to him, his marriage is threatened by the presence of Dennis Garland on the island while Nils himself is serving on a coast guard ship in the Pacific during World War II. Dennis reminds Joanna of her first husband, Alec, and in her loneliness she is tempted to stray.

Unaware of the crisis Joanna is going through, Nils had been aboard ship, "lying in sick bay, expecting to be told every time a doctor approached him, that he must lose his leg. And yet he had written her the sane, reassuring letters that had been her one link with the life they had known together." The doctors were unable to remove all the shrapnel from his leg, leaving Nils in both physical and mental pain. Upon his return, Joanna is heartbroken for his sake, knowing how his lameness must affect his pride. "Nils might face death with equanimity, but not lameness. And because he never spoke of it, never complained, it would go harder for him than Owen, who could swear freely about his missing fingers, and pity himself intensely and eloquently."

Nils reacts as always with stoic bravery, but the war has changed him nonetheless. He is distant and quiet, and pulls away from Joanna's affectionate advances. Joanna worries that he is angry about her friendship with Dennis when he rejects her love. Nils tries to explain how deeply the war affected him, saying, "it was a hell of a place for a fisherman to be! It was like tying down a gull. There was never a minute to myself, never a place to be alone—never a time when I wasn't under orders."

When Joanna breaks down after hearing this, Nils comforts her, saying, "Listen, dear, it's all over now. It's past. Don't think about it. Just try to see how it was to want to sleep at night when I'd forgotten how. After that first night, I was pretty discouraged. I'd lie here with my skin crawling, not wanting you to know I was awake." Nils and Joanna are able to talk through their anguish. Nils assures her that he never doubted her faithfulness, and that he was grateful she had Dennis for company. His body has started to heal since his return to Bennett's, and he has purged his soul of the restlessness that plagued him. Their love is renewed again. Elisabeth doesn't hesitate to portray such intimate conversations with sensitivity and compassion, further strengthening the reader's understanding of their relationship.

Nils's strength has been passed on to his son Jamie. In *An Answer in the Tide*, Jamie faces scandal and troubled affairs of the heart. In a 1991 review of the novel, Ron Brown, of the *Bangor Daily News,* addressed the question of Jamie's morality: "Jamie struggles with what he knows to be right and his own built-in value structure. This struggle eventually involves nearly all members of the community, as the island itself attempts to burn off its own fog of discontent to rectify its moral battles, trying to let the sunshine of harmony return again to Bennett's Island." Elisabeth isn't afraid to tackle these big issues, or to show the all-too-human side of her male heroes.

Critic Susan Berneis had her own interpretation of these male characters: "If there is an area of consistency in these novels it is in the characters of the heroes. Ogilvie seems to admire the taciturn, unemotional male who is deeply sensitive beneath a terse exterior. This is not to say that these men lack individuality or realism. Rather it seems that the writer began with a general type and fleshed him out to meet the demands of the story." (*Twentieth-Century Romance and Historical Writers*, 1990)

Certainly the Bennett men share these qualities. Elisabeth doesn't limit her male characters to one mold, however; she presents many different facets of the male personality. In Lyle Ritchie, she creates a man who is vulnerable to the demands of life, and makes mistakes. With Alick Gilchrist, Elisabeth explores a relationship where the man needs the woman as much as she needs him. Jennie is responsible for saving Alick, and the way he deals with this fact demonstrates his true nature.

Several Ogilvie heroes who embody these traits are profiled in the following chapter: Steve and Owen Bennett, Jamie and Nils Sorensen, Lyle

Ritchie, Giles Whitney, and Alick Gilchrist. All of these men, according to Berneis, "are consistent with their stations in life. Ogilvie does not focus on people of glamour, so sophistication and wit would be jarring characteristics to find in her heroes. Instead, they are workers and survivors, men to lean on. If the heroines do not lean on them very often it is because they are formed by the same forces that shaped their men. They must be strong rather than clinging to survive."

Elisabeth's heroines never feel the need to cling to anyone. They may need a strong shoulder once in a while, but they are made of sterner stuff than those created in what Elisabeth calls the "idiot-heroine" mode. Her women are shaped by their environment just as much as the men are. Elisabeth makes it clear in her article on background that the fierce island setting toughens its people, making them stronger for the hardships they inevitably will face. Of necessity, they must be strong enough to endure the dangers of the sea, the brutal winters, isolation and loneliness—and they must learn to rely on themselves as much as their neighbors.

Just as Elisabeth drew inspiration from the menfolk who surrounded her, she found exemplars of island women in her Criehaven and Gay's Island friends. Undoubtedly her mother, her Aunt Elizabeth, and other family members also inspired Elisabeth, but perhaps the person who provided the best example of the island woman was Dot Simpson.

Dot was a charismatic storyteller all of her life, and shared generously of her prodigious store of memories, both orally and on paper. Dot's tales provided a rich source of story-line ideas for Elisabeth, who is quick to point out that the best place to find Dot's memories is in her Janie series. In this autobiographical series chronicling the life and times of Janie Marshall and her family, Dot wrote movingly about her life as the oldest of nine children born to a hardworking lobsterman and his wife.

After Elisabeth observed and recorded details from real-life models, she went on to create characters straight from her own heart and imagination. Her range of female characters is broad, with Joanna Bennett Sorensen as the figurehead; no other personifies the Ogilvie heroine so well. Joanna, Jennie Glenroy, Philippa Marshall Bennett, Vanessa Barton, Rosa Fleming Sorensen, Thora Ritchie, Leslie Whitney—all of these women (profiled in the next chapter) exemplify the qualities Elisabeth values: self-reliance, strength, belief in doing what's right, and love and loyalty for their homes and families.

In *The Seasons Hereafter*, Vanessa gives an accurate description of the Bennett women: "The Bennetts went in for wholesome women, it appeared—

especially schoolteachers—who had a sense of humor and who never spent long nights in tantrums or nightmares or the unmoving, undreaming sleep that was worse than the other two. . . ."

Elisabeth has often said that she likes to write through the eyes of a female protagonist and to have things turn out right for them. In so doing, she never resorts to a narrowed vision or oversimplification. Her heroines are modern women. They are independent thinkers, and although loyal to their men, they are not afraid to dedicate themselves to a cause, even at some risk to themselves and their relationships.

It's not surprising that readers feel they are hearing Elisabeth's voice through these female characters, and perhaps none more clearly than in Joanna—the perfect vehicle to represent Elisabeth's passion for Criehaven. Like Joanna, Elisabeth is strong, feisty, and full of spirit; and like Joanna, Elisabeth loves the island with all of her heart. One can easily imagine her linking arms with Joanna, joining her effort to reclaim Criehaven's former glory.

11 🌺 CHARACTER PROFILES

THE WOMEN OF THE LOVERS TRILOGY—Philippa, Vanessa, and Rosa—all approach Bennett's Island with trepidation as well as a longing for redemption and peace. Varying images of a golden paradise greet the women—yellow, tawny rocks and an abundance of water, all bathed in a glowing light. The island is not only beautiful and welcoming, but it seems to radiate a healing power, the promise of relief after struggle.

Each woman has had to learn to be resilient and self-reliant for different reasons—Philippa as a widow and single mother, Vanessa as a survivor of a lonely childhood, Rosa as a woman undergoing a painful divorce. Each has come through the fire a stronger person, and is destined to find a new life on Bennett's Island. Elisabeth links the importance of place with character development, demonstrating that the two are intrinsically woven together.

The Bennett men featured in the Lovers Trilogy all share some key family traits. They are handsome and bronzed by the sun and sea; they are all supremely capable fishermen, and are fiercely loyal to their family and their island; and they all harbor strong feelings beneath their stoic exterior. Steve, the youngest of the Bennett brothers, may be somewhat in Owen's shadow, and Jamie is still a young man stretching his wings—but they all share a tremendous capacity for love, and once they find it, they put the whole force of their being into it.

In these three novels, Elisabeth gives the reader many different facets of love, like rays from a prism: in Steve, the gallant, wholehearted love destined to last for life; in Owen, the tempest of ill-fated passion, and in Jamie, the first tender shoots of a love that promises to grow fine and true. Elisabeth brings these men and women together against the island backdrop—a backdrop that, far from being neutral, often becomes a catalyst for the love stories that ensue.

PHILIPPA AND STEVE

When Philippa Marshall approaches Bennett's Island in *The Dawning of the Day*, she is looking for respite—a new home, a job to support herself and her son, and a place to grieve after the death of her husband. She is greeted with the shining image of the island as it appears on the horizon:

> When she turned toward the bow again, Bennett's Island had changed from a low blue mass to a definite shape composed of thick green spruce woods, steep rocky beaches wet in the shade and shimmering in the sun, and a sudden wide field of yellow grasses that seemed to stretch across the island to open sea.

Philippa steps onto the island and into the active life of island school-teacher, getting to know her students and the family with whom she is boarding. She barely gets settled when she is thrust into controversy with some of her pupils. Her life is complicated further by the entrance of Steve Bennett on the scene. Steve seems to fit the mold of the laconic and seemingly reserved fisherman who quietly goes about his business, as described by critic Susan Berneis. Even on their first meeting, however, he makes a good impression on Philippa.

> He was a spare, tall man with the deep coppery tan that comes to dark skin, his hair black as a crow's wing when he pushed back his cap. He had none of Young Charles's handsome arrogance, but the cheekbones and the lean squared lines of his jaw made him undeniably a Bennett. . . . He walked beside her, moving with a slow ease. A scent of washed and ironed cloth came from his shirt, and suddenly this scent carried a sense of overpowering masculinity with it.

Philippa is attracted to Steve, and he reciprocates her feelings. Their relationship deepens, and after a dance at the clubhouse, Philippa realizes her feelings for Steve have changed. "When he moved, she wasn't surprised. He took her by the shoulders and kissed her. It was as gentle, and as positive, as all his movements were." Philippa thought that this aspect of life had ended with Justin's death. Steve sets out to prove her wrong.

Elisabeth gently reveals the fact that there is much more to Steve than meets the eye. After the kiss, Philippa and Steve have an honest talk about their feelings. Steve openly tells her that he loves her, and Philippa responds with disbelief.

> "But you can't!" she said, desperately. "Love—what I call love— isn't like that. It's not sudden, it's slow. It doesn't hit you like a bolt from the blue. And even if it did—well, I have no illusions, Steve. There's nothing about me to fascinate a man all in an instant."

Steve calmly listens to her outburst, as she lists her weaknesses and failings. Then he quietly says,

> "You're a lot of other things. . . . You think they don't show, but they do. Mrs. Marshall's one person, but Philippa's another. She looks out sometimes, past the mother and the widow and the teacher."
>
> She didn't know what to say. His words enchanted her; she could not help a fierce and secret rejoicing that this was no dream, that this was actually happening to her.

Steve Bennett might not be as charismatic a character as his older brother Owen, but with these simple words, he charms the reader along with Philippa. Elisabeth has created a believable and moving love story with a startling depth of emotion. At the close of the book, readers are assured that Philippa and Steve's love will sustain them through whatever trials await them.

> There was no reason for any urgency to cut through their weariness. Their lifetime lay ahead of them. They sank into exhaustion with their arms around each other, as if into sleep, mutely grateful for each other with an emotion which for the moment had no concern with love or passion.

VANESSA AND OWEN

Although Vanessa Barton sees the same Bennett's Island as Philippa, her response is quite different. So much pain colors her knowledge of life that it is difficult for her to find peace anywhere. At the opening of *The Seasons Hereafter*, she is a wind-tossed soul, haunted by her experience as a foster child, when she learned to harden her heart to protect herself from disappointment.

Vanessa is not sure that she loves her husband, Barry. Even so, she is reluctant to leave the predictability of their life together on the mainland to go to unknown Bennett's Island. She is scornful of Barry's regard for the Bennetts, his new employers, and hates the thought of being beholden to them. In an argument with Barry, Vanessa reveals the shadow cast over her life by her forlorn childhood.

"The last thing I'd ever want is to be in solid with the Bennetts. I *hate* them."

"You hate them for having something." His voice was dry and cold. "Well, we've got a chance to have something for the first time. I can buy this house and a boat. We'll have a place where we belong."

"Not me. I'll never belong here."

"You'll never belong anywhere, then! You've always got it in your head that you're a state kid. You think it sticks out like salt rheum and makes folks shy off like you're contagious? You're the one that shies off. They don't know you're a state kid, and even if they did they wouldn't care."

The enigmatic Vanessa claims she isn't looking for a new life on the island. Change is not a positive thing for her—especially moving to such a dramatic, brilliantly lit new world, filled with openness. Her insecure childhood, fraught with disillusionment, has trained her to distrust everyone. She has always been waiting for something she vaguely calls "The Day—the birthday of her life"—when she will finally find happiness.

She doesn't expect to find it on this strange island, which threatens the balance of her hard-won, fragile existence.

In the house there was too much light, waves of light lapping across walls and ceilings. The windows were full of sky and clouds, gulls, and sometimes a black spatter of crows. The wind blew, and the sound of water was as unrelenting as the light. . . .

She doesn't know where to hide from the brightness, or the inevitable interaction with other islanders. She finds small comfort in the fact that their house is "the last one around on the far side of the harbor, with a high point of yellow rock and spruces rising up beyond the northwest windows." Inured to its beauty, Vanessa finds it nearly impossible to shed her past and open herself to this new environment. These passages foreshadow the fact that Vanessa is soon to face an awakening, caused by another source of inexorable light shining down on her previously dark and despairing life—the bright light of Owen Bennett.

Her intense dislike for the Bennetts only makes it more difficult when she falls in love with one of them. Owen Bennett enters her life in a deceptively simple way.

> Unsmiling and unspeaking they looked at each other, and her suspense composed of terror and delight was familiar; she knew at once that the tiger was here.
> "I'm Owen Bennett," he said finally.
> "Yes."

With that brief meeting, Vanessa's life is changed completely. She seeks Owen out at the wharf and in the harbor, drawn by his undeniable charisma:

> Where his brothers' and sister's smiles were warm, his blazed. Oh, and he knows it! she thought. He uses it.

Despite her awareness of his charms, she couldn't help but feel "the visceral excitement that was half-pleasant and half-sickening" each time she laid eyes on him. Soon, they are arranging clandestine meetings to be together.

After their first kiss, Vanessa is transformed. Has "The Day" finally arrived, in the form of this handsome lobsterman? Elisabeth portrays Vanessa's timid joy in this excerpt:

> Suddenly it came to her. The Day. This could be it. What she was born for, what she had been moving toward all the days of her life. She'd had to marry Barry, they'd had to live in a miserable crawl from one poor situation to another, so that he would be hanging around the Limerock waterfront at the right moment to meet Philip Bennett. That was why the Water Street House had to be sold, she knew now, goose-fleshed with awe; so she'd have nothing to hold her back. The Day. This was it.

Owen's passion matches her own. He confides that he has never loved anyone like he loves her, almost to the point of pain. He hates himself for being unfaithful to his wife, Laurie, and despairs that this love had to happen now, when he is fifty years old. These conflicting emotions cause him mental and physical anguish. "It keeps me awake nights and it makes me growl at my kids," he says. Vanessa also feels the painful physical impact of such emotion, yet is awed that he shares her love.

> A man felt this way about her, and it was a man whose touch took from her every defense. Many women wait their whole lives for this and it never happens, she thought.

Unfortunately, the flame from this love with Owen is not destined to burn for long. Although passion and a shared wild spirit tie Vanessa and Owen together, feelings of duty and loyalty bind Owen to his family, along with an awareness of his mortality. Owen experiences chest pains, and with his history of heart trouble, he is terrified. He has a revelation, realizing that if he is to die in any woman's arms, it has to be Laurie's. Both lovers are crushed almost irreparably by their separation. Elisabeth makes us feel their searing, unbearable pain. It is because she draws these characters so accurately and so completely that we care terribly about what is to become of them.

ROSA AND JAMIE

When Rosa Fleming comes to Bennetts Island, she is on a mission—to escape from the pain of her recent divorce and to forge a new life. Unlike Vanessa, she longs for change, and she is proactive in her search, even to captaining her own vessel to the island.

> She went well to the starboard of it and then made a turn to the east, and there, rising above her like a hill of gold in the sunlight, were the high yellow rocks of the western point of Bennett's Island harbor.

The golden image of the island, gleaming like a reward after hardship and sorrow, gives her a straightforward vision of hope.

Rosa plans to lick her wounds far away from the memories of her shame and humiliation: "It was a place where Con had never been and where nobody would know about him and her." She soon finds healing in work, as she goes out to haul lobster traps, and a sense of peace when she returns to the little nest she is slowly creating for herself. She appreciates equally the joys of solitude and sharing time with new friends. The island holds the possibility of romance for her as well, in the form of Jamie Sorensen.

Rosa is considerably more resourceful than Vanessa, who is always fighting her past; and she hasn't undergone the same degree of devastation as Philippa. She is a strong, determined young woman, and soon discovers that Bennett's Island is the perfect place for her to shed her unhappy memories. She keeps herself "pleasantly anesthetized . . . moving at a cautious, unjarring pace from one project to the other. The important thing was not to run out of projects."

Her friendship with Jamie starts as a pleasant diversion, and when he kisses her, she is both surprised and delighted. With this couple, Elisabeth shows us the hesitant early stages of love and attraction:

153

Jamie held her face and kissed her on each cheekbone, on her nose, and on her mouth. "There. I'm not putting pressure on you. I won't even come near you till you give me the word. But if you want me, just whistle.

It's lucky that Jamie is a patient man. He has to wait while Rosa goes through turmoil with Con, her ex-husband, as well as with a mysterious stranger, Quint, who is enmeshed in a violent conflict between the islanders and a fleet of invading fishermen. Rosa is ashamed of herself after she uses poor judgment in her dealings with both men, and is reluctant to face Jamie.

She has mixed feelings when he pulls alongside her and her cousin Edwin one day when they are out to haul. Jamie joins them for a mug-up, and Elisabeth introduces the idea of a future for Rosa and Jamie. Rosa stares at Jamie, thinking,

What grew between him and her—if she let it grow—would take time, but it would be sound and good. No doubt of that. Jamie wouldn't be coming to her for refuge; he was one of the most self-sufficient men she'd ever met.

Jamie is indeed self-reliant, but by no means without weakness. Elisabeth allows him his own trial-by-fire in the next Bennett's Island title, *An Answer in the Tide*, where he faces some of the same struggles of the heart that Rosa resolves in *Strawberries in the Sea*.

Rosa comes to a sense of peace after the humiliation she endures, and by the end of the book, the reader knows that she will be all right. She is going to stay on the island and face her future with a clear head and open heart.

Although each of these women may see the same island initially, their reactions to it are dramatically different. The way they will respond, and the paths they take, are indicative of their individual personalities. What the island has in store for each woman will soon be revealed, for each is shaped by its spell.

In all of her books, Elisabeth's characters seem to have a special communion with the natural world. No obstacle is too big to surmount if they are just able to "go out" and work through whatever it is they are facing. Elisabeth subtly puts forth the feeling that the island possesses great healing powers. No wound is too painful, no problem too large, if they can just listen to the murmuring of the wind in the spruce trees, sit on a broad expanse of rock warmed by the sun, and watch the surf tumbling in. The natural rhythms of the tide seem to hold a restorative power that is universal.

This is not to say that Elisabeth presents an oversimplification of life's travails. Often there are no easy solutions to the issues they face. However, it is this intermingling of the natural world—the background—with the characters' inner lives that is a constant in Elisabeth's writing. The characters' fates are part of the weave, their lives both influenced and changed by the world in which they live.

JOANNA AND NILS

No one more embodies the idea of "passion for place" than Joanna. As Elisabeth writes in *The Ebbing Tide,* "it amounted practically to a coastal tradition that no Bennett could retain his health and happiness for long away from the red rocks and wind-tormented spruces of their island."

Joanna Bennett Sorensen is arguably the most powerful female character created by Elisabeth Ogilvie. Her devotion to the island is matched only by her loyalty to her family. She easily gives her wholehearted adoration to her first husband, Alec Douglass, a charmer who arrives on the island ready to take up residence. Joanna is instantly intrigued and attracted to him, and their love quickly grows and leads to marriage. Soon after the wedding, she is shocked by Alec's betrayal; he is a gambler, and doesn't seem able to control his addiction, even when it threatens their future. A tragedy takes place, which changes the course of Joanna's life forever. She must be stronger than she ever imagined.

Patricia Morgan wrote an intriguing article about Joanna and the Tide Trilogy for *Down East* magazine in 1985, comparing Joanna to one of the most famous heroines of our time—Scarlett O'Hara. Skillfully comparing the two women, she noted that "Joanna Bennett of Bennett's Island is, at times, as obstinate and foolish and self-centered as Scarlett." Joanna and Scarlett also share "a fierce and proprietary love for a place, a land—a home. Just as Scarlett, in a scene memorable both in print and on film, raises her fist to a bitter orange sky and vows to restore Tara's glory and 'never be hungry again!', so Joanna is determined, even when it appears to be irrevocably lost, to regain the traditional way of life of her island lobstering village—and retain the Bennett suzerainty."

Morgan extended her comparison further, saying, "If one can accept this rough paradise as Joanna's Tara, the analogy becomes easier with the men in her life. Scarlett has her Ashley, Joanna her Alec. And if Nils Sorensen does not exhibit quite the charm of Rhett Butler, he does make a suitably quixotic gesture in returning to Bennett's Island after it seems that the battle for survival of the village has been lost."

This is not to say that Nils isn't a force to be reckoned with; on the contrary, he is the epitome of the Ogilvie hero. Stalwart and true, Nils has loved Joanna since they grew up together on Bennett's. He is only too aware of her vibrant spirit and her bigger-than-life passion for the island—qualities that double as her shortcomings. Her impatience and singlemindedness later contribute to one of the biggest crises in their marriage.

Nevertheless, Joanna soon finds that another sort of love is possible with Nils. Where Alec was an ardent first love, Nils offers a more temperate sort of romance. In Nils she finds a devoted suitor, and a life partner willing to rebuild the island with her. Theirs is a mature love, steadfast and secure, like a sturdy boat on the waves.

In *Storm Tide*, Joanna risks her new marriage to Nils by putting the island first. Patricia Morgan describes Joanna's fixation on the island: "[she] is obsessed beyond reason with maintaining the island's status quo. She is grasping, manipulative, self-righteous; unpleasant character traits also exhibited by Scarlett. Yet one may be moved . . . to feel compassion for these women—strong, driving and driven, forced by circumstances to wield power only through male intermediaries."

Joanna's obsession is evident when she tries to rally her brothers to her cause of restoring the island to its former glory.

> Her mind could only reiterate that Owen and Mark mustn't fight—they must work, like herself, for the Island. That must come first with them as it must come first with her. It was their past and their future. It was themselves.

Although some readers lose patience with Joanna's singlemindedness, Elisabeth makes no apologies for her heroine's passionate nature. As frustrating as Joanna's behavior might be, she never veers from the emotional course set for her in the very opening scenes of *High Tide at Noon*, when Elisabeth describes Joanna's grief over the island's demise:

> There were no boats in the harbor now, no lobsters in the lobster car that floated, an empty and rotting box, beside the empty and rotting wharf. There was no sound of saw and hammer from the workshops, no freshly painted buoys hung against weathered shingles, no

new traps of yellow wood piled high on the beach rocks. Bennett's Island was a desert island now, forgotten and scorned save by the woman whose footsteps sounded so strange in the emptiness. Joanna Bennett had come home.

Joanna is determined to revitalize Bennett's Island at any cost, and Nils understands this. He takes her as she is, and proves to be skillful in handling her outbursts. When tensions between them reach a fever pitch, however, Nils goes "ashore" (i.e., to the mainland) for a while to work on a boat, leaving Joanna to reflect on her actions. She is terrified at the thought of losing him, and when they are finally reunited, the dam breaks as Joanna releases the pent-up emotions of the past months:

> Joanna Bennett, sobbing like this! It was an incredible thing and she knew it; but the knowledge didn't quiet her. It was journey's end in more ways than one. For she was safe now; she was secure. She forgot shame and resentment and frustration in realizing that one certainty.

Elisabeth sums up their love for each other in a few beautiful lines, when Joanna asks Nils if he is ever coming home, saying:

> "Because if you don't want to go back to the Island . . . I'm never going back either. I don't care where you go. Only don't ever leave me behind again, Nils!"
>
> "You don't mean that, Joanna," he said, so near she could feel his breath on her cheek. "You wouldn't give up the Island for anybody."
>
> "I do mean it," she answered with a curious serenity, and knew that she was telling the truth. "Nils, wherever you are, that's my Island. I never knew it until now."

The way that Elisabeth deftly brings Joanna and Nils to an understanding and shared commitment to a dream is one of the finest parts of this book. The depth of love that Joanna feels for Nils surpasses anything she felt for Alec, or even for the island.

Nils and Joanna face yet another challenge in *The Ebbing Tide*, the third installment of the series. It is World War II, and most of the island men are off serving their country, including Nils. One would think Joanna would thrive under these conditions—independently keeping the island going while the men are gone. Surprisingly, this is not the case; Joanna finds herself quite vulnerable when Dr. Dennis Garland arrives. He reminds her of her first love, Alec, and she struggles with these feelings. Patricia Morgan wrote, "Just as Scarlett at last comes to realize it was Rhett she loved all along, so the Sorensen marriage is strengthened by the temptation Joanna endures while Nils is gone. The book concludes with the pair metaphorically sailing, after a rough passage, back into safe harbor."

In *The Dawning of the Day*, the fourth book of the series, we see signs of a changed and more mature Joanna, when she talks about the deep level of understanding and communication she and Nils have achieved. "Nils lets me get just so far with my vaporings, and then he starts hauling me back to earth again." This is a down-to-earth estimation of the ground they have traveled together since the early days, leading to this hard-won level of comfort and trust.

One of the charms and strongest elements of the Bennett's Island series is the reader's ability to grow up with Joanna, just as Elisabeth did. We witness the mellowing of her fire as she settles down into comfortable, though never dull, wedded harmony with Nils. She cares deeply for her children and stands steadfastly with them through storm and struggle. Her tenderness and devotion to her children is evident in the entire Bennett's series, from the very first description we have of her first child, Ellen, Alec's daughter.

In *An Answer in the Tide*, Joanna must support her son Jamie as he endures public humiliation, and in *The Day Before Winter* Joanna faces more struggles with the members of her extended family. At no point does she give in and allow society to drag her down. She consistently upholds the moral standards established by her parents, Stephen and Donna. In Joanna, Elisabeth has created a fully defined, thinking, feeling heroine of flesh and blood. Her passions and her fiery temperament, her steadfast love for her family, and her undying belief in her island home make her one of the best-loved of all Elisabeth's characters.

THORA AND LYLE

In *Waters on a Starry Night*, Elisabeth gives us one of her best portrayals of the simultaneous intensity and fragility of marriage. The central problem for Thora and Lyle Ritchie emerges very early in the book—they simply married too young. Thora often finds herself awestruck that she is mother to four growing girls:

That was the way everything always ended, with the children. Sometimes it seemed as if there had never been anything else, she had traveled from her own childhood to theirs, with nothing in between. She wondered if Lyle felt it too, if the boy she had seen walking away from her this morning was more than an illusion, a reality; sealed into the man's body, loaded with the man's burdens, and resenting his prison.

Thora is correct in her assumptions about Lyle, whose burdens soon become too much for him to handle. Thora is still in love with Lyle, despite the mistakes they've made and the poverty they face. But Lyle is struggling against the "prison" of debt and a suffocating sense of defeat—he feels their marriage is strained beyond the breaking point. When Thora tries to comfort him, he says, "There's nothing wrong—only a man gets his bellyful of failure after a while. He begins to think there's no use or sense in anything."

In Lyle, Elisabeth creates one of her most heartwrenching male characters. Trying to succeed and care for his family, but bowed down with the weight of so much failure, Lyle faces a turning point in his life. He must decide whether to remain true to his wife or, in an effort to forget his misery, succumb to the wily attractions of a lovely "summer complaint." With this novel, Elisabeth proves that even though she writes from a female viewpoint, she does not neglect her male characters. Lyle's struggles are sensitively portrayed with depth and empathy, his responses clothed in reality. He is not a cardboard figure of a man who strays. His suffering is just as real as Thora's, and like her, he must find answers on his own.

Thora finds it difficult to manage their financial burdens and meet the needs of their girls, all the while fearful that her husband is falling in love with another woman. The situation is complicated further when a stranger determines that Thora's book collection is rare and valuable. Thora's unwillingness to sell the collection is another source of strife in her marriage. The pain increases as Thora feels the void between herself and Lyle, where once there was such closeness and love. Thora doesn't crumble, however. She is always ready to take whatever action is needed in an effort to fix things.

> The situation had a sore familiarity, like the pain around an old scar; despair that was none the weaker for being so commonplace, and then the bracing-up, the turning eagerly to whatever was at hand with the illusion that you were doing something constructive.

When Thora feels overwhelmed by her situation, she does not sit idly by. She does battle with her ancient washing machine or cleans lamp chimneys or sometimes she grabs her jacket and "goes out." Like other Ogilvie heroines, she finds a constant source of healing and refuge on the island.

Thora is ferocious about protecting her marriage and family—her very life. Inspired by real-life young girls, Thora's children are beautifully drawn, yet Elisabeth doesn't paint an idyllic picture. She's not afraid to show family life, warts and all, in a description of a difficult morning:

> . . . as if the children felt her attention was not complete, they were contentious this morning. Chris slapped Nod, who roared as if she'd been maimed for life. Reprimanded, Chris went into a deep sulk which was so much like her father's that it would have been comical if Thora had not felt so bruised this morning. Beth had a crying spell, and Ann-Marie was so airily cut off from them all that Thora felt like shaking her.

The strain of mothering clearly adds another dimension to Thora's suffering, and makes us admire her all the more when she overcomes her difficulties.

The girls are aware of the changes in their once happy home. Ann-Marie is especially sensitive to what is going on between Thora and Lyle:

> "You don't wake us up singing, and Father's the way he is. . . . A year ago he wouldn't have forgot and sold the double-ender! And we had the Fourth of July picnic even though we were broker than we are now. And you and he talk to us but not to each other, and I know you don't sleep up there in the open chamber, I hear you get up and not come back—" She stopped, her mouth frozen open as if in horror at herself. Or at Thora's expression.

Thora deals with this as she does every conflict, facing it head on. She decides to be truthful with Ann-Marie, just as she is with Lyle. Thora's backbone of strength and fierce resolve to be true to herself—so similar to Joanna's—is evident:

> But even if she should shout it, it would make no difference because of what she had already said. And yet she had had to say it because she was Thora, and she knew no other lines but her own. She couldn't pretend to be anyone else but herself.

This conviction to be true to self is an underlying motto of each Ogilvie heroine.

Things come to a head when Thora finally decides to sell some of her books—too late as far as Lyle is concerned. His relationship with Vivian has progressed to where Lyle calls her a "sickness in his blood." Lyle decides that the only solution is to go to sea on a trawler, leaving the family behind. He advises Thora to move to the mainland, with divorce the ultimate death knell on the horizon.

To relieve her despair, Thora seeks solace in roaming her island home. Although these walks only provide temporary relief, they help her clear her head and search for solutions:

> Thora walked up to the house alone except for Missy, who came talking behind her. The silence was like balm on scorched flesh. She walked slowly to prolong it, her face lifted to the breeze that carried a deep-sea scent over warm earth and green hollows.

Elisabeth not only reveals the dearest thoughts and wishes of her characters with utter clarity, she also makes the reader long for similar refuge. This commingling of background with character both strengthens the plot and builds empathy for the characters.

In moments of ultimate despair, Thora cannot stand to stay in the house. On more than one night, Thora goes out to sleep in her daughters' "brush camp."

> She knew where she could sleep. Her weigela cave, the brush camp. She was sobbing a little from her haste and some appalling grief that had surrounded her all at once like that breath from the sea when she went into the woods by the wild apple tree. . . . Thora crawled into the brush camp and curled up on the spruce couch. Back to the womb, she thought wryly. . . .

At this point, Thora is facing an almost inevitable divorce from Lyle—it seems that their last battle has been fought and she has lost. Before the break happens, however, Lyle goes out to haul during a storm. When his boat is lost, Thora is sure he is dead and knows that life without him would not be worth living.

> The irony was that all the friendship and love in the world couldn't make any difference. Amy's loyalty now, the men's loyalty out on the water, couldn't save a drowned man. Her own love couldn't have held Lyle. . . . In whose arms could she wail now?

After what seems an eternity of waiting, the boat returns. The moment Thora knows that her husband has survived is one of pure joy. He tells her that when he was floating in the icy depths as his boat went under, he saw only Thora's face. Suddenly Lyle sees their youthful marriage as a wonder, saying to Thora, "We've grown together, you know that?" And she answers, "Like Siamese twins . . . we can't be separated."

Elisabeth by no means sets up this ending as a foregone conclusion of happiness. Much hard work will be required if they want to save their marriage. Thora will have to live with the knowledge of Lyle's feelings for Vivian, and he will have to live with the memory of what he has done. Regardless of all that has happened, they are united in their commitment to keep their family together. Elisabeth has depicted a marriage in crisis so acutely that the reader feels every emotion—cries along with Thora, questions along with Lyle, feels the daughters' torment, and rejoices at the end when Thora and Lyle are reunited. All is not settled; they will face more trials in the future. But they will face them together.

LESLIE AND GILES

In *Call Home the Heart*, we find another quintessential Ogilvie heroine and another portrait of a marriage. Leslie Whitney shares many qualities with Thora, Joanna, and the women of the Lovers Trilogy: a backbone of steel, faith in her mate, an understanding of the lobstering life, a deep love for her children, and an affinity with the outdoors.

This marriage is quite different from the one portrayed in *Waters on a Starry Night*, however. Leslie and Giles Whitney don't face as many obstacles as the Ritchie family. They are older and more secure, both financially and emotionally. The reader doesn't have an opportunity to know Giles as well as other Ogilvie heroes, as he is away much of the time fishing with his sons and son-in-law. The picture we do form of him is much like that of Nils or the Bennett men, clarified in an opening line: "As a Whitney of Teague's Island he was a fisherman born, who had to be in sight of the water when he wasn't on it."

Leslie understands that this is the only life for her husband, and she attempts to share this hard-won wisdom with her daughter-in-law Felice. Newly wed to Simon Whitney, Felice has dramatic ways and an exotic "otherness" that combine to get her into a great deal of trouble. It is this sensitivity that adds to the intense agony and abandonment she feels every time Simon leaves to go fishing.

As Elisabeth writes about Giles's passion for the sea, she explains the inner workings of all of her lobstermen characters. "Felice, he does love you. You're his woman. But he's a fisherman, and he's got to chase herring in the summer. You can't do a thing about it." When Felice asks Leslie if she wanted Giles to have the new boat, Leslie answers without thinking, "Yes, I did want him to have her, because he wanted her." And Leslie summarizes their shared fate when she tells Felice, "you and I have married a special breed of man and there's no use trying to change them." Some modern readers may find Elisabeth's heroines too old-fashioned, too committed to the dreams of their mates. The depiction of their solid union and understanding of each other is admirable, however, and enviable in today's climate of self-centeredness. Giles is wed to the sea as clearly as he is to Leslie. She understands and accepts that this is the only life for her men; her support of them is complete.

Just as Leslie accepts Giles's way of life, however, she expects him to do likewise. Leslie doesn't do anything by halves, and her nature is to right the wrongs she sees around her. Just as Joanna is consumed by her urgency to return Bennett's Island to its former glory, Leslie cannot rest until she helps those in need.

Leslie's call to do what's right takes hold as she tries to help Renie and her illegitimate baby, downtrodden and despised by the rest of the island. Leslie refutes the majority of the Sewing Circle, who do not wish to dirty their hands by helping Renie. She goes ahead and purchases a carriage for Renie's baby without the support of the group, finding admiration from some, and alienation from many. Ruel Whitney, Giles's cousin, is Renie's lover. For this family connection alone, Leslie feels compelled to help—but even more so because of her deep compassion for mother and child.

She is also moved by compassion to help her old love, Troy Teague, disgraced prodigal son of the island who has returned home decades after he scandalized the community. Leslie is sensitive to his plight, and willing to help, even when the Teagues turn their backs on him.

With a keen understanding of human nature, Elisabeth depicts the varied emotions of the islanders, and unravels a tangled snarl of human passions. As usual, all is not as it seems. Leslie's subsequent understanding of herself, and the transformation she undergoes during the summer, is powerful to witness.

Beyond being a dedicated fisherman, Giles is also a devoted husband, who stands ready to support and defend Leslie when she gets herself into trou-

ble with her various causes. At the close of the novel, he is with her, supporting her decision to help Renie and Troy, even at the risk to his own pride:

> "Well, mebbe it was my wife. It's just the kind of thing she'd do.
> I'm always asking her, For Christ's sake, can't you mind your own
> business? But there she goes, sticking out her neck to save somebody
> else's. I can't cure her of it unless I knock her over the head with the
> axe a few times, and I don't plan to do that even for the Teagues."

Here again, Elisabeth demonstrates her ability to juggle and eventually
resolve several various plotlines in one satisfactory, cohesive way. She subtly
brings together the island's out-of-place, forlorn characters, Renie and Felice,
and by uniting them, brings joy to both. She resolves the question of Troy's
tormented past, and reinforces the strength of Leslie and Giles's marriage.
Elisabeth seems to be saying something about the role of women in society,
and the strength of their resolve to persevere and survive despite the obstacles they face. There is an almost feminist edge to Elisabeth's writing, in her
message that the quiet power of women will not be ignored.

JENNIE AND ALICK

In Jennie Glenroy, the seeds of Elisabeth's feminist message have borne
fruit. Though, like the other Ogilvie heroines, Jennie represents many levels
of passion, she also demonstrates the growth Elisabeth has made as a writer.
In many respects, Elisabeth has created a thoroughly modern young woman
in the characterization of Jennie.

Writer Jack Barnes found Jennie "a marked contrast to most young
ladies at the beginning of the nineteenth century . . . a free-spirited, well-
educated young woman." Jennie becomes an orphan at age twenty-one and
goes to live with wealthy relatives in London. Nigel Gilchrist, a handsome
Cavalry officer, soon sweeps her off her feet. They marry and move to the Scottish Highlands to manage the family estate of Linnmore.

Elisabeth wastes no time in establishing Jennie's strength and sense of
moral courage. In *Jennie About to Be*, Jennie is shocked when she discovers
the truth about the Clearances—when landowners forced tenants from their
cottages in pursuit of profit—and shows her passion for justice when she
stands up to Nigel:

> "Don't you understand, Nigel?" She was resolved to speak rea-
> sonably and give him no chance to turn her emotions against her.

"You were—you are a part of the awfulness. I saw you doing those things, and there was no pity in you. You and your men were like soldiers sacking a captured village. . . . They're pulled up by the roots and thrown away. They're dispossessed, and so am I."

Jennie's disillusionment leads her to run away to the New World with Nigel's cousin Alick Gilchrist, who is fleeing the authorities in Scotland. Their journey along the Dark Mile is a long one, fraught with difficulty, and the "mindless rhythm of their walking" is evoked brilliantly:

> She walked behind Alick in a trancelike state. . . . Reality was the man walking ahead of her in coarse coat and breeches and scuffed boots. She had been watching those boots for years, it sometimes seemed; the dark pattern of the plaid folded over his shoulder had a ghastly familiarity, and the way the hair grew down his neck. The way the leather bag bounced softly on his hip.

When Alick's route to America requires that he have a wife, Jennie agrees to play the part, and together the "Glenroys" sail to New England. (The couple assumed an alias, fearing that Scottish authorities may be in pursuit.)

> She took Alick's hand and warmed it in both of hers. "I promised you a ship," she said, "and this is it. Now I promise you we are not going to drown. I will see you safe in America, with your own land under your feet."

As *The World of Jennie G.* opens, we find Jennie and Alick sailing toward the coast of Maine on the *Paul Revere*. Jennie has spent the month-long voyage teaching English to the Gaelic-speaking Highlanders on board, and now as they approach America, she is happy and proud to have fulfilled her promise—she has brought Alick safely to the New World, and a new life. They settle in the thriving town of Maddox, continuing to act as man and wife, with Alick working in the shipyard and Jennie as a governess. Jennie still plans to earn her passage back to England to be with her sisters, but things change when she discovers that she is pregnant with Nigel's child.

Alick is immediately supportive and wants to take care of Jennie and her baby. The passages where he shows his enduring love for Jennie are some of the most touching in all of Elisabeth's books. Alick and Jennie are soon involved in controversy with some town bullies, especially the cruel Zeb Pulsifer. They incur the disapproval of one of the town ministers as well. Through all of this, the Glenroys fight back, and Jennie is just as spirited as Alick in defending herself.

When it comes to helping others, Jennie resembles Leslie Whitney of *Call Home the Heart*. She is drawn to the mysterious Evans family the first time she sees them come through town. Convinced that Mr. Evans is brutalizing his wife, Jennie keeps a close eye on the family and tries to help them, with Alick's assistance. David, one of the young Evans children, ends up saving the Glenroys from a fiery death when he pulls them from a burning barn, the fire set by none other than the villainous Zeb Pulsifer. And when they are saved, they know that they will make their new life here on this farm by the river, in the town of Whittier.

Nancy McCallum of the *Journal Tribune* wrote about Jennie Glenroy's world, where "the individual is cherished, family bonds are tight, the wrongs of the world are pointed out, and life is an adventure seasoned with good humor, occasional sorrow, and deep passion." This is an apt description of not only the Jennie books, but of all Elisabeth's work.

The third installment of the series takes place seventeen years later, and covers one very eventful year in the lives of the Glenroy family. Opening in 1827, the "Godless Glenroys" are a wealthy, if often controversial, family living in Whittier (Thomaston), in midcoast Maine. Alick is running a successful shipyard, and Jennie has raised their five children to be independent thinkers.

When the third Jennie book was published, many critics were surprised at the clarity of Elisabeth's focus on women's lives during the 1800s, including the opportunities (or lack thereof) and issues they faced on a daily basis. Reviewer Karen Mather of the Brunswick, Maine, *Times Record* talks about how many of the female characters in the series exhibit uncommon courage and self-awareness during the worst of times. Not only Jennie, but characters like the woman doctor in town, and even Jennie's eldest daughter Priscilla, all possess the shared traits of honor and pride, and the ability to cope with all manner of trouble in an admirable fashion. Mather writes, "Jennie is a true heroine not because she endures fear and suffering but as a manifestation of the grace and dignity she maintains at every tragic curve."

Mather is referring here to the many tragedies Jennie must face through the course of the three novels. She confronts death in many forms—accidental, due to illness and murder, and even suicide. At each turn, she must deal with the crisis that faces them, and in so doing, she proves her mettle time and again. Elisabeth addresses some big issues in this third volume of the series, including women's rights, slavery, and questions of religion and spirituality.

The Glenroy children have gained a following among Ogilvie readers, who write to beg Elisabeth not to let the children grow up too fast. Readers are especially partial to Bell Ann Glenroy, the endearingly spunky apple of her parents' eyes. Bell Ann is comparable to the adorable Nod Ritchie from *Waters on a Starry Night*.

Elisabeth provides such a lively and realistic description of the irrepressible Bell Ann, that we can almost hear her childish tones and see her rambunctious gamboling around the yard. Elisabeth's understanding and love for children ring in every phrase:

> Bell Ann was still at the manic stage. The dowsing had been both mysterious and dull for her, with everyone hushing her, and she'd seen no witch on a broomstick. But the way home had been glorious. She had lost one hair ribbon, her dress was soiled, she was scratched, her shoes were wet, her stockings falling down, and she had green apples in her pockets. She was almost too hoarse to speak, but she kept talking anyway.

Jennie, Joanna, Thora and Leslie equally demonstrate another important component of Elisabeth's characters—their commitment to family. Their fierce love for their mates and their children are the bedrock of their existence.

PART IV

Selections from Her Early Writings

12 ❧ *Soliloquy by a Cat*

This charming poem, published in The Manet *in 1934 (twelfth grade), exhibits Elisabeth's delicate use of words and imagery, her affinity for animals, and her unbounded joy in the seasons and the natural world.*

Oh, springtime is a mystic thing
Whereof a thousand poets sing.
It is the most delightful time
To rhapsodize in song and rhyme.
To me it is the time of year
When first the little snakes appear.
The poets tell of butterflies
That flutt'ring o'er the crocus rise.
I grant that they are pretty things
With fragile bubble-tinted wings.
But, O to catch those bits of gauze
Within my eager-reaching paws!
And poets idolize spring flow'rs—
My mistress prates of them for hours.
She's talking now—so I retreat
And find them really very sweet.
But heavens! she will lose her head
To find me in the tulip bed!

13 ❧ *The Delightful Guest*

When originally published in The Manet *in 1934,"The Delightful Guest" was prefaced by the following editor's note: "This story, although sentimental and improbable, has a charming atmosphere of fragile and beautiful old age. The descriptions are remarkably lucid, and the general tone of the story is warm and pleasing."*

IT WAS SPRING IN Miss Gabrielle's garden. Not that it wasn't spring outside, too, but it seemed to make a specialty of decorating Miss Gabrielle's little walled place. Though a good many people would sniff at calling this secluded spot a garden, it was one undoubtedly.

There were four apple trees, growing informally instead of geometrically; they were in blossom and the air was full of creamy-rose petals. And old-fashioned flowers—red and white striped tulips, michaelmas daisies, and iris in lavender and blue, and tawny yellow, grew in great unrestrained clumps. The air was heavy with lilies-of-the-valley and lad's love. There were no prim paths, but single flagstones dotted the grass which was Miss Gabrielle's pride—it was so thick and green. And all around this lovely spot there was a wall of faded rose-red bricks.

Miss Gabrielle sat in a green wicker chair under the chiefest of the apple trees. Through its snowy branches she regarded the uncertain blue and white of the April sky. There was a thrush somewhere; at his sudden rapture Miss Gabrielle felt a sort of sweet wistful sadness.

"Gabie, you're not getting sentimental," she accused herself. "You're not thinking of dear dead days beyond recall!" But she was, unconsciously. She sighed, then abruptly sat up with a quickening of the pulses. She had the same feeling she used to have as a child—a conviction that at any moment something strange and delightful was going to happen. It had been company or a hummingbird or jam for tea, but now company, besides the butcher's boy and the postman, was unheard of, and there were always humming birds in her undisturbed garden, and she had long since outgrown her love for jam. Nevertheless her heart beat faster and she looked around excitedly at the quaint gate in the wall.

No one appeared at the gate but there was a scraping noise somewhere, and precisely at the moment that Miss Gabrielle turned to look in its direction, which seemed to be in front of her chair, she saw a dark head, a pair of shoulders and finally a whole body appear on the wall. And there sat a young man, swinging his legs and regarding her with somewhat frightened amazement.

Miss Gabrielle was also astonished and startled. Then, with a flush in her cheeks, and without rising, she said, "Good afternoon."

"Good afternoon," he answered back, nervously. By his voice he was a very young man indeed. He leaned forward and added anxiously, "I say, I'm awfully sorry I barged in this way—I had no idea there was anyone here?" Which sounded strange but he was so visibly embarrassed and sincere that Miss Gabrielle said reassuringly, "Do come down before you fall! And I like company."

He smiled suddenly. "Thanks—thank you!"

He slid off the wall and landed with a thud on the grass. He crossed to her quickly, put his hands behind his back and looked down at her from his great height, speaking breathlessly.

"This is awfully decent of you—you see I was coming down the road from town and I saw your wall and—well, I've always had an insatiable curiosity for the wrong side of a wall—and I saw the tops of the trees—and—here I am!"

"What a dear boy he is," thought Miss Gabrielle. She said graciously, motioning towards a chair, "Won't you sit down?"

He accepted promptly, but sat on the grass instead of on the chair, crossing his legs and leaning his elbows on his knees. A mist arose in Miss Gabrielle's eyes. All her life she had longed for boys in her garden. At first, sturdy rosy youngsters in tight blue jerseys that showed the curves of their hard, independent, yet lovable little bodies. Then boys growing tall and fair, in worn tweeds, and bare brown, scarred knees, a superfluity of arms and legs and a ridiculous, uncertain, lilt in their voices. And now—the stranger hugged his knees and beamed at her from blue, bright eyes under dark brows—the left one quirked in absurdly familiar fashion. He was by no means a handsome boy—his nose had a bump in the middle and his mouth was wide—but his teeth gleamed and his skin was darkly glowing against his white scarf.

She found herself speaking. "This is a delightful surprise to me. I have so few visitors."

He was looking around with enchanted eyes. "Is it real or isn't it? I thought gardens like this existed only in books!"

Miss Gabrielle smiled again and contentedly studied the blue blazer, piped with white with a white monogram on the breast pocket. Some sort of school uniform she thought, then suggested, "Perhaps you'd like to explore."

He jumped up eagerly.

"May I really?"

"Of course," said Miss Gabrielle. "I'll let you go alone—I think it's much more interesting to discover things by oneself."

He plunged his hands in his pockets. "I say, you are a jolly sport!" He turned away and sauntered across the grass, whistling a tuneless fragment of song. When he had disappeared Miss Gabrielle said to herself "Perhaps he's a burglar—but if the way to a man's heart is through his stomach a good tea might be of some use." She smiled up at Janet, who, unconscious of the guest, had brought out tea for one, laid attractively on a wheeled tray.

"Tea for two, Janet, with some of the little plum cakes you made, and please put some jam in the little ming bowl—the yellow one."

"For two, Miss Gabrielle?" Janet's plain face was astonished. She lifted severe eyebrows, half-opened her straight dour mouth.

"A young gentleman is calling, Janet. Please hurry."

Janet, burning with curiosity, switched off with an indignant whirl of starched skirts; Miss Gabrielle quivered with excitement as she made sure that there was plenty of sugar—boys liked sugar—and put a spray of apple-blossoms in her hair, like a maiden going to meet her lover.

When the visitor returned, Janet had already made the necessary additions, had returned to the house, and had stationed herself at a convenient window. She caught her breath sharply when he came into view, for there was something in his easy lounging poise that reminded her very much of some-one who had stood, in that same spot, leaning against the twisted trunk of an apple tree.

Miss Gabrielle, meanwhile, was extremely happy. He had come back with shining eyes, and flushed.

"A dovecote too! Now I know it can't be real! And does the tiger cat bother the doves?"

"Not at all. Please sit down and have some tea with me."

Talking continuously he sat down and opened his snowy napkin with calloused, capable, brown hands. "I never was in a place like this before. Are *you* real? You look like a Dresden china figure," he added boldly.

Miss Gabrielle's cheeks became as pink as the fragile old teapot from which she filled his cup.

"Please, please," she murmured, passing it to him.

Over the cakes he became confidential. Amusing and entertaining de-tails flowed in a continuous stream—his family, his school life, his childhood, his friends. Miss Gabrielle was entranced.

"They still think I'm the baby at home," he stated heatedly. "I'm nine-teen. Sometimes I think I'm rather old for my age but maybe I'm wrong. Alaric—the one that's in India—is no end hipped on himself." With utmost gravity he licked a crumb from his finger. "I hope I'll never be like that."

"My dear, you will never be like that," thought Miss Gabrielle. "Not as long as you are so confident and delightful and friendly."

They talked. Long gold lines came across the wall. It grew cool and a faint breeze scattered the creamy-rose petals on a silvery head and a black one.

Suddenly the boy was up. "It must be late!" he exclaimed, drawing his black brows together. Suddenly Miss Gabrielle knew. She didn't have to be told his name . . . she knew, as surely as she knew her name.

With a contagious, surprised laugh, he cried out, "We don't even know each other's names?"

"My friends call me 'Miss Gabrielle'," she said gently. "And you're—"

"Michael Storm. My father used to live near here. Perhaps you knew him."

Miss Gabrielle sat very still. He approached her and she held out her small, fragile, hand. He took it in his big brown one, saying, "I've had a jolly time!" His eyes were eloquent. "I'm coming again—sometime."

Miss Gabrielle would have spoken, but he bent swiftly and kissed her cheek. Suddenly she was smelling heather . . . soap . . . vigorous young hair . . . he stood up, she saw his bright, dear blue eyes smiling down at her, through a mist—he was gone.

Janet saw him vault the gate and wondered. Miss Gabrielle stayed dreaming in her chair, staring at the napkin he had dropped on the grass. All at once she was filled with an all-consuming ecstasy. . . . Michael Storm had left her without a word years before . . . but he had come back . . . to kiss her good-bye.

14 ❧ *Summer Girl*

This short story, set on Bennett's Island, was first published in Woman's Day *in July 1944, the same year as* High Tide at Noon.

JOEL ROWED ACROSS the harbor from Grant's lobster car, whistling as if he hadn't just put in six hours without a break at the same oars, hauling his string of pots all the way around the ragged, rocky shores of Bennett's Island. He had a right to whistle, he thought, making the old double-ender fly across the smooth harbor waters. The fifteen dollars Grant had just paid him for his lobsters would more than make up the fifty he needed. And he had the rest in his dungarees right now, no need to go home and take it out of the dresser drawer. He could walk right up the beach to Mark Bennett's fish house and slap down the fifty on the work bench, and his money would be as good as any fisherman's money on Bennett's Island. Yessir, he'd just about bet that fifty that there wouldn't be any cracks about whether he was dry behind the ears yet when he laid the spot cash out in front of them. They'd know Joel Radway had his feet braced at last.

The shabby peapod with the tall young boy standing up at the oars slid by a big green powerboat moored in the shelter of the high rocky wall of Eastern Harbor Point. The man scrubbing the gunnels with an old broom yelled, "Put the steam right to her, Cap'n Joel!"

Joel bent all his strength to the oars. Sure, he could make this old tub go, but wait till he had that brand-new one of Mark Bennett's under his feet. His heart beat faster, his wide mouth twitched in a grin of sheer delight. If he could make fifty dollars as quick as this, with the spring crawl falling off—it was June already—what would he make when the fall spurt began, and in the new double-ender? Next year he'd be able to have a powerboat.

Before I'm seventeen I'll have me the new double-ender, he said to himself, without doubt or hesitation. Before I'm eighteen—a powerboat.

From now on nothing could stop him. He was on his way. He wanted to sing out loud, shatter the bright June silence with his voice, but he contented himself with a flying leap over the side as the pebbles grated under the boat. With a mighty splashing he hauled the peapod up on the beach and made her fast.

Yessir, Mark was in his fish house all right, standing in the doorway, looking kind of unfamiliar in his tan shirt and pants. Just like he was waitin' for me, mused Joel, grinning at his own queer ideas. Because he hadn't said anything to Mark about the peapod. He wanted to surprise everybody by walking in there and handing out the fifty dollars, just like that. Cripes, but he felt like yelling, like a wild Injun or something! Sure, it was kind of tough, thinking Mark was selling off all his gear because he was in the Army now, and might never come back to the Island alive, or all whole again. But this morning nothing could dim the dancing lights in Joel's eyes, blue-green under his old yachting cap—like the sea in October, his mother used to say when he was a little kid. And nothing could quench the invincible gaiety of his wide mouth, whose grin slashed his flat brown cheeks with dimples, and made people say, "That Joel's got the darndest grin!"

He took his bait box with the empty bags in it out of his old boat and lugged it up the beach to his father's bait shed. He wasn't in any hurry to get over there and see Mark. He wanted to savor this moment. Pretty soon it would all be over, and the new peapod—there she was, upturned in the beach peas and primroses, freshly painted, glittering white and sleek—would be his. The actual moment of taking out the money would be too quickly gone.

Besides, Lucia Harkness was hanging around there talking to Mark. Funny about a uniform. Lucia had never paid much attention to any particular one of the Island boys. She was a tomboy—always had been, ever since the Harknesses first started coming to the Island in the summers. Look at her now, in faded old dungarees Joel would use to clean his shotgun with, and that yellow mop of hers strung back in pigtails to keep it out of the way. . . . But Mark was a soldier, so she was hanging around him.

Girls! Thought Joel. He shook his head and spat eloquently on the beach stones. His old man wasn't anywhere around the shore—it was dinner time. The whole place looked empty, the curving beach white under the high blue sky of June, the punts and dories yellow and green and orange down at the edge of the tide, the harbor as pretty as a piece of blue silk, the gulls perched half asleep on the yellow harbor ledges, and behind the village the spruce woods so tall and dark against the sky.

The Island was a pretty place. He'd always known it was pretty, even in winter with snow flying across the yellow fields, and the wind always shrieking. But today it looked special. Anything would look special to him today. He put his hand in his pocket and felt the smooth leather of his billfold. Fifty dollars. Yessir!

He tried to walk slowly towards Mark's fish house, but his long legs acted in a hurry on their own account. Lucia Harkness was still there. Well, she could see him hand over the money too, and maybe from now on she'd stop looking at him with that funny little quirk to her mouth that made him so clumsy and foolish.

"Hi, Joel," Mark Bennett said. Lucia looked over her shoulder.

"Hi, Joel," she said.

He said, "Hi, kids." Funny, on account of the fifty dollars he almost liked Lucia. She still had freckles but they were tiny ones. She wasn't so skinny either —she kind of filled out her striped jersey. Her eyes were clear, wide, and brown, gazing steadily up at him. But today he didn't mind what he called her "uppity look."

"How's lobsters?" she asked him.

"Good. . . . Don't hurry," he added jauntily, as she began to walk away. He wanted her to see how a man had worked for his money, to be able to hand out fifty dollars as if it was a dime, and buy him a new boat.

"It's dinner time," she said. "Aren't you hungry? I am." She gave the bottom of the peapod a little pat as she went by it. Lady, that's my vessel you're layin' hands on, Joel thought, his heart thumping with his happiness.

"Good kid, Lucia," he said generously to Mark, as they watched her go across the marsh.

Mark nodded. "Funny kid, though. Wants to have a few pots out this summer to play around with. She's crazy about this place. I told her she'd better start looking around for a fisherman to marry, and she said she wouldn't mind."

"I betcha they got some lieutenant or somethin' all picked out for her to marry, Ted Harkness bein' a major in this man's war," said Joel. "Lobsterin', huh? She'll find out it's work and no play when she gets a nice crop of blisters and a kink in her back."

"She bought ten pots from me this morning," said Mark, "and—"

"Forget the wench," said Joel grandly, and took out his billfold. "I got a little matter o' business to discuss with you, Private Bennett." Try as he might, he couldn't keep his eyes from the peapod. The little beauty! When he had her, nothing could stop him.

The words bounced out in spite of his wish to be deliberate. "I'm buying your peapod, Mark. Fifty dollars is your askin' price, ain't it?"

"Sure, fifty's right, Joel," Mark said slowly. "You never told me you had your eye on her, though. Never spoke for her. . . . Gosh, Joel, if I'd known you wanted her—why didn't you tell me before?"

Joel felt sick. It began with a cold emptiness in the pit of his stomach and spread all through him. His face was hot, though, and his eyes burned as if the June sun were too bright for them. He looked down at the billfold, open in his hands.

"You sound like you've sold her, Mark," he said. "Who is it?"

"Lucia Harkness," said Mark.

Joel put his billfold back in his pocket. He knew Mark kept looking at him, and his face grew hotter. Mark was sorry for him, that was it! He looked straight at Mark through the foggy feeling in his eyes, and said, "Well, fifty dollars to raise hell with. Guess I'll go to town!"

"If you'd just spoke for her—" Mark began again.

"Aw, forget it, Mark," Joel said. "I don't really need her anyway."

But when he turned away, he didn't look at the peapod. All the time he'd been looking at it before, when he was watching Lucia Harkness pat it, he'd been thinking it was his. And it was hers. Hers. It belonged to a girl, and a summer girl at that. A girl who wanted it to play in. A girl who—why did it have to be her?

He went back to his father's fish house, and out on the little wharf built spindle-shanked over the rocks. With his back against a hogshead of bait, he dangled his rubber boots over the quietly moving water below, and stared out at the harbor.

He'd earned every cent of his fifty dollars with his hands and his back and sweat; that was what it meant to be a pod fisherman, rowing miles every day, rowing in circles to set the trap just where you'd hauled it, fighting against the wind that blew you out of your way while you were pulling up a trap. Sometimes your back ached like a toothache on the last end of a day's work, and those pots in Long Cove like to weighed six tons each, when you got them by the bridle and hefted them to the gunnel. But he hadn't kicked, when he thought of what his money was going to do; it was that thought which made him whistle when he rowed away from the car to leap ashore like a circus acrobat. Right now he didn't feel like ever whistling or leaping again.

Lucia Harkness. He looked back to a time when Lucia couldn't have been more than nine, and he was ten, sailing his [model] boat from the flat rocks at the edge of the harbor, on the other side. Ted Harkness—he wasn't a major in the Army then—had bought a little punt from Jud Gray, and painted it up bright blue for Lucia, and taught her how to row. She rowed all around the harbor in it, a skinny little kid in shorts and a jersey and sneakers, and Ted and Marian never worried about her. She could swim like a little fish, they said.

So there was Joel, sailing his boat at the edge of the harbor, and Lucia in her little blue punt. She'd rowed across to him, and watched his boat for a while, and then asked him to get into the punt.

"We can sail your boat way out in the harbor then," she said.

More than anything else in the world, Joel wanted to go. He knew he couldn't, but there was a way to get out of it without Lucia's knowing that he wasn't allowed in a punt. . . . Only his mother hadn't given him a chance to shrug his shoulders and say he didn't want to go. She had called down from the clotheslines, where she was hanging sheets, "Joel, don't you dare get into that punt! You know your father don't allow it—you'll be fallin' overboard first thing!"

She went into the house. Joel, his face burning, wished Lucia would go away. He hated her for being there and knowing he couldn't go around in a punt, when he was a boy, and older than her at that. He felt like hitting her.

"Can't you swim?" she asked him, her brown eyes wide.

"Who the hell wants that kind of foolishness?" he said roughly, and was glad when she looked surprised and hurt. He shoved the punt away from the big flat rock. "You take that pretty-painted clamshell and stay away from my side of the harbor, you hear? 'Cause I'm liable to mess it up some."

She looked very small and dignified as she pulled on the oars. "Don't worry, Mr. Joel Radway," she said carefully. "I won't even *speak* to you again!"

And she didn't. Not that summer, anyway. Later they spoke, but they never played together, and by the time he was twelve or thirteen, he worked with his father all summer long and she was just a pesty girl, as pesty as his sister and his cousins, and all the other girls he knew.

When he was fourteen he wanted to go to the dances at the clubhouse; some of the big girls were swell, letting you take them on in a square dance or a waltz, and that was how you learned. His mother sent off for new white ducks for him, and white shoes. But he wouldn't go, after all, even when the music of the accordion and fiddle floated across the field to torment him where he lay in bed, trying to read western stories.

He wouldn't go, because Lucia Harkness always went, and she'd see him trying to learn, and he would know by her look that she was laughing inside herself. It would have been different if they hadn't had that punt between them. But she'd been able to swim, and row alone, before he could; and by God, she wasn't going to laugh at him because she could waltz before he could!

And now she had the peapod. He'd worked and sweated for it, and Ted Harkness had probably sent her fifty dollars and said, "Buy it." It wasn't fair! The blood rushed up hotly under his skin. He wished he had the peapod right there, he could take it to pieces with his two hands so that nobody would ever have it!

But he knew he wouldn't do anything. He would paint over his old one, and fub along in it until it was time to take up his pots. He felt very tired as he got slowly to his feet and started toward home, a tall boy with narrowed, unfriendly eyes and a sullen mouth. A boy who looked as if he never whistled.

Even paint couldn't do much for his double-ender. It even made her look worse, as if she were trying to perk up alongside the unscarred glossiness of the new boat. The way Lucia kept it tied up beside his, you'd almost think she knew how it made him feel. But she didn't know, because nobody but Mark Bennett had known Joel wanted the boat, and Mark had gone back to camp a few days after the sale.

The first day Joel went to haul, after he finished the painting, Lucia Harkness was hauling too. She had her traps set outside the breakwater. Joel had a few set there too, but this morning he rowed straight by; they could wait till he came back, and she wouldn't be fooling around there.

He watched her covertly as he rowed by. She was strong for a girl, standing up there with her feet braced, but she had to work hard at it. The peapod was rolling some, in spite of the calm June sea. Slyly, his mouth twitching, he swerved a little closer, and then swore. No wonder she was stuck!

All his bitterness leaped out at her then, glad of an excuse. "What's the big idea of settin' your pots right on top of mine?"

She jumped, and dropped the warp, turning to look at him with her eyes very big in her flushed, wet face. "Is that yours I'm fouled up with?"

"You're darn right it's mine, and I ain't got so many I can afford to cut mine off so you can go free." He rowed close, his eyes narrowed and hard, his words chopping themselves off. She didn't look uppity now—she looked scared, and it was good enough for her, playing around at a man's work and getting in a man's way.

She sat down wearily. "Well, cut mine off, then."

He shipped his oars and lit a cigarette, putting out an instinctive hand to keep the two peapods from rubbing together. "It's none of my business," he said casually, "but how much did Mark soak you for this tub?"

She looked surprised. "Fifty dollars."

"I suppose your old man gave it to ye—birthday or somethin'." He watched her narrowly. There was a speck of blood on her lower lip where she'd been biting it, and her fair hair was wet and curly around her forehead. She took hold of her oars as if she didn't like the way he spoke.

"You'd better cut off my trap if you're going to. I earned the money. I worked in a hardware store after school and Saturdays."

Joel hid his surprise behind sarcasm. "Worked, huh? I thought all you did up there in Boston was run around to parties and eat ice cream."

He began to work over the tangled warps. The sun was warm on his back, and there was no sound but the soft wash of water under the peapods, and a gull calling overhead. So Lucia's voice came out cool and clear in the silence.

"Did I ever do anything to you, Joel?"

"Huh?" he grunted. "What are you talkin' about?"

"Nothing much. Only I get to wondering what makes you so disagreeable. I can't remember a time when you were even polite to me. Everybody else on the Island likes me. I'd just like to know why you can't be civil."

He straightened up from the tangle of rope. "So you'd like to know, would ye?"

"Yes, I would." Her eyes didn't leave his, and he felt the curious rush of heat to his face, the raging tide of anger he'd felt when his mother told him he couldn't go in the punt, the nights when he lay in bed listening to the music at the dance, the day Mark told him Lucia had bought the peapod. And there she sat, looking at him as if she thought he was the clumsiest damn' fool God ever made.

He threw the two buoys overboard and picked up his oars. "I'll tell ye," he drawled. "I'm not like the rest of the Island. I'm not one to suck around these here high-and-mighties that come down in the summer time and think it's a hell of a lot of fun to be nice to the natives."

He saw her cheeks redden and her eyes darken, and he felt a savage pleasure in it. That had taken the wind out of her sails, all right! She'd know better than to bother him any more. He pushed on the oars and sent the pea-pod flying across the glassy-smooth blue water. As he reached the high rocky arm of the next cove, he looked back over his shoulder and saw her, still sitting there.

He laughed aloud. But as he began to haul he felt his old ugliness settling over him again.

June slipped suddenly into July, and the lobsters slacked off. Joel lived by routine.

Lucia Harkness tied her peapod up at the other side of the beach now, next to Bill Ames. Joel saw them there sometimes, Bill acting as if he thought Lucia was pretty good, even in the patched old dungarees and those ungodly homely pigtails. And she'd laugh back at him. When she laughed, her mouth wide and her eyes crinkled up, she looked different. Joel figured he was the only person on the Island she never talked to like that, easy and relaxed and ready to grin. In fact, she didn't speak to him at all now. He was glad of it. They'd know better than to fool around after him, summer girls like Lucia Harkness. . . .

There was a day when he didn't get out till after the mailboat had come and gone. Most of the powerboats were gone from their moorings when he lugged his baitbox down the beach and put it aboard. It was like living on an island that was all his own, and that was what he wanted these days. A place where no one would speak to him and he didn't have to look at people—especially one person. Even if he didn't have to speak to her, he didn't want to look at her, either. A person hadn't ought to hate like that, he thought sometimes—it was like poison in him. But he couldn't help it.

He hauled along the west side, towards Sou'west Point. There was no other boat in sight anywhere. He might have been alone in the world and it suited him fine. He could be happy if he were really alone, he thought. . . . And then, as he came around the rocks into Sou'west Cove, he saw Mark Bennett's peapod drifting, alone—and empty.

His first thought was of horror, until he remembered that Lucia Harkness was a strong swimmer. He rowed towards the empty boat, put out a hand to it, and stared into it. The oarlocks hung down inside and the oars were placed neatly together, and at the sight of them, Joel was suddenly furious.

He rowed ashore, towing the other peapod, and pulled them both well up on the beach. The grassy barren slopes of Sou'west Point rose above him, and there was nothing to see there—nothing alive. When he reached the top of the slope he looked around, and he saw Lucia Harkness in a little hollow between the curves of the ground. She was lying on her face. Her dungarees were rolled up above her knees, and her legs looked long and brown in the sun.

Joel started towards her, his wrath forming words for his tongue. She didn't seem to hear him, or move, even when he stood over her and said, "By God, I'd ought to give you a hidin'. You know where your peapod was?"

"Where?" She didn't lift her face from the short grass.

"Driftin' out to sea. You were so damn' set on havin' her, and you can't even take decent care of her—leavin' her where the tide could catch her! Serve you right if I'd let her go."

"Why didn't you?" she said drearily, and sat up. He was startled to see how she looked, eyelids swollen and red, her mouth unsteady. She had a handkerchief in her hand. Then she tried to get that uppity look back again. "Thanks for catching her for me, Joel. I guess I didn't pull her up high enough."

"I guess you didn't." He felt very big and tall, towering over her, and then he forgot about how he felt as he saw the tears rush out of her eyes like the tide coming in, and the way her face crumpled. She turned away from him, and he shrugged. Maybe he'd taken her down a peg. He sure hoped so. . . . He started to walk away, and then hesitated.

Suppose it wasn't him or the peapod? Perplexed and queerly angry, he went back. "Look here, you sprained your ankle or somethin'?"

"No!" Her voice was muffled and shaking.

"Well, you don't have to cry any more—the peapod's safe now."

"It isn't the boat. Now go away."

"Excuse me!" said Joel elaborately.

She sat up quickly and tossed her hair out of her eyes. "What do you care what the matter is, anyway? You'll be glad when you find out. You'll be glad I won't be around any more being high-and-mighty and nice to the natives!"

He'd never seen her upset, and he enjoyed it. He squatted on his heels and looked at her closely. "You better tell me," he said.

"Sure, I'll tell you, and make you happy, Joel Radway. I'm going away, next boat. My mother had a letter from my father this morning." She was flinging the words at him like stones. "He's been transferred to California, and that's where we're going, right away."

"California!" He was amazed. "Gosh! You cryin' about goin' there!"

"I'm crying about leaving here, if you want to know. I s'pose you can't understand that, Joel Radway."

"Gosh." He stared at her. "You ever been to California?"

"No, and I don't want to go there." The tears were running freely again and her voice was all choked up. "I thought all winter long about coming here, and now I'm here, and I don't want to go away from it—so far away from it—ever." She lifted her shaking chin. "I s'pose you think I haven't any right to love this island better than any other place in the world."

"Well, nobody told you you can't come back on it again."

"Don't you see? California's such a long way, and I have the awfulest feeling about it . . . as if I can never come back again." She looked at him with drenched brown eyes. "Don't you see?"

He didn't know why he felt like this—maybe it was the same thing that made him pick up his sister's kitten after he'd stepped on its tail, and stroke it. Anyway, Lucia looked so kind of small, all huddled up there with her chin shaking, and he couldn't blame her for feeling like that about the Island—it made him mad sometimes when his sister was always talking about getting away from it.

He put his arm around her clumsily, and said, "Hell, California's not so far. I figure on seein' it for myself, some day."

"Honest?" She stared at him eagerly through her tears, and it made him think crazily of sunshine breaking through a shower. "You mean it?"

"Sure! And I guess nobody's goin' to keep me from comin' back here when I get my mind made up to it."

"Yes, but—" Her chin quivered again. "You're a man. Nobody can stop you from doing what you want to do."

You're a man, she'd told him, and it was the first time in his almost-seventeen years that anyone had called him a man—except himself. And it was true, too. He was a man, and nobody could stop him from doing what he wanted to do, whether it was going to California, or putting his arm around a girl. It also dawned on him that this was the first time he'd ever put his arm around a girl, and it had to be Lucia Harkness. He felt like laughing at himself.

"Lucia, don't cry," he said awkwardly, close to her ear. "The Island'll always be here. Maybe the war will be over before long, and you won't have to stay out there."

It was queer to be so close to her that he could see each separate wet lash, and the fine soft down on her cheeks, and the little white scar at the corner of her mouth. "You really think I'll be back, Joel?" she asked him. "And you really mean you're coming out?"

"Sure thing," he said. "Why not. And maybe the Army'll send me out there free of charge, couple more years."

And then she was grinning, her mouth wide so he could see her glistening little white teeth, her eyes crinkling as she tilted her head back. Her laughter rang out, excited and shaky, but true.

"Gee, will I be glad to see you walk in! Look, Joel, as soon as we get there I'll send you my address."

"All right," he said. He took his arm away. "Now I got to be gettin' to work." He felt queer. When she was laughing, she didn't need to be stroked like a kitten. Somehow, when she'd been crying, he'd felt big and a man, he could shelter her with his arm, and she would turn to him, and listen, and believe. Now she was the girl who had bought the peapod. His peapod. He stood up, drove his hands into the hip pockets of his dungarees.

"I s'pose you'll want to show off one o' them down-in-Maine stump-jumpers to your friends," he said, and left her.

He hauled all the way around the Island, his teeth clamped savagely together, and when he came back to the harbor, from the east'ard, there she was in Mark's peapod, just outside the harbor mouth. He swore to himself as she rowed towards him, and looked at her suspiciously as she came alongside.

"Race you in," she said. "Come on, Joel."

"What you been doin' all this time?"

"Fooling around." She reddened. "Just rowing around, getting blisters."

"I suppose you'll be rowin' that peapod around in California waters before long." Well, he wouldn't have to look at it any more, or her either. . . . "All right, I'll race ye."

The peapods sped across the harbor and Joel didn't let up any, just because she was a girl. He took a grim satisfaction in seeing her get out of breath. She was panting when they reached the shore. He pulled up his own boat, made her fast, and started off across the beach. But she came hurrying after him, slipping a little on the beach stones.

"Hey, Joel, wait a minute! I want to speak to you."

They didn't have anything to say to each other, except good-by and good riddance. . . . He waited, scowling.

"Joel," she said. Her head came to his shoulder; her face turned up to him, sunburned across the nose, eyes steady on his. "I want you to do me a favor. I can't take my peapod with me. . . . That's one of the things I was crying about. But if you're taking care of her, I'll know she's all right."

He had to be ugly to her. "Sure you ain't thinkin' you're doin' me a favor?"

"Mark told me not to let her get dried out," she said steadily. "He said she'd last a good long time if I kept her in the water. And there's nobody I'd trust her to but you."

"What about Bill Ames?"

"Bill Ames is a nitwit . . . Joel, please, I know you don't think much of me, but you're the only person I'd want to take care of my peapod."

"I'm a hell of a guy. Don't even know how to be civil . . . shouldn't think you'd ask me anything." He walked away, but she kept beside him, her voice soft and persistent. "Joel, you're not a hell of a guy. I never thought so! That's why I asked you once why you hated me . . . if you were anybody else, I wouldn't care whether you hated me or not. But I had to know why you didn't like me."

There was something in her very breathlessness that halted him at last. "What are you talkin' about, Lucia?"

She said bravely, "It doesn't matter if I tell you now, because I'm going away next boat, and maybe you'll never see me again. So I'll tell you. Joel, sometimes when I meet you in the road, I think my heart's going to stop beating. And then when you look at me the way you do, I feel like dying."

There was nothing to say. He could only stare down at her, seeing nothing but her face turned up to his. He had never felt like this before in his life; like laughing and crying together, like holding on to something because his legs felt funny, like shouting. This was it, then. This was why he hated her. Only it wasn't hate. Not hate, but something quite different, something he'd been scared to look in the face . . . The sun was caught in her hair, making light all around her head, and there were tiny speckles of light in her eyes as she looked up at him.

Light in his eyes, too. He could hardly see. . . . There was somebody walking down the beach past them, people moving here and there. He had to do something. His hand closed without hesitation on her elbow and turned her towards the road. He was a man, and nobody could stop him from doing what he wanted to do.

"Damn' hot," he said. "Let's get a bottle of pop over at Grant's, and then we can talk about me takin' care of the peapod."

"Yes, Joel," she said in that soft, breathless voice, color coming and going in her face.

"Of course," he added carelessly, "I'll have to get somebody else to take care of her, when I start out for California."

PART V

Plot Sketches
of Published Work

BENNETT'S ISLAND

2½ miles from Sou'west Point to Eastern End Cove

What isn't woods is ledge (all around shores) and field.

To "The Rock"

Sou'west Ledges

Sou'west Point

Bull Cove

Cranberries and Wild Strawberries

High Ledge

Spruce Woods

Goose Cove Ledges

Goose Cove

cemetery

Barque Cove

Harbor Ledges

Western Harbor Point

The Homestead

Charles

Nils and Joanna

Marx

Big Wharf

Windward Point

Owen's wharf

School-house Cove

Schoolhouse

Harbor Beach

Eastern Harbor Point

Ice pond

Owen

Barn

Long Cove

To Brigport

Woods

Stephen

Eastern End Cove

To Tenpound Island

Pudding Island

Shag Ledge

OTHERS

① Fennell
② Clubhouse
③ Rosa & Jamie
④ Percy
⑤ The Well
⑥ Dinsmore [the Bennetts]
⑦ Philip
⑧ Harmon
⑨ Campion
⑩ Barton [Vanessa, etc.]

Paths ....

N S E W

MAP BY A.B. VENTI FROM *AN ANSWER IN THE TIDE*

15 🌺 THE BENNETT'S ISLAND SERIES

It's a profession of its own, being a Bennett or a Bennett's Islander.

—The Seasons Hereafter

ELISABETH IS BEST KNOWN FOR this series of books about life on a remote island in Maine, her signature work. Inspired by the island of Criehaven and its year-round fishing community of the 1930s and '40s, these nine novels tell the story of the stalwart Bennett family, with Joanna as the central character. While Joanna shares many of Elisabeth's feelings and responses to life, Elisabeth describes her as a composite character, with traits drawn from many women she has known through the years. Joanna and other main characters in the Bennett's series are profiled in more detail in Chapter 11.

The larger series can also be viewed as consisting of three related trilogies, which is how they are grouped in the following plot descriptions. (Also see the Young Bennetts series descriptions beginning on page 252. Many of the same characters appear in those young adult novels.)

The Bennett's Island novels have captivated readers for more than half a century, and the Tide Trilogy books have also been published in England and Denmark.

Though Elisabeth is often asked if she will write another Bennett's Island book, at this time she feels that she has completed the cycle and that any additional installments would be repetitious.

• • •

The Bennett Family

Jamie Bennett took possession of the island of Racketash in 1825. Racketash was officially named Bennett's Island when it received a post office. Charles James (aka Jamie I) and Pleasance Marriot were great-grandparents of Nathan and Stephen Bennett.

Nathan Bennett married Mary M.
    Their children: Jeffrey, married, living in Texas
                Rachel, married, living in Midwest
                Hugo, married Vivian Haliburton, living in California
                Haliburton Bennett ("Hal")

Stephen Bennett married Donna B. (came to teach school)
    Their children: **Charles** married Mateel Trudeau
                Charles, drowned
                Donna, married, living on mainland
                Pierre, married, Merchant Marine
                Hugo, island lobsterman
                Betsy, attending college
            Philip married Lisa Filippi
                Sam, adopted, attending high school
                Ross, adopted, attending island school
                Amy, adopted, attending island school
            Owen married Annie Laurie Gibson
                Joss, through college, working away
                Holly, attending college
                Richard, attending high school
            Joanna married Alec Douglass (deceased)
                Ellen, married, living in Massachusetts
              married Nils Sorensen
                Jamie, married Rosa MacKinnon Fleming
                  Sara Joanne
                Linnea, through college, traveling in Sweden

Mark married Helmi
   Mark (aka "Young Mark")
Stephen married Philippa Marshall
   Eric, Philippa's son, teaching in Peace Corps
   Robin, attending high school

(All wives are from the mainland, except Mateel Trudeau.)

OTHER EARLY BENNETT'S ISLAND FAMILIES

The Sorensens: Gunnar and Anna
  Karl (his wife died young)
    Sigurd (living on mainland)
    Nils (Bennett's Islander)
    Kristi (living on mainland)
    David (living on mainland)
  Eric

LATER FAMILIES (since World War II)

The Fennels: Matt, Sr., and Nora
  "Young Matt" and Carol Fennell; one son
The Bartons: Barry and Vanessa; one daughter
The Percys: Ralph and Marjorie; two sons
The Dinsmores: Rob and Maggie; two daughters
The Harmons: Myles and Nan; two daughters, one son
The Campions: Sky and Binnie; two sons, one daughter
   Terence and Kate (Kathy); several Campion children
   (Sky and Terence are first cousins; their children
   are second cousins.)

(From *The Day Before Winter*, 1997)

THE TIDE TRILOGY

High Tide at Noon (1944)

The whole world shone and was fragrant. The path lay before her, streaked with cold shadows and yellow sunlight. On her right hand tall dark trees had their precarious foothold among the rocks. Far below them the water curled itself in flashing eddies, and the seaweed moved languorously with the tide. A bluejay swooped noisily across the path before Joanna, and was lost in the woods on the hillside that rose with its lichened boulders, its spruces, and its little sun-filled glades on the other side of the path. The bird was the color of a jewel, the sea was full of diamonds, the day itself with a gemlike radiance. This is a day to be happy in, she thought, and remembered her mother singing, "oh, the sunshine, blessed sunshine," in the kitchen at breakfast time. Her serene content had brought a lump into Joanna's throat, and it was difficult for her to swallow her toast.

Called "evocative" and "timeless," the first book of the Tide Trilogy introduces Joanna Bennett and her family on Bennett's Island. Growing up with several lively brothers who sail and fish, Joanna finds it difficult to fulfill the typically feminine role of the time. Strong-willed and vibrant, she attracts the attention, and eventually, the love, of three men: her old friend Nils, the conniving Simon Bird, and charming Alec Douglass, whom Joanna marries.

The dust jacket from an early edition of this classic proclaims, "The sea brings to Joanna her lover and husband, and it is to the sea she turns, the glorious high tide at noon, when she is in despair. How Joanna develops from a turbulent tomboy into a mature and courageous woman determined to keep the island a complete and beautiful world, is told here with exciting vividness."

In this first book, Elisabeth introduces us to Joanna's devotion to her island, which will prove so significant in later installments of the series. *The New York Times Book Review* (April 16, 1944) captured the essence of Joanna's feeling for the island: "Joanna loved it better than any of them. In part because, as the only girl in a family of husky young lobstermen, some of the freedom of its roughly adventurous and independent life was denied to her."

Other critics had equal praise for the novel. Sterling North of *Book Week* announced, "there can be no doubt that Miss Ogilvie has a brilliant future," while David Tilden of the *Weekly Book Review* pronounced the Bennett family "particularly engaging." These characters would continue to live and flourish through the course of eight more novels.

Storm Tide (1945)

The Bennett family's story continues in *Storm Tide*. This is one of the most controversial books of the Bennett's series, for it is here that we feel the full force of Joanna's single-minded passion for the island—strong enough to threaten her relationship with husband Nils.

Eleven years after her marriage to Alec ended in tragedy, Joanna marries Nils Sorensen and plans to live on Bennett's Island once again, after an extended absence. She longs to return the island to the thriving lobstering community it once was, and her determination to fulfill this goal soon becomes an obsession. Nils shares her dedication to this cause, but finds that Joanna often places it before their family life. Just before their marriage is about to crash on the rocks, Joanna realizes the crisis that she has brought about and takes steps to avert it. Together, Nils and Joanna find a solution, learning a great deal more about each other along the way.

This book generates a great deal of discussion among Ogilvie readers, causing them to argue for and against Joanna's viewpoint. Some find her ferocity for the island cause overwhelming, and her treatment of Nils unfair. Others argue that Joanna remains true to herself, no matter what. Indeed, part of her love for Nils is tied up with the fact that he also loves the Island and wants to return it to its former glory. Elisabeth explores all the nuances of this situation in *Storm Tide*. This novel earned the New England Press Association Award for best novel in 1945, and the Northeast Woman's Press Association award in 1946. It is one of her most powerful books, and well deserving of the recognition it has received.

The Ebbing Tide (1947)

The demand for more stories about the Bennett clan did not diminish, and Elisabeth obliged with *The Ebbing Tide*. Although she never originally intended to write a series about this family, she had material left over after writing the first two books, which she felt deserved expression. She decided to continue and let readers see the characters marry and have children of their own. The islanders soon became like family to her, with their stories clamoring to be told.

In this third book of the Tide Trilogy, called by critic Virginia Kirkus "generous, communicably sympathetic reading," Nils has gone to fight in the second world war, leaving Joanna to handle life alone on Bennett's Island. Dennis Garland, a newcomer to the island, finds Joanna intriguing, and she returns those feelings. Their friendship threatens Joanna's future, and she has to work through emotions from the past, including memories of her first husband, before she can continue living her life with Nils. An excerpt from the novel summarizes her inner conflict:

> . . . sometimes she found herself wondering what she would do if she should glance out the harbor window and see Dennis coming. The very fancy caused a sickening constriction in her breathing, and so she did not think of it often. She thought instead about how it would be if she should see Nils coming up the path.

The day finally comes when Nils walks up that path, and finds Joanna waiting for him. The bond they have shared since Joanna's early years has held strong through the turmoil Joanna experienced during Nils' absence. By the end of the Tide Trilogy, readers feel that their love can survive anything.

THE LOVERS TRILOGY

The Dawning of the Day (1954)

This first installment of the Lovers Trilogy finds newly widowed Philippa Marshall of Boston hoping to begin a new life as the schoolteacher on Bennett's Island. Leaving her son Eric behind while she gets settled, Philippa creates a life for herself, getting to know the islanders and their children. She seeks peace of mind, which she desperately needs, but discovers that life on the island is full of challenges and complications. There are deep and long-standing resentments and jealousies among some of the families, and she must fight slanderous attacks and malicious gossip to win the respect of the island children and her new friend, Steve Bennett.

The tension between the Bennetts and the Campions finally erupts in violence when the Campions cut loose a Bennett lobster pot. Philippa is drawn further into the lives of her students, particularly in defending the forlorn Webster children from the harassment of Perley. (One of these children, Edwin Webster, later reappears in *Strawberries in the Sea*.) Philippa turns to friend Steve Bennett for support, and finds more than just a shoulder to cry on. When a death occurs, she must decide whether to stay on the island or leave forever.

Elisabeth has used lobster wars many times in her novels; such battles still happen today over fishing territory. Her depiction of the life of a school-teacher on the island is based on her knowledge of real-life teachers who came to Criehaven.

The Seasons Hereafter (1966)

The Bennett brothers hire lobsterman Barry Barton, who brings his wife Vanessa with him when he moves to the island. It's not an easy life for Vanessa, whose childhood experiences as a foster child have made her wary of change and suspicious of others. She views Barry's enthusiasm with scorn, and especially fears the intrusive curiosity of the islanders. She has no way of knowing how drastically her life will change when she meets the charismatic Owen, one of Joanna's dashing older brothers. This book chronicles their tragic tale of love and loss.

Elisabeth wrote in detail about this novel in a professional article, "Background, The Most Important Character," explored in Chapter 10. Many Ogilvie readers feel that this is one of Elisabeth's most powerful novels, de-picting an almost Shakespearean drama between lovers. Vanessa is one of her most complex female characters, and this novel is the rare exception to Elis-abeth's rule of having things come out right for her heroines. Vanessa, like Philippa and Joanna before her, does not run away from her problems. Al-though damaged by a childhood filled with sadness, her resilient spirit enables her to continue her quest for joy.

Vanessa and Owen's story continues in *The Summer of the Osprey*.

Strawberries in the Sea (1973)

> *The man in the wilderness asked me,*
> *How many strawberries grow in the sea?*
> *I answered him, as I thought good,*
> *As many as red herrings grow in the wood.*
>
> —Old nursery rhyme

This book, the sixth of the Bennett's series and the third in the Lovers Trilogy, introduces us to Rosa Fleming, an important character on the island. Devastated by her recent divorce, Rosa takes the family boat to Bennett's

Island, hoping to hide there and lick her wounds. She is young and healthy, however, and soon discovers she has much to live for—making friends, playing her guitar, and going out to haul a small string of traps. Another source of happiness is her new friend, Jamie Sorensen.

Rosa is happy to have her cousin Edwin Webster there with her, and remembers with gratitude that it was Philippa who discovered that Edwin was deaf and made sure he got the education he needed (in *The Dawning of the Day*). Edwin provides constant support as Rosa deals with her ex-husband, her confusing friendship with Jamie, and a crisis between island lobstermen and the purse seiners.

Rosa is one of Elisabeth's most independent and admirable heroines, finding the strength not only to survive, but to prosper on the island. Her growing friendship with Jamie Sorensen continues into the next book in the series, *An Answer in the Tide*.

An Answer in the Tide (1978)

> *When all else fails, we find an answer in the tide.*
> *We hear the rote resounding softly from the shores of*
> *the island of the heart;*
> *In every body cell a compass points us home,*
> *And we become again the creatures that we were,*
> *sovereign and apart.*
>
> —Elisabeth Ogilvie

In the next installment of the Bennett's Island series, Jamie Sorensen faces a moral dilemma and ultimately a crisis of identity. He becomes involved with a married woman, Eloise, and gallantly comes to her rescue when she convinces him that her husband is abusing her. Life is complicated further by another love interest for Jamie—the lady lobster buyer, Bronwen—and a potential trap war.

Joanna and Nils are deeply concerned for their son and try to help, but Jamie must resolve the situation on his own. Rosa proves to be a true friend to Jamie, offering support and solace, as do all the members of the Bennett clan. The undeniable island virtues of family loyalty at all costs, hard work, and an adherence to an unwritten moral code, are all present in this book.

This seventh volume of the Bennett's series addresses some weighty moral topics, and Elisabeth welcomes the opportunity to present the island as a microcosm of society.

The Summer of the Osprey (1987)

This book picks up where *An Answer in the Tide* left off. The islanders are suspicious when off-islander Felix Drake purchases a house and wharf and arrives in a fancy new lobster boat filled with expensive gear. That he is "from away" is cause enough for doubt—but when he begins to lobster for sport and refuses to sell his catch to the island buyer, he generates further distrust.

Drake has also brought along a beautiful and mysterious young woman whom he keeps hidden in his home. He describes her simply as a friend who has experienced traumatic circumstances and needs seclusion. As the summer goes on, it becomes evident that the beautiful lady is pregnant. As the birth becomes imminent, the threat of a hurricane adds to the suspense. The situation demands the intervention of the island women, and understanding is born along with the baby boy.

Elisabeth masterfully weaves a multi-layered plot in this novel. Along with the suspenseful mystery of Drake and the woman, there is a stabbing at a dance, one Bennett family's worry over losing an adopted son, and Jamie Sorensen's close call with death. Here Elisabeth continues the love story of Owen and Vanessa (*The Seasons Hereafter*), along with that of Jamie and Rosa (*An Answer in the Tide*), giving the reader a satisfying view into the lives of all the main characters of the series.

The Day Before Winter (1997)

The story of the Bennett's Islanders picks up during the Vietnam War era. A new family arrives on the island, along with cousin Hal from California, who comes to renew family ties. Joanna is caught up in the ensuing tensions that surround both of these situations. Hal is enamored of island life and soon becomes a very popular figure. However, the islanders find that beneath his smooth surface he is hiding many problems.

Critic William David Barry summarized the action:

> Young Hal seems to be a free spirit looking, in typical 1960s fashion, for himself. Charming and likable, but estranged from his father, he finds a safe harbor and is looked upon as a perfect sternman for the stave-up Owen Bennett. Hal impresses young and old alike and makes plans to design a cabin. But times are changing, and motives and situations are not as they first appear.
>
> By book's end, life on the island goes on much the same as it al-

ways has, though several lives are changed forever. Ogilvie, as ever, is a keen and subtle student of human nature and interaction. *The Day Before Winter* is a masterful and engaging study from start to finish.

With this ninth installment, Elisabeth feels the Bennett's Island series has come to a natural conclusion.

16 ❧ GENERAL FICTION

ELISABETH HAS WRITTEN SEVERAL general fiction books that are not part of a series. These are some of her best-loved novels, and contain romance, intrigue, a strong element of family ties, and the vivid settings for which she is famous. In these books, Elisabeth addresses a wide range of issues with a singularly perceptive eye. From the conflict of lobster wars, to family struggles, to the plight of a couple that married too young, her range of emotional understanding is wide and true.

Poems inspired the titles and themes for some of these five books. A great fan of poetry, Elisabeth has found ideas for her work in poems (and in *The Oxford Dictionary of Quotations*). She has also included her own poetry and that of her brother Allan in various works.

Rowan Head (1949)

> Rowan Head. It had a lifting, arrogant ring; one time it was a harsh, cold sound to her, like jade-cored breakers rushing in from the sea to crash in glistening white thunder over granite cliffs. At another time it was like music, stirring enough to cause a turmoil of expectant excitement in the blood.

When a companion is needed for Felice Cameron, an elderly lady who is living in the past, Dr. Tolman suggests Miriam Chase. Miriam soon finds herself involved in more than just caring for Mrs. Cameron, when Felice's three sons provide a source of additional conflict.

In an article that appeared in *The Saturday Review* on September 17, 1949, critic Henry Beston wrote of this complex family:

Barth, being temperamentally the rather grim son of the spirit of place and the family tradition, and the next in line, Giles, being a vital and good-looking *mauvais sujet,* with overtones of the genuine blackguard. An old, completely mad mother and a kind of ghost of an artist younger son (who nevertheless resolves the crisis of the action) move in the background of the tension. . . .

The Cameron family was once the primary boatbuilding family of Robbinsport, but they lost everything when the shipyard was sold to the Bradshaws. One tragedy after another strikes the household, until a final act brings both destruction and revelation. The strength of Miriam's character is tested as she seeks to return peace to Rowan Head.

Beston described *Rowan Head* as a novel in the tradition of the Brontë sisters. "It is long since American writing has had so Brontë-like a novel. This romance is one with *Jane Eyre* and *Wuthering Heights*, and like its predecessors, displays the same power to keep the drama in full suspense. The life within the house, moreover, and the life outside it are both presented with a realism which is only heightened by the romantic quality of the plot. The scenes between the brothers are particularly well done. Elisabeth Ogilvie has given us another most interesting study of our world."

Rowan Head was a selection of the People's Book Club (Chicago), and as a result there are many editions of this book available in bookstores and on the Internet.

Call Home the Heart (1962)

Troy Teague leaves his beloved island home as a young man, due to an affair between his father and their hired girl. For twenty-eight years, the islanders believed Troy to be responsible for the hired girl's disgrace. When Troy returns, he befriends Renie, a young, unmarried woman, and her child, but is again accused of indiscretion. It is only after his unexpected death that the truth can finally be told.

This novel features Leslie Whitney (profiled in Chapter 11), a wonderful heroine in the classic Ogilvie tradition. Reminiscent of Joanna in her strength and integrity, Leslie tries to do "good works" on the small island, known for its long-running feud between the Teagues and the Whitneys. She struggles against the biases of the small community and tries to help Renie, Troy, and her own daughter-in-law, who is trying to adjust to married life.

Leslie's words echo those of many other Ogilvie's characters, when it comes to describing her love for the island:

In winter or in summer, in the soggy brown-and-gray weeks that sometimes settled spongily in March, or in the bone-chilling rawness possible in November, there was always beauty here, a comfort for the soul, a sense of ease as if one were returning to one's own country.

This book, set on Brigport (Matinicus), was partly inspired by a real-life tragedy that occurred on that island, when a son was forced to take the blame for his father's behavior, to save the family name. The Teague family history is based on the fascinating history of Ebenezer Hall, found in Chapter 6.

There May Be Heaven (1966)

Ah, take the season and have done,
Love well the hour and let it go;
Two souls may sleep and wake up one,
Or dream they wake and find it so,
And then—you know.

—From "Felice," by A. C. Swinburne

Like Philippa Marshall in *The Dawning of the Day*, Claire Carradine has come to an island to escape the pain of her husband's death. Robert, Claire's brother-in-law, convinces Claire to take her daughter, Nancy, and go help Aunt Mag. Life in a Maine lobstering village appeals to Claire. She soon meets likable Finn Judson, who becomes a good-natured, comfortable companion. Their friendship intensifies, and Finn begins to consider a lifelong relationship with Claire.

The four Judson brothers disrupt the couple's happiness with their jealous cruelty. Claire soon finds herself drawn into controversy when, in a fit of anger, Finn's brother Rafe rams Finn's boat. Oldest brother Cleon does nothing to prevent the trouble. Finn is convinced that his brothers hate him and that it goes beyond mere jealousy. He breaks away to be with Claire, causing dramatic changes in their lives.

This novel contains a classic example of the infamous lobster wars, which can go on for decades and still occur today as lobster fishermen compete for their fishing territories.

Set on Gay's Island, this novel contains several references to the real-life geography of the St. George peninsula and environs. Nancy goes to visit on a farm up on Appleton Ridge, a scenic area northwest of Rockland. Salisbury Point, christened Saltberry Point for this novel, was granted to Richard Salisbury in 1628.

Waters on a Starry Night (1968)

> *The Rainbow comes and goes,*
> *And lovely is the Rose.*
> *The moon doth with delight*
> *Look round her when the heavens are bare—*
>
> *Waters on a starry night*
> *Are beautiful and fair.*
> *The sunshine is a glorious birth,*
> *But yet I know, where'er I go,*
> *That there hath passed away a glory from the earth.*
>
> —From Wordsworth's "Intimations" ode

When Thora and Lyle Ritchie married as young teenagers, they were deeply in love and ready to shelter each other from the ugliness of life. As they grew up, however, they grew apart. Thirteen years later, they have four young daughters and are struggling to make ends meet. The stress is beginning to tell, and when lovely Vivian Perth returns to their coastal Maine town for the summer, Lyle can't help but be flattered by her interest. Another stranger from away enters their island sanctuary and brings more conflict with him.

Elisabeth portrays a family at risk with a deep understanding of the realities of marriage. Thora and Lyle's struggles (profiled in Chapter 11) are portrayed eloquently and with compassion. The children provide a moving counterpoint to the main plot.

The setting for this book is Gay's Island, and the Ritchie children were modeled on real-life girls who stayed with Elisabeth and Dot for a while at Tide's Way (as told in Chapter 4).

Lyle Ritchie also appears in *The Road to Nowhere*, as the lobsterman who picks up the girls in his boat.

• • •

READER COMMENT

More than thirty years ago, with my children sleeping quietly after a siege of illness, I sat down and opened a book entitled *Waters on a Starry Night* by Elisabeth Ogilvie. Whistles should have shrieked and foghorns blared to signal the beginning of a new adventure! From the first sentence, I was engrossed in this book and transported to an unknown island off the Maine coast. If raising children in a landlocked Connecticut town was a challenge, how much more difficult life was for Thora and Lyle Ritchie, who had to take their children to the mainland to catch the school bus, dealing with slippery ladders, frosty-cold mornings and fractious outboard motors on the way. The children are described so well that one can't help but smile at their joys and feel sad at their disappointments. This book provides a fine description of the life of an island lobstering family, and for me, was the first step on a delightful journey through the world of Elisabeth Ogilvie's books.

—Kathie Crane, New York

A Theme for Reason (1970)

> *Dear love, for nothing less than thee*
> *Would I have broke this happy dream,*
> *It was a theme*
> *For reason, much too strong for fantasy,*
> *Therefore thou wak'd'st me wisely; yet*
> *My dream thou brok'st not, but continued'st it.*
>
> —John Donne

For nine summers, Alexia (Alix) Horne and Shane Mannering lived together at Gib's Cove on the fictional Maine island of Tiree. Separated from his wife Cathleen, but unable to divorce her due to religious beliefs, Shane is devoted to Alix and their stolen time together each year. His early death at his daughter's wedding breakfast plunges Alix into despair, leaving her with the desire to end her own life. In this, she even surpasses Vanessa of *The Seasons Hereafter* with her degree of emotional torment:

This wasn't depression. It was an enormous indifference. A nothingness, as if all her apparatus for feeling, smelling, tasting, and hearing had died when Shane did. . . . Waking up in the dark, confused and thick-tongued, she would orient herself by thinking, *Shane is dead. He died suddenly and I wasn't there.* It meant nothing. It was just words. . . . She had some idea that if she could hammer the facts into her consciousness like nails into the flesh, she would suffer great agony, and that would be better than this vacuum. But no matter what she said to herself, nothing happened. She was merely oppressed by her own dullness and apathy.

Alix returns to Tiree, where she plans to commit suicide—but soon finds that other people's problems interfere with her plans. She becomes involved in the lives of Jonas, a loner on the island, a young girl named Karen, and ultimately, Shane's own daughter, Bunny. Alix also finds solace in the beauties of nature and soon finds that her healing has begun; she does indeed have a life without Shane. The way Elisabeth describes Alix's slow ascent back into the world of the living is skillful and moving. Again, as with all of her work, Elisabeth's union of characters with background reinforces the plot and ultimate impact of the story.

In *A Theme for Reason*, she again uses the lines "A ceiling of amber, / A pavement of pearl" from the poem "The Forsaken Merman," also referenced in her young adult book, *Ceiling of Amber*.

17 ✿ MYSTERY / SUSPENSE

You don't have to be a murderer or an adulterer
to write about one. . . .

—Elisabeth Ogilvie

ELISABETH HAS SAID THAT one of her very favorite genres to read or write is mystery, in part because of the challenge of solving the puzzle. She has proven herself very successful in writing suspense fiction, where her sense of place and deep characterizations combine with her understanding of the genre to create rich and absorbing tales.

In a 1970 article about suspense in fiction, Elisabeth reminisced about her first published mystery story, "A Woman's Reputation" (*Redbook*, 1962):

> [It] was written as therapy. I was housebound with a broken leg, and a series of family disasters had made it impossible for me to concentrate on any serious writing. One day when I was alone in the house I looked out at the seine dories anchored in the cove and thought, "Suppose someone rowed up to one of them and found a dead body in it?"

Within an hour she'd developed the victim, the murder suspect, and the background, then spent all summer finishing the story, fleshing out the characters and working on the resolution. True to her habits, she then put it away and didn't look at it until the following spring, when she "tidied it up [and] sent it off." To her delight, *Redbook* bought and published it.

Commenting on "A Woman's Reputation," Elisabeth also reveals much about her heroines in general:

[In "A Woman's Reputation"] a demure wife has a secret craving for drama and thus causes her own and her lover's deaths; the heroine finds out the truth by accident, and then she is [herself] endangered. But none of these women are in the idiot-heroine tradition: I have no patience with females who know by the pricking of their thumbs that something wicked this way comes, and then insist on barging into places where a self-respecting cat would have the common sense not to go.

Elisabeth Ogilvie shows her versatility in all of her mysteries, allowing the reader to revel in her glorious landscapes. In fact, she almost lulls the reader into a sense of peace before introducing elements of intrigue, suspense, and fear. In their 1996 profile of Elisabeth in *The Gothic Journal*, Gina and Dara Haldane compared her style to river-rafting:

For a good portion of the journey, the reader drifts along, dreamily savoring the starkly beautiful scenery, occasionally encountering snags and curves, and sometimes being startled by a grim sight, perhaps the corpse of an animal thrown up on the banks. Sometime after the halfway point, the white water predominates, gaining rapidly in intensity and ferocity, until at last the rafter is white-knuckling his paddle, hoping to reach the pull-out point in one piece.

Elisabeth adds authenticity to her mystery novels with extensive research, working with the local constable, state policemen, the county medical examiner, doctors, and other professionals where necessary. Elisabeth has also assimilated into her work her interests in the natural world, conservation of wildlife, archaeology, and many beloved cats and dogs (*Weep and Know Why*, for example). *The Devil in Tartan*, set in Nova Scotia, reflects her interest in her Scottish heritage, as does *The Silent Ones*, set on the Isle of Lewis.

No Evil Angel (1956)

Love is a familiar; Love is a devil,
There is no evil angel but Love.

—William Shakespeare

This novel is unusual for Ogilvie because it features a male protagonist, Ross Fordyce, the son of John Fordyce. "Mr. Johnny" is patriarch not only of the Fordyce family, but also of the islanders of Landfall. As wicked a villain as

Elisabeth has ever painted, Mr. Johnny dominates the islanders with fear, his control over them strengthened by the fact that many islanders owe him money at his store. Elisabeth doesn't shrink from vividly portraying Mr. Johnny's evil exploits, from womanizing to drinking. Mr. Johnny's cruelty is never more apparent than when he leaves the island as soon as his frail wife, Viola, dies, not even staying to take care of her funeral arrangements.

A short time later, he returns with a beautiful new wife named Christine, a flamboyant ex-actress who doesn't hesitate to use her charms on both Fordyce sons. Although Ross hates her initially, he can't resist her wiles, and falls in love with her. Meanwhile, the island is increasingly tormented by Mr. Johnny's tyranny, and it becomes apparent that almost no one will escape unscathed.

Elisabeth gives us a thorough characterization of Ross, the plainer, "bookkeeper" son, who, in the tradition of Nils Sorensen and the Bennetts, has a stern moral sense and the courage to uphold his values.

The Witch Door (1959)

Megan Atwood finds herself at a crucial turning point, forced to make a decision she has long been postponing. Richard Hendries, old family friend turned love interest, has proposed marriage. She must decide whether to divorce or declare dead her husband Craig, who abandoned her seven years before. Her son Chris's feelings have prevented her from taking action thus far. Chris is violently opposed to her union with Richard, maintaining fierce loyalty to his father.

During their annual summer visit to Fairweather Island (modeled on Gay's Island), Megan and her children, (Chris and daughters Shelley and Emily) are shocked when Craig suddenly joins them there. Showing no remorse and making no attempt to explain, Craig expects Megan to welcome him back with open arms. While Megan is immune to his charms, Chris is not. Craig uses his son's devotion to prolong this summer visit. Megan is unable to oppose, seeing what it means to her children.

That this decision will bring heartache, damage other families, and ultimately cost someone's life, is not immediately apparent, but the fact that Craig is hiding a deadly secret is. As the situation worsens, Megan must find a way to save her children, her love for Richard, and herself. (*The Gothic Journal*, 1996)

Bellwood (1969)

Bellwood seems like a dream come true when Caroline Brewster begins her job as governess at the lonely mansion on the sea-bound cliff on the outskirts of Somerset, Maine. The surroundings are breathtaking, she loves her young charge Tim, and she is fascinated by Tim's father, the handsome Rees Morgan. Caroline is sure she can help Rees forget the tragic death of his wife, ease his suffering, and unravel the real reasons behind their withdrawal from the world.

Rees tells Caroline that he has purposely isolated his son in an effort to protect him from society's cruelty. Caro initially follows his direction to refrain from teaching Tim anything that would cause frustration. She soon realizes, however, that Tim is naturally bright, and she begins to doubt Rees's claim that Tim will never develop mentally beyond his current age of five. Caro realizes that other dark secrets are hidden beneath the seemingly placid surface of life at Bellwood.

The Gothic Journal declared of *Bellwood,* "Ogilvie's lyrical descriptive style fuses perfectly with gothic elements in this exciting suspense novel. It features well-rounded characters and a highly satisfying resolution."

Elisabeth wrote this book to try her hand at creating a gothic novel, "filled with mysterious dwellings and equally mysterious dark and brooding heroes." It's a genre that never seems to diminish in popularity. "This book began as a joke," she says, "the big old house and the young governess and the whole thing. I did it kind of for fun, to see if I'd like working in that style. It turned out better than I expected; it's even been published in France."

Elisabeth also used the setting of Somerset for *The Face of Innocence*.

The Face of Innocence (1970)

Suburban housewife Susan Linden has a secret in her past. Eighteen years ago, she was eighteen-year-old Leslie Danton, billed as a reincarnated Egyptian princess by her mother Olivia, who painted pictures of her daughter's past life. Now happily married for fifteen years to Richard and living with him and their children in Somerset, Maine, Susan thought she had left her past behind. She is shocked when an art exhibit arrives in town, accompanied by her ex-fiancé, David.

David claims they are still destined to be together and that the life Susan has created with her family is neither real nor lasting. David's desire to win her back only grows, as does the danger element for Susan. Insights into Susan's past are revealed through flashbacks. Her lonely childhood contrasts sharply with her adult life. Her loving husband, Richard, displays some of the same qualities readers have come to know in the Bennett's Island men—quiet strength and unwavering commitment to his family.

Part of Elisabeth's inspiration for this novel came from a real-life woman she knew who painted scenes of ancient Egypt, supposedly while under spirit control (although Elisabeth believes it was self-hypnosis). In an article for *The Writer*, she said of this novel:

> The heroine is a "Band Mother," a PTA member, and her husband owns a hardware store. Within a quiet suburban setting, she meets her private horror face to face. She lives a nightmare, while attempting to keep up with the rhythms of daily life, and when the trouble is over, very few people in the town know that she's been involved in anything.

Elisabeth often thought she should use her childhood neighborhood as a setting for a book. The town of Somerset is based on her memories of the calm suburban town of Dorchester, Massachusetts.

Weep and Know Why (1972)

> *Margaret, are you grieving*
> *Over Goldengrove unleaving?*
> *Leaves, like the things of man, you*
> *With your fresh thoughts care for, can you?*
> *Ah! As the heart grows older*
> *It will come to such sights colder*
> *By and by, nor spare a sigh*
> *Though worlds of wanwood leafmeal lie:*
> *And yet you will weep and know why.*
> *Now no matter, child, the name:*
> *Sorrow's springs are the same.*
> *Nor mouth had, no nor mind, expressed*
> *What heart heard of, ghost guessed:*
> *It is the blight man was born for,*
> *It is Margaret you mourn for.*
>
> —Gerard Manley Hopkins

After losing her job as well as her boyfriend, Mirabell accepts the invitation of her aunt and uncle to stay at their home, "The Shallows," to watch their dogs while they are away on a trip. Her childhood chum, Barnaby Taggart, is staying nearby at his grandfather's, and she looks forward to becoming reacquainted with him. In the beautiful setting of Cape Silver, Maine, she plans to enjoy the summer while taking stock of her life.

Vandalism, terrifying noises, and sinister happenings soon put an end to hopes of relaxation, and bring about drastic changes for all involved. Rumors abound that Barnaby is linked to the crimes, and a mysterious couple nicknamed the "Peter Rabbits" (because of their rather large teeth) add touches of both humor and intrigue.

Elisabeth wrote about the setting for this book in "Suspense and a Sense of Place" (*The Writer*, September 1976). The inspiration was Gay's Island, with a few changes in the terrain.

> In *Weep and Know Why*, the action takes place on a nature preserve. Because of its isolation, it is possible for two people to disappear and their bodies be hidden. Because the place attracts geologists, ornithologists, botanists, and marine biologists, nobody in the area questions the credentials of two supposed archaeologists searching for traces of a prehistoric people. And because wildlife refuges attract poachers, this leads to still another murder.

The Australian terriers in the story, Girl and Digger, were modeled on Elisabeth's real-life dogs at the time, Jill and Sherman. They were full of personality, and Elisabeth remembers how Jill used to roll her eyes at Sherman.

Barnaby and Mirabell's story continues in *The Dreaming Swimmer*.

Image of a Lover (1974)

> *She, sleepless in summer, one midnight will discover*
> *In a mirror, by candlelight, the image of a lover.*
>
> —Elisabeth Ogilvie

Miranda Muir, raised by an uncle on Drummond's Island, invites her friend Seafair Bell home for the summer of 1896. Although Seafair plans on spending the time giving piano lessons to Miranda, she becomes more involved with the family than she ever imagined. Miranda's three cousins, Patrick, Andrew, and Ian, all take a liking to Seafair. The dances, picnics, sailing,

and island life in general make for an interesting summer, and allow her to re-
capture the carefree happiness she thought she had lost when her mother died.

The follies and passions of romance soon lead to tragedy. Seafair falls in
love with Patrick, who is obsessed with Miranda, but Miranda is interested
only in flirting with other men on the island. Mere unhappiness is replaced
with madness, and their peaceful island idyll becomes a nightmare.

Joyce Harris, senior feature writer for the *Dallas Morning News* and a
Mug-up newsletter subscriber, shared her thoughts about the novel, along
with some correspondence from Elisabeth:

> *Image of a Lover* is perhaps the darkest of Elisabeth Ogilvie's
> novels. Its terrifying portrayal of love turned to jealous insanity is ut-
> terly convincing and utterly heartbreaking. This theme of a beloved
> person gone mad would turn up again, in a different but equally dis-
> turbing context, in 1989's *When the Music Stopped*.
>
> As a "Gothic" romantic-suspense novel, *Image of a Lover* also has
> charms befitting its period setting. The vivid descriptions of village
> life on a remote Maine island just before the turn of the century have
> great authenticity. . . .

Elisabeth herself also has commented on the novel's authenticity:

> *Image of a Lover* confines all the action to what is possible and ap-
> propriate in an island community in the year 1896. The daily business
> of the place, its events and amusements, all belong to that era. The
> characters are not 1976-people dressed up in period costumes, think-
> ing and behaving like 1976 people. They are 1896-people, strongly in-
> fluenced by the mores of that time, even when they are in rebellion.

Criehaven is the real-life model for Drummond's Island, described as
being a three-hour journey from Rockland. Elisabeth wrote to Joyce Harris in
February 1986 about her inspiration for the novel:

> I drew on my mother's experiences when she spent summers on
> a Maine island from the 1890s on, as a teenager and then as a young
> married woman before WWI with my brothers. The young years were
> full of the events and characters I described (not the murders).
>
> Later I was taken there, and as a teenager just before WW2, I
> joined in the same kind of fun. Kids today don't know what they're
> missing, but it's still possible to do some of the same things on a few

islands where TV depends on a generator in the shed and is therefore expensive, especially when the lobstering is poor!

She made an interesting additional comment in this letter: "It is especially nice to hear from someone who likes other books besides those in the Bennett-Sorensen saga, because I put my heart into them to the same extent."

Where the Lost Aprils Are (1975)

> *Dead memory that revolves on doubtful ways,*
> *Half harkening what the buried season says*
> *Out of the world of the unapparent dead*
> *Where the lost Aprils are, and the lost Mays.*
> —from "Relics," by A. C. Swinburne

April is a time of horrible memories for Miriam, and even her interesting job in New York City can't alleviate the pain. Each spring, she is forced to relive the agony associated with this harrowing month. Her decision to spend some time in the small town of Parmenter, Maine, to try and unravel her background only causes more disruption in her life.

Miriam is searching for her father in Parmenter, along with answers to her past. Her quest is complicated when she falls in love with Rory Barstow, a talented singer. He loves her as well, but his mother has other plans for her son. She also holds many of the answers Miriam is searching for—but is quite unwilling to share them. With consummate skill, Elisabeth weaves a complex mystery that reaches its crescendo in a burst of flames.

> All the time I was working on *Where the Lost Aprils Are*, I was thinking of it simply as a love story. But readers reacted to it as a suspense story, so I've been analyzing it as objectively as possible (I keep wanting to rewrite or delete)—to try to see how I plaited three strands into one tight braid of suspense.
>
> The three strands are these: Miriam's parents' story, . . . Miriam's own story, . . . and the town of Parmenter, the new dimension; not only a theater for events but, as always with my work, a major character without whom the others would have no existence.
>
> I came to the conclusion that *Where the Lost Aprils Are* is a suspense story after all, because Miriam is in suspense all the way through the book. She has been in suspense ever since her mother told her that she was illegitimate but not who her father was. And

when Miriam finally does know the truth, she is still in suspense, because her life is left hanging in a kind of limbo until she can come to terms with the ghosts of her past. (*The Writer*, September 1976).

This book began as an outline for a movie script written by Mollie Mc-Neill, an English friend of Elisabeth's. The scenario didn't sell, so Mollie sent it to Elisabeth to see what she could do with it. From this original idea, Elisabeth created the novel. After it sold, Elisabeth not only dedicated it to Mollie and her husband, but also decided to share half the royalties with Mollie, by this time a widow.

Other inspirations included a real-life enormous house fire, the poetry of Swinburne, and a recording of great Scots tenor (and personal favorite of Elisabeth's), Calum Kennedy, singing "My Love Is Like a Red, Red Rose." The name of the town, Parmenter, was the last name of one of Elisabeth's classmates at North Quincy High School.

The Dreaming Swimmer (1976)

> *I think the danger of the ocean lies*
> *Not in the storm, but in the mermaid's eyes;*
> *She closes them for kisses, unaware,*
> *Enfolds the dreaming swimmer, and he dies.*
>
> —Allan R. Ogilvie

In this sequel to *Weep and Know Why*, we meet up again with Mirabell and Barnaby Taggart. Now married for two years, they live at Cape Silver with Barnaby's visiting cousin, nineteen-year-old Sara Brownell. Stranger Cory Sanderson buys the old Darby house for $100,000 in cash, and moves right in. He does not welcome any overtures of friendship, closing himself off from the rest of the world. Sara refuses to accept his misanthropy and gets to know him secretly. She rejoices when she makes inroads toward friendship—until his house burns down and he disappears.

One violent action follows another, making the entire community unsure of just whom to trust. Suspicions are aroused by eccentric caretaker Lorenzo Darby, and even by Max Kemper, Sara's love interest. Everyone tries to solve the mystery of what happened to Cory Sanderson—until one afternoon on Cat Island, when the action reaches a dramatic crescendo. Elisabeth is at her best in this chilling novel of suspense, which contains enough twists and turns to satisfy any mystery reader.

One of the novel's violent crises involves the death of a pet. In a 1985 interview for *Down East* Magazine, Elisabeth stated that the death of an animal is truly disturbing to her. She used this device in *The Dreaming Swimmer,* where a pet dog gets shot in the head. His owners, Kyle and Deirdre Boone, have just let him out for his usual midnight run when they suddenly hear him barking in the woods. Kyle whistles for him, but he doesn't come. Upon investigation, Kyle finds Prince lying dead behind the carriage house, greatly increasing the level of suspense.

The setting for this story is Gay's Island, with a few changes in terrain.

A Dancer in Yellow (1979)

> *"O! There is sweet music on yonder green hill, O!*
> *And you shall be a dancer, a dancer in yellow,*
> *All in yellow, all in yellow,"*
> *Said the crow to the frog, and then, O!*
> *"All in yellow, all in yellow,"*
> *Said the frog to the crow again, O!*
>
> —Old English nursery rhyme

Astrid and Gray Price are leading a happy life in their small Maine coastal town. They live with their two small sons in a close-knit community, where Gray works in the family construction business. Astrid is shocked when Gray confides that he is tired of being the youngest of the three Price brothers, without any autonomy. She immediately supports him in his desire to go out on his own.

Things seem to improve, but Astrid soon learns that Gray's job worries were only masking the real trouble—an affair with their teenage babysitter, Dorri Sears. Beautiful and stubborn, Dorri sees in Gray a way to escape the stultifying small-town life she abhors. When Dorri and Gray disappear, some of the townsfolk feel it's for the best. The way Elisabeth resolves the mystery makes for one of her most disturbing and unusual suspense novels.

"I do love to write a straight murder story," Elisabeth told *Down East* magazine in 1985. "I ask a doctor all the medical questions; for *A Dancer in Yellow*, for example, I had to find out how bodies are going to look after they've been two weeks in the hot summer right up under the roof of a fish house—what color they're going to be."

When asked whether she finds it difficult to write something so repugnant, Elisabeth laughed and said, "No, not if I don't care too much about the characters— and I don't kill off the ones I like! That may sound strange, but the things I do find it uncomfortable to write about are cruelty to animals or children. . . . In [*The Dreaming Swimmer*] a dog was killed. This was a particularly dastardly act, and I felt bad doing it, but it was good for the story."

The Road to Nowhere (1983)

Jule Moreton has been busy finishing her high school education and trying to support herself on the mainland. She is also trying to forget her nightmarish childhood, where she and her foster sister Roz were never allowed to have any contact with the outside world after they moved to Osprey Island. "There Beatrice 'Mummie' Moreton had ruled the girls and Jondy, her ineffectual mate, with the proverbial iron hand, alternating abuse with terrifying silences. There Jule and Roz had endured the sordid misery of their childhood." (*The Gothic Journal*, 1996)

Roz escaped the island with stolen household money, abandoning Jule to their psychotic mother. Roz found wealthy relatives, the Deverells, and now has a new life. Jule anticipates that Roz can give her back some of the funds she had used to escape their miserable childhood home. Roz does not welcome Jule, who soon suffers mysterious mishaps. "Beginning with Jule's 'accidents,' the pace accelerates, sweeping to a grisly climax. Author Ogilvie offers striking characterizations (particularly of the grotesque 'Mummie') and a dark, complex, yet understandable, plot." (*The Gothic Journal*)

The Road to Nowhere was loosely based on a true story. The real-life "Mummie" was quite a character. Her husband was very good-natured and charming, but apparently under his wife's thumb entirely. Like Jondy in the book, the real-life husband never stood up to his despotic wife.

Lyle Ritchie, of *Waters on a Starry Night*, shows up as the man who picks up Roz from the island. The Deverell's cook, Martie Foster, also appears in *Rowan Head*, and Jule's cat, Hodge, appears in *Ceiling of Amber*.

The Devil in Tartan (1980)

> *From the lone shieling of the misty island*
> *Mountains divide us, and the waste of seas—*
> *Yet still the blood is strong, the heart is Highland,*
> *And we in dreams behold the Hebrides.*
>
> —"Canadian Boat-Song" (from the Gaelic)

Twenty-four-year-old Noel Paige and her stepbrother Robbie travel to Brierbank, Nova Scotia, for the summer. Her mission is to complete the Kendrum family genealogy that Robbie's father began before he died. The family can trace their roots back to Scotsman Angus James Kendrum, son of the fifth Earl of Strathcorran, killed at the Battle of Culloden in 1746. One of the Kendrum men in the family is the legitimate sixth Earl of Strathcorran, but no one knows for sure which one, as no written records were kept. Noel becomes involved in the drama when violence begins to eliminate family members just as a gathering is to take place. Someone is trying to get rid of those who have the strongest claims to the Earl's title.

Reviewer Jack Barnes wrote that the "dreams, extrasensory perceptions, ghosts in the night, and premeditated murder make this novel a thriller." This novel is fascinating both for its suspenseful content and its connections to Elisabeth's own family background.

The inspiration for *The Devil in Tartan* came from Ogilvie family history. As described in Chapters 1 and 2, Elisabeth's brother Gordon researched their family's ancestry. The characters in this novel echo Elisabeth's own ancestors, who made their way to Georgia for a time before emigrating to Nova Scotia. Gordon once told Elisabeth that he'd been thinking about their family history so much, he even dreamed about it. She worked that dream into her novel, where Noel also becomes deeply involved in her family research. Gordon used some of the same family history in his novel, *Jamie Reid*.

The Silent Ones (1981)

Dr. Alison Barbour, of Hazelhurst College in New England, decides to search out her family after finding a photo of her great-grandmother, Christina MacLeod. Alison has inherited the red hair of her ancestors from Torsaig, Isle of Lewis, in the Outer Hebrides of Scotland. She also wants answers to the mystery of Christina's departure from the Isle of Lewis, and feels the Standing Stones at Callanish hold the key.

Alison becomes enthralled with the Standing Stones while exploring the beautiful island landscape. She also soon becomes involved with Ewen Chisholm, a local writer who has a similar obsession with the Standing Stones.

A cast of unscrupulous characters all seem to be searching for the Book of St. Neacal, a long-lost literary artifact. Small annoyances during the trip "pale for Alison when she discovers a body within the circle of the Standing Stones. Like the mists cloaking the severe landscape, a miasma of intrigue

and violence settles over the story, with Alison a likely future murder victim."
(*The Gothic Journal*, 1996)

> She saw Norris. He was lying almost at her feet, and his eyes were
> open. At first she thought he was looking at her, that it was a morbid
> practical joke and he was going to start laughing in a moment. Then
> it was as if a drawn shade had suddenly snapped up in her brain and
> let in a brutally unsparing light. She saw that the open gray eyes were
> blind. They were dead eyes. His fair hair was darkened and stiffened
> with blood. Where the blood had run from his nose and mouth it
> looked black. The tan trenchcoat was streaked and stained with dirt.
> She didn't scream. She heard herself whispering inanely, "Some-
> body come. Something is terrible."

Pamela Marsh, reviewing the novel for the *Christian Science Monitor*,
touched on the components that make every Ogilvie book so satisfying:

> For readers who once in a while like to forget their own world
> and pull a story around them like a blanket, it's hard to beat novels
> by the ever entertaining Elisabeth Ogilvie. Her heroines are young,
> usually beautiful, unusually intelligent, possessing hidden depths of
> self-reliance. Danger, when it comes—of course it comes—has unex-
> pected twists. Her heroes are romantically impenetrable. And don't
> forget her settings. Oh, those marvelous vivid settings.

Marsh concluded with a comment that *The Silent Ones* provides "that almost
forgotten commodity—a good read."

Elisabeth, like her heroine, traveled to Scotland to search out her family roots on the Isle of Lewis, specifically her maternal great-grandmother,
Peigi MacLeod. The Standing Stones at Callanish on the Isle of Lewis provided
inspiration as well. Elisabeth gathered material for this novel during her first
trip to Scotland in 1979, when she spent five months there.

This is a particularly fine mystery, and it gained popularity and rave reviews in Scotland. To research the novel, Elisabeth corresponded with the
Procurator Fiscal (equivalent to a district attorney in the United States) so she
could properly describe the procedures used to investigate a murder in Scotland. (Elisabeth notes that Scottish law has some Roman law mixed in with
English; Scotland is the only country that allows a verdict of "not proven," as
well as "guilty" or "not guilty.") When this book was published, Elisabeth sent

a copy to the Procurator Fiscal to thank him for his help. He enjoyed the book so much that he wrote a glowing review for the *Stornoway Gazette*. Although *The Silent Ones* was not published in Great Britain, many residents of the Isle of Lewis have acquired copies. As a result, Elisabeth has many fans in Scotland.

When the Music Stopped (1989)

> *I shall never be friends again with roses,*
> *I shall hate sweet music my whole life long.*
> —From "The Triumph of Time," by A. C. Swinburne

When sisters Marianne and Emma Esmond return home to their small coastal village of Job's Harbor, everyone is talking about what happened sixty years ago. At that time Marianne ran off with a married man, who stole from the people of the area by cleaning out the bank's vault. Now, with their return, the two women have reinstated Sunday afternoon musical socials at their home. This brings a spark of new life to the people of Job's Harbor, including writer Eden Winter, who is intrigued by their past. At one of the musical afternoons, Eden meets Nick Raintree, a mysterious newcomer who seems intent on disrupting her romance with Glen Heriot, a local man.

When a sudden, violent tragedy tears the fabric of the town forever, Eden is plunged headlong into the horror and finds herself intimately connected with the players involved.

The character Eden Winter shares her creator's addiction to writing and her fondness for the Brontë sisters. Eden writes chapters of "Gothic novels set in Maine," to be devoured by her friend, Fee, and even feels that she receives supernatural guidance:

> With the help of the Ouija board we were convinced that the Brontës were dictating to me. I think we assisted the board to reach its conclusions, but we would never admit it; I did think the Brontës might have picked me to carry the torch, if they could have. But whenever I read the stuff over a few months later, I knew I wasn't their nominee.

Elisabeth feels this is one of her best mysteries. The idea for the book germinated when Elisabeth heard a brief news item about two elderly women, both musicians, found dead in Dorchester (where Elisabeth lived until she was nine years old). With typical humor, Elisabeth once suggested that would make a catchy title —"Dead in Dorchester." The Dorchester murderer, apparently looking for drug money, gave himself up right afterward. Elisabeth changed the setting to Maine, and when she began writing the novel, she wasn't sure who would be the killer.

Reviewer Jack Barnes once remarked about Elisabeth's suspense novels that, "just as readers are lulled into a state of euphoria, perhaps by the distant chorus of gulls blending with the eternal rote, she will very likely jolt them back to reality with a shocking scene and ensuing moments of suspense. . . ." Indeed, Elisabeth doesn't spare the reader any horror in the grisly details of this story, but, as always, her setting and her characters become real and satisfying, and we inevitably care deeply about both.

In several geographical references, *When the Music Stopped* can be correlated with the Jennie series. Glen's ancestors came from Scotland, and Eden proposes to Glen a trip to the Hebrides, to which he agrees. Mentioned are the islands of Mull, Iona, Tiree, Barra, and Skye. Other common threads include the Harris tweed jacket, fishing, lobstering, and bagpipes. The town of Job's Harbor is also mentioned in *Jennie Glenroy*.

READER COMMENT

When the Music Stopped is one of my favorite Ogilvie books, and I understand it is also one of Elisabeth's favorites. The story is interwoven with mystery and scandal from long ago, as well as glimpses into the lives of many of the people of Job's Harbor. In addition to the wonderful mystery, I enjoyed the closeness of Eden to her grandparents. I love the fact that she is living in part of the family homestead, and that she has ties to the past in her interest in Marianne and Emma Esmond. Even though this is a suspenseful mystery, Elisabeth still creates the same type of mood as in the Bennett's series.

—Kathy Walker, Illinois

18 ❧ THE JENNIE SERIES

IN HER FIRST FORAY into historical fiction, Elisabeth chose what seemed a natural venue: Scotland, beautiful land of her ancestors. This country had always fascinated her, and from her travels there (described in Chapter 8) she was inspired to write several novels, including *The Silent Ones,* the young adult novel *Too Young to Know*, and the Jennie series.

Consisting of three published books and a fourth one in the works, this series focuses on a brave young woman who in 1809 travels from England, to Scotland, and then to the New World.

JENNIE'S FAMILY

Parents: Priscilla and Carolus Hawthorne
  Their daughters: Sylvia, married William, son Carolus Jerome
                 Ianthe
                 Eugenia (Jennie)
                 Sophie

Jennie married Nigel Gilchrist (deceased)
                 Priscilla
        married Alick Gilchrist (aka Jennie and Alick Glenroy)
                 Alexander and Carolus (twins)
                 William
                 April (deceased)
                 Bell Ann

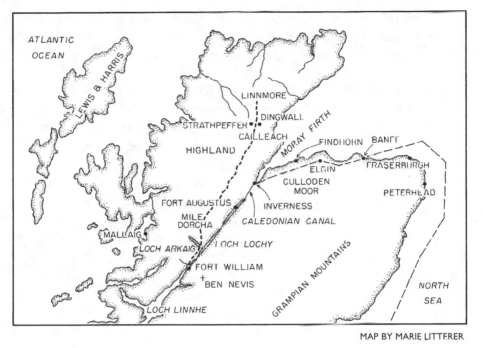

MAP BY MARIE LITTERER

Travels with Jennie
(Locations shown on map)

- Born Eugenia Hawthorne at Pippin Grange in the Kyloe Hills near the North Sea, in England.

- Lived with aunt and uncle in Brunswick Square, London.

- Married Nigel Gilchrist, sailed to Inverness, Scotland, by way of the North Sea, past the towns of Peterhead and Fraserburgh, on to Banff; stayed at Inn in Elgin. Sailed up the Moray Firth past Findhorn, with its bay open to the firth, past Nairn and Culloden Moor, to Inverness and through the Caledonian Canal. Traveled to their home, the Gilchrist family estate Linnmore, located in the western Highlands of Scotland two days north of Inverness. (When the ship docked at Banff, they were invited to ride with friends in a chaise-and-four as far as Inverness. There, Linnmore staff met them with a wagon to take them the rest of the way.)

- Ran away with Alick Gilchrist to Fort William, sailing from there to Maine aboard the *Paul Revere*.

Writing the Jennie books was a different experience for Elisabeth. Having never lived in Scotland, she needed to do much research—through reading and travel—before she could begin writing the story:

In writing *Jennie About to Be*, though I knew much Scottish history and have been to Scotland, there was plenty I didn't know. So I had to find out what flora and fauna my people could expect to find on their long walk through the Highlands, what surprises the weather could come up with, and what mysterious phenomena might occur, like the Great Grey Man, and so forth. (He was suspected of being a ghost.) ("The Practice and the Passion," *The Writer*, 1985)

The route that Jennie and Alick walked in this first Jennie book was based on an actual walking route called the Dark Mile. "Through guidebooks and maps I traced out a rough route for the walkers, though I didn't use actual place names until they reached their destination, which was and is a real town [Fort William]. By keeping the mountains and lochs anonymous, or inventing names for them, I allowed myself freedom for my imagination and kept myself from making glaring errors of ignorance. And then there were those paintings and photographs, into which I had thought myself so completely." (*The Writer*, 1985)

They went out around a stony mound, and some distance before them a deep, forested crease appeared between two hills. She guessed that they were heading for it. Instinctively she looked back. Already a mile or so of uneven terrain had hidden the general location of the hollow, but now the loch had disappeared, though she thought she could still see the osprey hanging over it. Far away across the billows of moor that brightened and darkened under sun and cloud, there was the line of the great old pines against the sky.

She filled her eyes with them to imprint them for always on her memory. Then she turned and hurried to catch up with Alick.

For the Maine portion of the series, Elisabeth found historical information in *Eaton's History of Thomaston and Rockland*, including a recounting of the Highlanders' arrival in Maine in 1802. General Knox had advertised in Scotland for settlers for his new town. They arrived and made quite a stir, dressed in their kilts and plaids and speaking Gaelic. Many of these Scots later

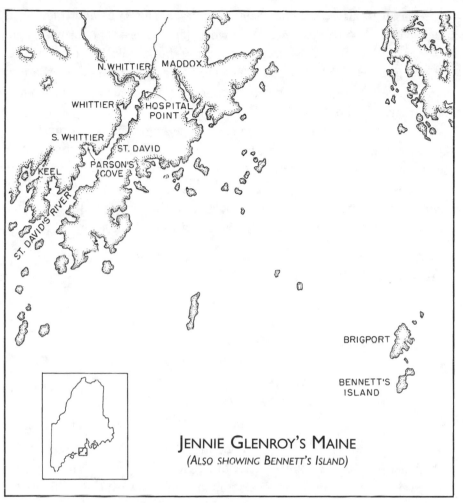

JENNIE GLENROY'S MAINE
(ALSO SHOWING BENNETT'S ISLAND)

MAP BY MARIE LITTERER

moved to Nova Scotia. The town of Maddox is based on the real town of Thomaston, Maine, near Elisabeth's home of Cushing.

In her exhaustive research, Elisabeth delved into what life was like during the early nineteenth century. In researching the third Jennie book, Elisabeth read the journals of Hezekiah Prince, Jr. (1822–28). "They were having such a grand time," she told interviewer Jack Barnes in 1989, "going sailing in the summer, and in the winter they would go to Waldoboro, dance all evening, have a midnight supper, and get back by daylight." ("Elisabeth Ogilvie: Maine's Prolific Writer," *New Hampshire Sunday News*)

Elisabeth also researched Scottish culture. One Highland tradition is touched on in *The World of Jennie G.*, when Jennie presents Alick with a gift of a razor. He is very uneasy accepting her gift, but thanks her. Later at supper she finds a penny by her plate, "For the blade," he said. For any sharp or pointed object given you, you pay the donor a penny a blade or for each point, lest a friendship should be slashed or pierced.

The Gaelic used in the Jennie series (see Appendix 2) was mostly obtained from reference books, but Elisabeth also researched the language when she visited a primary school in the Outer Hebrides. There, they put the English words along with their Gaelic equivalents around the top of the schoolroom walls, similar to what some schools do in this country with the alphabet. She noted that Gaelic speakers use perfect English, as a general rule.

Jennie About to Be (1984)

Whether we be young or old,
Our destiny, our being's heart and home,
Is with infinitude, and only there;
With hope it is, hope that can never die,
Effort, and expectation, and desire,
And something evermore about to be.

—William Wordsworth

Jennie Hawthorne is living in London with her aunt, following the death of both her parents in 1809. Jennie is homesick, and not eager to join the husband-seeking ranks, until she meets and falls in love with Nigel Gilchrist, a dashing Household Cavalry officer. Jennie marries him and moves to the Scottish Highlands, where Nigel is to manage the family estate of Linnmore.

Her newlywed bliss soon turns to horror when she witnesses the cruel Highland Clearances—when longstanding tenants (subsistence farmers) were evicted to make way for more profitable flocks of sheep. Jennie joins Nigel's cousin, Alick Gilchrist, to fight against the Clearances, but to no avail. Their efforts end tragically, and they have no choice but to escape together, into the unknown. Jennie and Alick flee on foot, heading south through the Highlands. They spend nights in caves and survive on vegetation and wild life. Along the route leading to Fort William—and ultimately America and a new life—their relationship develops from a mutely distant one, to a partnership marked by mutual understanding and respect.

Reviewer Jack Barnes didn't doubt Jennie's ability to prevail in the New World, writing, "Fortunately, Jennie possesses the courage and pertinacity of a Joanna Bennett of Bennett's Island." He described the first Jennie book as "a powerful novel that may surpass anything Elisabeth Ogilvie has written." *Jennie About to Be* was so well received that McGraw-Hill asked her to give top priority to a sequel.

Elisabeth says about this book, "I wanted [the novel to be set] before the War of 1812, but still deal with the situation in Europe at the time of Napoleon. Landed Scottish gentry took advantage of poor tenant farmers to drive them off and convert acreage to grazing land for sheep at a time when most of the young men were in Portugal and Spain fighting the Peninsular War."

The World of Jennie G. (1986)

> *Not in Utopia, subterranean fields,*
> *Or some secreted island, Heaven knows where?*
> *But in the very world, which is the world*
> *Of all of us,—the place where, in the end*
> *We find our happiness, or not at all!*
>
> —William Wordsworth

Jennie and Alick's story continues on the brig *Paul Revere*, as the two sail toward the coast of Maine. Jennie feels responsible for Alick, believing it is due to her actions that Alick must now flee the authorities and escape to New England. When the trip's patron requires all immigrant men on board be married, Jennie willingly acts as his wife on the voyage. They settle in the small town of Maddox, and begin a life together under the assumed name of Glenroy.

Unlike other Scottish immigrants from the ship, Jennie and Alick speak English, yet even they become targets of hostility from some of the townspeople. Their new life, although full of hardships, also brings rewards. Alick finds work in the shipyard, and Jennie as a governess. Jennie intends to earn her passage back to England to rejoin her sisters, but her plans are for naught when she is faced with an undesired pregnancy—and an even deeper connection with the mysterious Alick Glenroy.

Many readers have formed an attachment to Alick, just as others have to Owen Bennett. The love story that develops between Jennie and Alick is one of the most romantic in all of Ogilvie's work.

Jennie Glenroy (1993)

> *"A land of love and a land of light."*
> —From *Kilmeny*, by James Hogg

This third book of the series opens in 1827. Jennie and Alick are now married, and sharing their love with five children. Alick is the owner of his own profitable shipyard, and Jennie is busy caring for the family. Despite their many causes for joy, however, they undergo a year filled with tragedy. Jennie tries to find a way to help her sons, who are mistakenly accused of a horrible crime. Her oldest daughter falls in love, and proves to be as independent as Jennie herself had been during her youth. In the end, Jennie and Alick must deal with consequences from the past they thought they left behind. As always, they deal with it together, with an intense devotion to each other.

Jennie describes her feelings about Alick in a paragraph toward the end of the book, when she fears for their future. This passage is reminiscent of Thora and Lyle Ritchie's marriage in *Waters on a Starry Night*.

> But for a couple who had grown as inseparable as two seeds in the core of an apple, to have the fruit brutally riven apart as by an axe— she felt as if the house itself had shuddered in an earthquake.

Reviewer Karen Mather, of the Brunswick *Times Record*, appreciated Elisabeth's descriptive powers, calling the opening scene "detailed with all the freshness and sundrenched color of a watercolor seascape." She praised Elisabeth's attention to detail in "[how] the era is rendered. The language is also remarkable due both to the interspersing of Gaelic sentiments as well as its oblique modesty." She also highlighted the author's extraordinary awareness of the lives of women and the various issues they faced at the time.

Even though the Glenroy family must survive much tragedy during the course of this book, this does not "reduce the novel to a level of despair," wrote Mather. "Rather, the story's tension is skillfully developed from this perilous background." And she found Elisabeth's portrait of Jennie to be multidimensional and complete, noting, "Jennie is a true heroine not because she endures fear and suffering but as a manifestation of the grace and dignity she maintains at every tragic curve."

Continuing the Jennie Series

Elisabeth reports that the fourth Jennie novel (still untitled when this book went to press) will recount the adventures of the Glenroy family over the course of one year. Its plot picks up where the third installment leaves off:

> I'm not going to spend much more than a year, because I don't want the kids growing up too fast. Bell Ann is ten, and William is fifteen. I have a history of Maine, and it says that [during that period] they were always having a fit about keeping up the militia, because people began to think less and less of it. William is worried that they're going to do away with it entirely before he turns sixteen and can join.
>
> Jennie and Alick allow Priscilla to go to Europe to stay with her aunt, to be apprenticed to a French dressmaker. She is so sure she's going to have a shop when she comes home, after being gone for a few years. Carolus is in college majoring in botany, and Sandy has a chance to go on a ship with Captain Whittier, who is well respected in town. Captain Whittier takes his own grandson and Sandy along, more or less to give them practical experience during a trip to the Caribbean. They are all very anxious about slavery, and want to get into the Revenue Marine (which later becomes the Coast Guard).

Elisabeth feels committed to continuing the story of the Glenroys for a while yet, noting that she has enough material for several more novels.

19 ❧ YOUNG ADULT NOVELS

ELISABETH HAS ALWAYS had an affinity for young people, expressed not only in her personal life but in her juvenile novels. She began writing for young people in 1954, when she was asked to contribute to a series of books on statehood. In *Whistle for a Wind: Maine 1820* she spun a story about the Bennett patriarch, Jamie Bennett, that included an exciting adventure and the history of Maine's birth as a state. She was off and running, and went on to write more young adult books, fifteen in all.

Except for *Whistle for a Wind*, all of her young adult novels have contemporary settings. All were written for teenagers on the brink of experiencing life, with elements of romance, danger, and intrigue, along with opportunities for choice. Elisabeth writes about real topics of vital concern to young people.

Elisabeth told *Something About the Author*, "I've enjoyed . . . the letters I get from the [younger] readers a great deal. Many of my adult books are favorites of teenagers who have gone beyond the juvenile classification." She shares more of her thoughts on writing juvenile novels in the following essay, written for the Spring 1999 *Mug-up* newsletter.

ON WRITING JUVENILE NOVELS, by Elisabeth Ogilvie

I had never been interested in writing about juveniles, even though I had juvenile characters in my adult books. Joanna was only fifteen in the first part of *High Tide at Noon.* When a Scribner's editor approached me about doing a juvenile book for their statehood series—each story would take place in the year a state came into official existence— I saw it as a challenge.

My hero, Jamie Bennett, came at once to life and I placed him on Brigport, with the island known as the "south island" [Bennett's Island] lying out there with a few people living on it. Jamie wouldn't be a child, but an older teenager with the responsibility of being the man of the house, since his father had been "impressed" by the British Navy when he was out fishing one day during the war of 1812—and to all intents and purposes he was dead.

I used to imagine doing a historical novel, but it seemed like a lot of work and research while one Bennett's Island novel after another kept crowding me. Well, here was a historical story with early Bennetts in it; it would be the story of how the "south island" became Bennett's Island. (In a later juvenile, the modern Jamie and his cousins go over to Brigport to poke around on the site of the old Bennett Homestead.)

I've also written several other juveniles with Bennett's Island characters. Whittlesey House, the name for McGraw-Hill's juvenile section when it was born, wanted "young adult" books, and this was what I liked; people who are still legally juveniles but have to make serious decisions that will affect their adult lives.

Whistle for a Wind (1954), a good folk phrase about the weather, was the obvious title for the first book. I did a lot of historical research about that period, studied up on the fishing habits of those days and on ships and shipping as the great Age of Sail began. A paperback called *Sea Terms Come Ashore* still provides a lot of color for me, as many of the expressions are in use today by older men, more or less whimsically as tribute to the ancestors who lived that deep-sea life. And some of them are still in use, an ageless language.

Whistle did so well, I wrote others in between the adult books, and Whittlesey House bought them all. I began including a mystery now and then, and some life-threatening situations, even though decision-making was always important. I began thinking about adult mysteries; the juveniles were a good training ground.

A fact (sometimes sad) of publishing is [that sometimes] an editor with whom you've become friends, retires, and is replaced by someone who's not the least interested in your background; in fact, won't give it houseroom, and isn't a bit nice about saying so. This happened to the last juvenile novel I sent to Whittlesey House (and she wasn't even polite! I wonder how long she lasted). Fortunately the parent company was stable, and in forty years I've been friends with every editor I had....

I haven't written a juvenile for a long time.... But I've always been glad that Scribner's editor asked me for a story set in 1820. I have not written another hardcover juvenile since *Come Aboard and Bring Your Dory!* [Published in 1969; the title is an expression of welcome from the great days of the Grand Banks fisheries]....

I did write a few paperbacks for Scholastic, in a Young Love series; the fad for these lasted only a few years and then it changed to Horror, in which I was not interested. Still, the books I did write [for that series] gave me more training, and [allowed me to include historical research, as in *My Summer Love*, 1985] when people were discovering marvelously painted walls in old houses, and seeing them as priceless. In another [book], I used my experience of time spent in Scotland (*Too Young to Know*, 1982). When the editor asked me to write Young Love stories—first romances, really—she suggested the problems an extremely beautiful young girl might encounter. Never having been that, or even remotely approaching it, I [at first] thought a beautiful teenager wouldn't have any problems.

I began asking questions of the teenage girls I knew, and found the young beauties have a different set of problems, sometimes beginning in the first grade, and not only from other youngsters. The book was a success, and brought me letters from lonely kids as far away as Australia. It's simply called *Beautiful Girl*—the experience was short in years, but the royalties were great! And I learned something new, as I do from all my work....

THE YOUNG BENNETTS SERIES

Whistle for a Wind: Maine 1820 (1954)

There was an old superstition that one could raise the wind by whistling. At least to whistle for a wind might help to keep up one's courage or allay one's impatience, when actually there was nothing else one could do.

—George David Chase, *Sea Terms Come Ashore*

Elisabeth Ogilvie was asked to write this book about Maine as part of a series entitled The Strength of the Union, edited by Erick Berry. The goal of the series was to show how each state contributed to the Union. Other titles in the series covered Utah, Connecticut, Florida, and Minnesota.

This novel is set on Brigport, the real-life island of Matinicus, a well-known part of the Bennett's Island series; Elisabeth also used this setting in *Call Home the Heart*. In this story we meet Jamie Bennett, the patriarch of the Bennett clan. In typical Ogilvie fashion, the story revolves around a central crisis or mystery—and, true to form, the hero must make important, life-altering decisions.

When Jamie's father, Charles Bennett, is taken from his ship (impressed) by the British navy one day while out fishing, his children respond to their mother's needs by staying close to home. The younger children, Sylvia, Larkin, and the twins Margery and Albion, enjoy living on Brigport, but Jamie longs to travel and see the world. His sense of responsibility keeps him home supporting the family by fishing.

The island folk find that "wreckers" are at work, luring ships onto the rocks in order to abscond with their cargo. The skipper of the ship *Cynthia*, Captain Jeremy Thorne, is killed in one such raid. Shortly after, his brother Roger applies for the schoolmaster position. With Jamie's help, Roger is able to bring his brother's killers to justice.

This book simultaneously presents the history of the Bennett family in 1820 and the story of how Maine became a state on March 15 of that year, when the District of Maine was finally separated from the Commonwealth of Massachusetts.

How Wide the Heart (1959)
A Steady Kind of Love (Scholastic edition, 1979)

Ellen Douglass, daughter of Joanna and Alec Douglass, has returned home after graduating from high school on the mainland. She applies to art school in Boston and is accepted, but shortly after returning home she begins to question her plans for more schooling.

Robert Villiers, considered an inaccessible "summer complaint" (summer resident) by most of the islanders, has rented Owen's fish house in Schoolhouse Cove. Ellen meets him and is attracted to the mysterious stranger, whom she finds fascinating. At the same time, Ellen's romance with childhood friend Joey Caldwell, three years her senior, intensifies when he asks her to marry him. Watching her married cousin who has a small child makes Ellen's choice even harder, as she longs for a child of her own.

Ellen is torn between making a decision to become a lobsterman's wife or to follow her artistic abilities and attend school once more. Elisabeth writes about Ellen's struggle with sensitivity and understanding. She provides for the reader not only another view of the Bennett family, but an insightful rendering of the decisions young adults must face on the path to adulthood.

The Young Islanders (1960)

Eric Marshall and his cousin Jamie Sorensen, both thirteen years old, plan on pooling their money to purchase a lobster boat and engine. They concentrate on saving the money they earn as peapod fishermen, hauling a string of fifty traps. Everything is going as planned until they meet up with the MacKenzies of Brigport. Jeannie MacKenzie and her brothers are out to make trouble for Eric and Jamie in any way possible. Neither of the cousins can understand why they are being treated this way, and try to befriend the MacKenzie children despite their animosity.

When an elderly Bennett's Island lobsterman is found injured and unconscious, and some of their own traps have been interfered with, the cousins decide it is time the MacKenzies are forced to face up to the damage they have wrought.

This book is filled with the wonders of island living and the excitement of lobstering. Elisabeth ties this story to *Whistle for a Wind* by including some Bennett family history, referring back to the origins of the family on Brigport.

READER COMMENT

My fourteen-year-old daughter, Jenny, and I have only recently become devoted Elisabeth Ogilvie fans. She is an avid reader, and these books are so very appealing and safe to read. What a real treasure these books are to us! Our memories of sharing them and a "mug-up" of hot chocolate will always be with us.

—Barbara Brown, Maine

Ceiling of Amber (1964)
Until the End of Summer (Scholastic edition, 1981)

> *We shall see, while above us*
> *The waves roar and whirl,*
> *A ceiling of amber,*
> *A pavement of pearl.*
>
> —From "The Forsaken Merman,"
> by Matthew Arnold, 1849

In this last of the Young Bennetts books, nineteen-year-old Clarie Tanner comes back to Bennett's Island to help her family after her father's unexpected death. Determined that she and her younger brother can carry on the family lobstering business so that their mother Margaret won't have to give up their home, Clarie finds that she faces fierce competition from Owen, Charles, Mark, and Ross Bennett. In Clarie, Elisabeth creates another heroine who is strong and able to stand up to adversity, even in her youth. The way Clarie deals with the Bennetts and supports her own family in time of trouble is another example of Elisabeth's strong island characters.

We also again see poetry running like an ever-present thread through Elisabeth's work. The scene where Margaret reads the poem "The Forsaken Merman" to Brian and Clarie recalls Elisabeth's mother. Just as Maude recited poetry in the kitchen with Elisabeth and her brothers, so does this mother share thrilling lines of verse with her own children:

> "Give me the book." Clarie remembered the poem, she too had read it in the ninth grade at Limerock High. But she was not prepared for the physical thrill of hearing it now, in her mother's low voice, with the storm outside. She scooped up Hodge the cat and settled down in the rocker with him, shutting her eyes.

Elisabeth shares her own feelings about the importance of reading and writing when Margaret urges Brian to work hard on his poetry paper. A reluctant Brian asks why he can't just focus on math and history, and Margaret answers, "Because you'll be taking English in high school . . . and because it's your language, and you're going to know how to read it and write it and speak it."

(Lines from "The Forsaken Merman" are also quoted in *A Theme for Reason*, and a cat named Hodge also appears in *The Road to Nowhere*.)

OTHER YOUNG ADULT NOVELS

Blueberry Summer (1956)

This is the first of two novels about teenager Cass Phillips, set in a fictional Sandford Center on the coast of Maine. At sixteen, Cass is overweight and convinced she is unattractive. To make matters worse, she is forced to give up a summer job to care for her brother, Peter, and the family home when circumstances call her parents away. Instead of a vacation and a new summer job, she finds herself responsible for Peter, the family's animals and blueberry fields, and a host of related concerns.

Her situation brightens when she meets Adam Ross, a pre-med student from Massachusetts. Cass suddenly has an incentive to make some big decisions about her future. She loses weight, improving her appearance and disposition, and she matures along the way, considering life from a different vantage point. She decides to make the most of her summer romance with Adam before he heads back to school in the fall.

In a special section devoted to "Reading for Older Girls," a reviewer for the *Christian Science Monitor* wrote on May 10, 1956:

> It was an enlightening summer for Cass. One of the biggest things she learned was that when things seem stacked against you, it's often largely your own fault. She found out, too, something about boy friends, and what to look for in the right one . . . and about taking responsibility, about being loyal to friends and [being] completely just to strangers and friends alike. Elisabeth Ogilvie is a writer of adult as well as juvenile books. It shows. She has a seasoned, professional touch that is interest-compelling from the start.

The Fabulous Year (1958)

In this sequel to *Blueberry Summer* we have the continuing story of Cass Phillips as she begins her senior year at Sandford High. Things are back to normal after Cass's summer of transition, and Cass's life centers around the select Calpurnia Club, a group of elite girls who set the tone for the school. Even though her boyfriend, Adam, has begun his first year of medical school, their relationship intensifies. Both Cass and Adam find that when they are apart, it actually brings them closer together. Cass continues to mature and comes to realize that the things she thought were so important in life—the

Young Adult Novels

search for popularity with the Calpurnia Club, for example—are not as important as the real struggles some of her classmates face.

Elisabeth doesn't neglect the importance of setting in her young adult novels. When Cass and her friend Rory Fraser go to Pemaquid to see the surf, Elisabeth evokes all the beauty of the scene with her trademark style:

> At Pemaquid there were a few other people among the massive rock cliffs to watch the great seas roar in and explode in fountains of white, but not enough to take away the exhilarating sense of wildness. The gulls screamed thinly overhead, gliding and turning on the wind. Cass could think of nothing but the moment: the savage, brilliant beauty all around her, the suspense of watching a man photograph an oncoming breaker and then run before it caught him. She and Rory went down over the rocks until spray flew over them and wet their faces. Cass tasted it with a delight that hadn't changed since the first time she stood up in the bow of her father's boat, letting the white spray fly over her. It was native to her; the high, shrill calling of the gulls pierced her through, as a Scot is pierced to the heart by the unexpected sound of bagpipes.

Becky's Island (1961)

The Conrad family spends each summer at Greyrocks, their summer home on the coast of Maine. Wanting some time to herself, Vicky takes the dory to Pigwiggin, one of the islands in the Fingerlings. Here she finds Jude and Tamar, two children of neighboring Becky's Island. Returning them to their home, she is horrified by the poverty she finds there: "She wanted to get away from this desolate island and these desolate people as fast as she could. She was so depressed by them that she felt awful."

Vicky soon finds she can't forget the haunting images of the children and their hard life on the island. When Jude and Tamar fall ill and their father asks her to visit them, she agrees, bringing them gifts and fruit. After spending just a short time on the island, Vicky knows she has to do something to help. She begins with teaching the children songs and telling stories; she finds them eager to learn, and with dedication and hard work, Vicky helps build a school on Becky's Island, along with introducing other basic improvements to their lifestyle.

In *Becky's Island*, Elisabeth gives us a fictionalized version of a fascinating chapter of Maine history, based on the real island of Malaga, in Arrowsic, near Bath. *Becky's Island* is set in about 1960, but the real-life scandal at Malaga erupted in the early 1900s. In *The Maine Islands in Story and Legend*, Dot Simpson told about Malaga's dramatic history of "degeneration, miscegenation, incest, and general nastiness."

James McKenney, called "King of Malaga" (King Harry in *Becky's Island*) at the time, "was of Scottish descent [and] it is said he ruled his people like a dictator," wrote Simpson. "Why the Malagans degenerated into such a sad state is easy to understand. Misfits on the mainland, rejected by society for one reason or another, withdrew to the nearby island, and in time became a sort of salt-water Skid Row. The derelicts clung together without any moral guidance; their children grew up uneducated. Intermarriage was common, and so was no marriage. After a time there was a large percentage of mentally retarded and physically unfit islanders."

A kind family of summer folk decided to help the islanders by establishing a school. "All through June, July and August of 1908 the Lanes' daughter Cora [Vicky Conrad in Ogilvie's book] rowed across from Horse Island on every good day to teach the children. She started them off with singing lessons and thus aroused their interest and enthusiasm." Teaching them the basics led to the building of a school, with the help of generous contributions from individuals and groups in Maine and Massachusetts.

Turn Around Twice (1962)

> *I have been here before,*
> *But when or how I cannot tell;*
> *I know the grass beyond the door,*
> *The sweet keen smell,*
> *The sighing sound, the lights around the shore.*

—From "You'll Be Back and Older,"
by Dante Gabriel Rossetti

Burnley Wilder is a shy sixteen-year-old, unsure of herself in social situations and the victim of constant teasing. When she wins the grand prize in the Rye-Crunchy *My America* Essay Contest, she is shocked. Her choice of prizes is either $3,000 or an island off the coast of Maine. Although her siblings doubt her common sense, she chooses the forty-acre Hopkins Island, off Port George, as her reward.

The family plans to vacation there, until Mr. Wilder's aunt in Illinois falls ill and the parents are obliged to go there instead. The young people travel on their own from Kendall, Massachusetts, to Port George, Maine. Staying at the New Ocean House in Port George (based on the Ocean House hotel in Port Clyde, south of Rockland), they meet the owner's son, Mont Cady. He takes them to the island, where they stay despite the islanders' efforts to scare them off. They meet the grandson of the island's founder, finding his legacy in paintings done by his father. Claiming the island plunges the young people into intrigue and mystery and brings unexpected romance into Burnley's life.

Elisabeth successfully combines her understanding of young people and her love of the mystery genre in this novel. The idea of a budding young writer winning an essay contest and choosing to own an island are elements drawn from Elisabeth's own life.

Masquerade at Sea House (1965)

When Monica and Martin Christie decide to spend two weeks of their summer on Sea Island, it is simply to experience what their father, Mark, had told them about his youth. Mark had spent a great deal of time on the island, staying with his best friend, Tom Sanborn, at his family's cottage. Now both Mark and Tom are dead, and Monica and Martin decide to explore the island as uninvited houseguests—and impostors.

Monica and Martin fool the Brices, the caretakers of Sea House, into thinking they are part of the Sanborn family. Odd things soon begin to happen—items disappear and strange noises are heard at night. They eventually find a secured room filled with stolen items, and soon they are on the trail of the thief. The time they spend on this family-owned Maine island involves crime, suspicion, and romance.

The character Mont Cady is also found in the previous book, *Turn Around Twice*.

The Pigeon Pair (1967)

The Snow twins' father, Steve, has affectionately dubbed them "The Pigeon Pair." This term comes from the fact that pigeons often lay two eggs in a single nest, one egg producing a male and the other a female. Eighteen-year-old twins Ingrid and Gregory are just two of five siblings who are on their own a great deal after the death of their mother, Kitty, during her sixth pregnancy. (The Snow children were all named after movie stars from films Kitty had enjoyed: Ingrid Bergman, Gregory Peck, Elizabeth Taylor, Montgomery Clift, and Rock Hudson.) Ingrid becomes a mother figure when she returns home from high school in Augusta to help care for the family.

Steve is very independent and chooses to work his own jobs as he sees fit. As a result, the family lives a precarious hand-to-mouth existence in a run-down camp on a back road in a small Maine coast town. Greg and Ingrid have dreams for a better life, imagining their family living in the old Snow house on the main road—what they believe should have been their legacy. They plan to save money to purchase the house. When it is sold privately to a family from New Jersey, Ingrid is disappointed, while Greg expresses his anguish by trashing the property, landing himself in deep trouble. With grit and determination typical of Ogilvie characters, the family works together to overcome many significant obstacles.

The New York Times Book Review of May 7, 1967, contained praise for Elisabeth's sensitive portrayal of a young girl's awareness of her family's hardships: "Ingrid's struggle to better herself and her family will give readers an insight into another aspect of what the war against poverty can mean.... The special merit of this novel lies in its catching a glimpse of contemporary teenage problems that are bigger than those of growing up."

Come Aboard and Bring Your Dory! (1969)

This novel has a theme similar to *The Pigeon Pair*—young people working together to survive and prosper. After Mr. and Mrs. Cameron die within two months of each other, their six children decide to stay together and live as a family. The two older ones—Geordie, almost twenty-one, and his sister Lucy, just out of high school—feel that they can hold the family together rather than let relatives separate them.

At age seventeen, Penn falls in love and marries before finishing high school. Genie, not quite fifteen, finds that her close friendship with Ralph Morey defies his mother's desires. The ten-year-old twins, Peter and Phillip, suffer from divided loyalties following an enjoyable vacation with Uncle Bill and Aunt Nora Sylvester. Family ties are stretched to the limit with many trials and tribulations, but the Cameron siblings hold together and see it through. Elisabeth imbues this young adult novel with the same values that permeate her adult works—the strength of family, and the moral standards that she feels are so important.

The phrase "Come aboard and bring your dory," a fisherman's welcome meaning "Come in and set down," had been taught to the children by their father, who fished in the Grand Banks.

YOUNG LOVE SERIES

Beautiful Girl (1980)

When Scholastic Publishing Company's Young Love series editor asked Elisabeth to write these stories about first romances, she suggested that this first one might explore the problems an extremely beautiful young girl might encounter.

From the age of four, April Adams knew she had a special beauty. Friends of her parents, as well as relatives, would speak of her as "adorable," but when she begins referring to herself as adorable, beautiful, lovely, or breathtaking in the presence of her parents, she learns that it is not appreciated. Finding it difficult to be friends with both girls and boys, she decides everyone is against her due to her looks.

April eventually joins the thespians in school, and becomes friends with fellow actor Jason Barrett. When she meets Jason's older brother Nick, April is enchanted, and also flattered by his attention. When she finds her beauty is still working against her, a family friend who is painting her portrait offers a willing ear and some wise advice: "You'll have to come to terms with your own beauty before you can expect anyone else to, " he counsels. His encouragement strengthens her resolve to fight injustice and shows others what is behind her beautiful facade.

Elisabeth hadn't been sure what the reaction would be to a book on this topic, and she was surprised to receive a great deal of mail from young people who were touched by the story and had strong feelings about its message. Students at North Quincy High School thoroughly enjoyed this book when they read it in 2001 (page 25).

A Forgotten Girl ... and a Forgotten Time (1982)

When Val's and Alix's father, Richard Raeburn, finds he was actually born as Thomas Yardley, their lives change drastically. Richard's father, also named Thomas Yardley, was an only child who died during World War II. His widow returned home to Virginia, where she gave birth to her son, Thomas. She later married Richard Raeburn, who legally adopted Thomas, giving him his own name.

When Grandfather Yardley's will is read, a lawyer in Limerock contacts Richard, telling him that he was mentioned in the will. His inheritance is half of Dunbar's Island, twenty-five miles off the coast of Maine in Penobscot Bay. Val and Alix are allowed to go and stay there, as their lawyer assures the family that Mrs. Bancroft, an elderly lady living at the opposite end of the island, will provide some sort of supervision.

What the girls do not know prior to their arrival is that Mrs. Bancroft doesn't want them there. Life on the island is completely different from the life they knew in New York State. The family background involves them in deep mystery and finally romance.

Too Young to Know (1982)

Mary Kate, the youngest of the three Morgan children, has always been "her daddy's girl," until she accompanies him on a business trip to the Isle of Lewis, in Scotland. There she finds that Kenneth Morgan is busy with more than just consulting for an oil company and that his work with assistant Jean Cameron involves more than just business.

Trying to find a life for herself, Mary Kate meets and befriends Fiona Mackenzie, as well as others on the island. Her new friends are quite different from the friends she had back home; life is complicated further when she finds herself falling in love with Rob Munroe. Their love for each other grows, leading Mary Kate to decide that she wants to live on Lewis forever. But will her father allow it? Elisabeth realistically portrays this archetypal story of a young woman growing up and falling in love.

My Summer Love (1985)

Diana managed to fail all of her junior high classes by having fun instead of studying. Now summer has arrived, and it means playing catch-up in order to graduate with her classmates. Her mother makes arrangements with a widowed friend, teacher Madge Thornton, to tutor Di. In return, Di will care for the two younger Thornton children, Roger and Tabby. Even though Di resents being shipped out to the boonies, she at least anticipates the change of scene.

Upon her arrival at Hawthorne Farm, the Thornton homestead built in

1694, Di finds that the property is in the midst of turmoil, with family heirs feuding over whether to develop it into Hawthorne Estates, Inc. Di soon becomes involved in the family's effort to save the farm, with help from older son Mac Thornton. By accident, Tabby begins peeling back a corner of loose wallpaper in an attic room; soon, Di and Roger help, revealing marvelously painted walls.

When the paintings are shown to Mac, he suggests they be kept as a secret to show their mother. They soon uncover not just a small painting, but walls and walls of scenes from around the Hawthorne Farm—paintings that could prove to be the answer to saving the farm.

20 ❧ SHORT STORIES

Elisabeth's stories from *The Manet*—North Quincy High School's literary magazine—show a marked bent for adventure, for lively dialogue in the tradition of some British writers of the time, and for lyrical description.

It's interesting that her very early work focused on male heroes, while her later books always featured strong female characters. She was likely influenced by the books she read during her school years, which featured a predominance of male characters. Elisabeth was already exploring themes of adventure and family, and the importance of background.

Her gift for description was already evident, along with her ability to create a mood and a strong sense of background. In "The Power and the Glory," we hear Elisabeth's strongly evocative voice as she describes "the shining blue-pottery sky" and the eyes of the soldier's young love, Kathi: "Her eyes were gray-green, like the sea in winter, and unafraid under the shelter of her lashes."

"A Delightful Guest" was called sentimental by the editors of *The Manet*, but was also acclaimed for its lucid descriptions and warmth of tone. Elisabeth wrote another story similar to this one, which was published in the *Boston Post*. Apparently the newspaper continued the contest it had offered when her mother Maude was young, and like her mother, Elisabeth won the two-dollar prize.

"A Case of Mistaken Identity" (eighth grade, 1930)

"My parents having died, I started out on the road at the age of twelve to become a vagabond." With these opening lines, Elisabeth begins an adventure story that may have been inspired by some of the children's literature she was reading at the time. Her sense of character and dialogue is already apparent, as well as her sense of place. Her hero leaves the village of Arzon for Paris and sails to San Francisco—all in the course of this short story.

"Davey's Pirate" (ninth grade, 1931)

Young Davey, having lost his uncle guardian, is dreading the thought of living with Mrs. Hawkins. A friendly whistling man named Ron comes along and invites him aboard his yacht. Davey throws convention to the wind and accepts, becoming part of Ron the Hijacker's journey, and a life of rum-runners and danger. It's a boy's paradise, as Davey learns to handle a gun with skill, work aboard the yacht, and swap stories with the pirates.

"Legs for Rupert" (ninth grade, 1931)

In this story Elisabeth's characters could be from a period British drama, complete with appropriately elegant titles like Lord "Binks" Asherton and Lord Barnington. This is a tale about a young boy who befriends a wheelchair-bound man and becomes involved in the love affair between the man's doctor and his fiancée.

"Night-Errant" (eleventh grade, 1933)

Basil Thorndike is in love with the fiery, redheaded Jennifer Storme, but she wants nothing to do with him. Seeking a way to win her love, Basil confides in his father's secretary, the dashing Guy Westlake, who convinces Basil that the secret is to make Jen jealous. What follows is a delightful comedy of errors, filled with Elisabeth's bright humor. This story features skillful illustrations of the lead characters done by one of Elisabeth's friends.

"The Power and the Glory" (twelfth grade, 1934)

A captain fears assassination and orders one of his young soldiers to take his place in the parade. The story traces the journey of this soldier, his bitterness at the captain's cowardice, and the soldier's own willingness to die with honor. One can feel the influence of Elisabeth's upbringing in this story, as she explores the themes of bravery, cowardice, and unquestioning service to country.

"Mon Meilleur Noel" (My Best Christmas) (twelfth grade, 1934)

A fictionalized account, written in French, of a young girl's unexpected Christmas vacation spent on an island (most likely inspired by Criehaven).

"The Delightful Guest" (twelfth grade, 1934)

In this story (reprinted on pages 172–76), Elisabeth creates elderly Miss Gabrielle's garden, a place of soft, tranquil beauty. Gabrielle is wistful and wishing for company, so she is delighted to discover a young man perched on her wall. A hint of remembered romance enters in when she realizes he is the son of an old lover, and the gentle kiss he gives her upon departure lights up her face and fills her with joy.

"Meet Mr. King" (twelfth grade, 1934)

Elisabeth and fellow student Noyes Farmer interviewed British singer Dennis King as part of an assignment (see Chapter 3 for more details).

SHORT STORIES WRITTEN FOR NATIONAL MAGAZINES

"And Then It Will Be Spring" (*Everywoman* magazine, 1940s)

It was a long hard winter, and suddenly it was spring—a time to fall in love, but there wasn't a soul around. A young woman overcomes hardships on a rugged Maine island.

"Summer Girl" (*Woman's Day,* July 1944)

Set on Bennett's Island, this story (reprinted on pages 177–88) tells of the friendship between young lobsterman Joel Radway and summer girl Lucia Harkness.

"Eighteenth Summer" (*Woman's Day,* July 1947)

A sensitive love story about a young woman who falls in love with a lobsterman, and the subsequent choices she must make for her life. Elisabeth's skillful use of flashback is featured in this story.

"Hubert and the Eternal Feminine" (*Woman's Day,* March 1950)

The groom expected to live happily with his new bride, but had not envisioned life with her two cats. A touching, humorous story filled with Elisabeth's love of animals.

"Scobie" (*Woman's Day,* August 1951)

This charming story (reprinted in *Maine Speaks: An Anthology of Maine Literature*) speaks of the faith of childhood. A mysterious transient fisherman named Scobie and his pet pig Barnaby, change the lives of three young children.

"A Weekend with Ebony" (*Woman's Day,* August 1952)

Lacy is left alone by her parents to care for the house and Ebony, her pet sheep. What ensues is an adventurous weekend beyond what she had imagined, involving some frightening strangers, a new understanding of her friend Enos, and the bravery of Ebony.

"A Woman's Reputation" *(Redbook,* October 1962)

This lengthy story (billed as a "novel") focuses on a woman accused of murder and seen as guilty by the townspeople she trusted. Unfortunately, the only person who knows the truth has disappeared. Elisabeth wrote this story, her first effort at writing short suspense fiction, while recuperating from a broken leg.

"Island of Shadows" (*Good Housekeeping*, November 1969)

Kendal Blain is torn between two men—a calm widower who seems to have become more friend than lover, and a rugged, masculine islander who makes her heart skip a beat. How can she be sure of her feelings for either one? Set on a beautiful island twenty-five miles from shore (probably modeled on Criehaven), this story is filled with both romance and suspense.

"Reach for the Dawn" (*Good Housekeeping*, February 1981)

A condensed version of *The Silent Ones* (see page 218).

21 ❧ NONFICTION

ARTICLES ABOUT MAINE ISLAND LIFE

"The Lobsterman's Wife" (*Boston Transcript*, June 1946)

To most of us lobster is a luxury food, but to the lobsterman's family, it is their livelihood. This wonderful description of the lobstering life is reprinted on pages 98–102.

"Last Waltz on Criehaven" (*Island Journal*, Volume 13, 1996)

A description of life on Criehaven, then and now, reprinted on pages 66–75. This essay traces the Criehaven community from a lively population of year-round fisherfolk and summer residents in the 1930s and '40s, to the small summer colony of today.

AUTOBIOGRAPHY

My World Is an Island (1950)

I could go on and on about evenings when the sun set directly at the Friendship end of the Gut, and turned the water peach and rose and lavender, and we dipped the oars in pure color as we rowed along, leaving eddies of gold behind us; the birds made sleepy sounds in the alders and birches that grew down close to the water, and the fish hawks from Howard Head soared and piped high in the sky, on the last foray of the day, while the gulls flew homeward two by two.

In 1950, Elisabeth took time off from her fiction to write this book about her new home, Tide's Way, on Gay's Island in Muscongus Bay. Warm, affectionate, and often humorous, this depiction of life on an island is filled with references to the natural world and the animals that were so special to her and Dot Simpson. Once again, an island becomes a character in its own right, as Elisabeth acknowledges: "Perhaps [the book's] strongest feature is its quiet and gentle tone, that and the way it makes the island the chief character. . . ."

Writing in 1990, when Down East Books published the reprint edition, Nan Lincoln of the *Bar Harbor Times* noted that *My World Is an Island* celebrates Elisabeth's love affair with islands, beginning in adolescence with Crie-haven. Lincoln found that Elisabeth maintains a light touch with her sense of humor and down-to-earth recollections of daily life, mixed in with rapturous poetic descriptions of her surroundings.

Critiquing the book for the *Saturday Review of Literature* in 1950, Ruth Moore wrote, "So pleasant does Miss Ogilvie make her island sound that she may well start a seaward movement among people who have not yet lived on an island. . . ." The *New York Herald Tribune*'s Ernestine Evans commented that Ogilvie "makes a case for all islands as more manageable than larger frames of reference, and she takes your mind off continents and millenniums and exploits her own content with persuasive vivacity."

Reviewing the reprint edition of *My World Is an Island* in 1990, the *Bangor Daily News* placed the book in the "worth repeating" category:

> Her autobiography tells of her move to . . . Gay's Island and her purchase of a home there which she called Tide's Way, because the success of her first novel made it possible. It covers her first four years on Gay's Island, beginning in 1944, and of her struggles to repair, adapt and explore the terrain of this place. . . . Yet you sense she would choose no other way of life. She also has the consummate gift of making the reader understand why.
>
> In this book she already was honing her rare skill of describing the droll antics of the family pets, which then included sheep and goats as well as sundry dogs and cats. She can etch in a single sentence the joy and imagination of children as they discover the wonders of this new world; a facility which served her well in later novels.

My World Is an Island was also published in England.

READER COMMENT

I was thrilled when I first met Elisabeth—a first cousin to my husband's mother—and visiting her in her mainland home was very memorable. She was so unpretentious and direct, and I envied her for the simple way of life she enjoyed—staying on the mainland all winter and rowing over to her island for the summer. What an idyllic way to live! I enjoyed *My World Is an Island* because it really spoke of what made up the days and weeks of her life. I felt I knew her so much better after reading it.

—Beverly Lawson, Colorado

PROFESSIONAL ARTICLES FROM THE WRITER

"Background—the Most Important Character" (July 1966)

Elisabeth writes about the importance of setting in her novels, outlining her technique and advising fellow writers on how to make their writing come alive for readers.

"Suspense in Fiction" (January 1970)

A rich and vivid background can help create suspense and "soak a scene with menace," Elisabeth explains, using examples from her gothic novel, *Bellwood* and her short story "A Woman's Reputation." She talks about how she is always filled with ideas for potential story lines, even when walking the dog at night.

"Suspense and a Sense of Place" (September 1976)

Elisabeth discusses the combination of suspense and setting in this article, which mentions several of her novels: *The Face of Innocence, Weep and Know Why, Image of a Lover*, and *Where the Lost Aprils Are*. She places the most emphasis on this latter novel, exploring the techniques she used to create suspense.

"Speaking of Magic Carpets" (September 1981)

This articles discusses how to capture your chosen environment on paper with authenticity. Elisabeth focuses on her Jennie series, and her passion for Scotland. She also explains that even if you are unable to physically visit a place, detailed and careful research can be sufficient to create a believable background.

"The Practice and the Passion" (April 1985)

Elisabeth advises fellow writers on how to be careful observers in order to capture every nuance of an environment. She not only discusses her own enduring love affair with words, but also carefully outlines her writing process and recommends spending at least one half-hour each day on practicing the art of description.

PART VI

Appendixes

❧ CHARACTERS IN OGILVIE NOVELS

A

257

Bennett, Richard	AN ANSWER IN THE TIDE	son of Owen and Laurie
	THE SUMMER OF THE OSPREY	
	THE DAY BEFORE WINTER	16 years old
Bennett, Robin	AN ANSWER IN THE TIDE	daughter of Philippa and Steve
	THE SUMMER OF THE OSPREY	
	THE DAY BEFORE WINTER	
Bennett, Ross	CEILING OF AMBER	son of Philip and Liza
	THE DAY BEFORE WINTER	
Bennett, Sam	STRAWBERRIES IN THE SEA	son of Philip and Liza
	AN ANSWER IN THE TIDE	
	THE SUMMER OF THE OSPREY	
	THE DAY BEFORE WINTER	16 years old
Bennett, Sophia	WHISTLE FOR A WIND	daughter of Lydia and Charles
Bennett, Stephen, Sr.	HIGH TIDE AT NOON	Joanna's father
	STORM TIDE	
	THE EBBING TIDE	
Bennett, Steve	(All 9 Bennett Island books)	Joanna's brother
	HOW WIDE THE HEART	
	THE YOUNG ISLANDERS	
Bingham, Todd	WEEP AND KNOW WHY	Irenie's fiancée
	THE DREAMING SWIMMER	
Bird, Ash	HIGH TIDE AT NOON	Simon's brother
Bird, Flora	HIGH TIDE AT NOON	Mrs. George
Bird, George	HIGH TIDE AT NOON	father of Simon and Ash
Bird, Simon	HIGH TIDE AT NOON	Ash's brother
	THE SUMMER OF THE OSPREY	
BisBee, Tom	THE WORLD OF JENNIE G.	Eliza's father
BisBee, Eliza	THE WORLD OF JENNIE G.	cares for MacKenzie children
Black, Harrison	WHEN THE MUSIC STOPPED	Julian's attorney
Blackwell, Claudie	BLUEBERRY SUMMER	13-year-old problem
	THE FABULOUS YEAR	
Blackwell, Clem	BLUEBERRY SUMMER	18-year-old problem
	THE FABULOUS YEAR	
Blackwell, Flodie (Florian)	BLUEBERRY SUMMER	16-year-old problem
	THE FABULOUS YEAR	
Blake, Detective Sgt. Dan	THE DREAMING SWIMMER	Maine State Police
Blake, Donna	COME ABOARD AND BRING YOUR DORY!	Georgie's interest
Boone, Deirdre	THE DREAMING SWIMMER	Mrs. Kyle
Boone, Kyle	THE DREAMING SWIMMER	neighbors
Boyd, Alicia	THE FABULOUS YEAR	troubled classmate
Boyd, Izzy	WHISTLE FOR A WIND	a wrecker
Boyd, Mrs.	THE FABULOUS YEAR	Alicia's mother
Boyd, Reuben	WHISTLE FOR A WIND	sailed with Charles
Boyd, Tim	WHISTLE FOR A WIND	a wrecker

Bradshaw, Averil	ROWAN HEAD	Elliott and Ben's sister
Bradshaw, Ben	ROWAN HEAD	son
Bradshaw, Elliot	ROWAN HEAD	eldest son
Bradshaw, Vaughn	ROWAN HEAD	bought shipyard
Brewster, Caroline (Caro)	BELLWOOD	governess for Tim
Brewster, Eric	BELLWOOD	Caro's brother
Brewster, Mindy	BELLWOOD	Mrs. Eric
Brice, Cora	MASQUERADE AT SEA HOUSE	Mrs. Elmore
Brice, Elmore	MASQUERADE AT SEA HOUSE	caretakers of Sea House
Brice, Homer	MASQUERADE AT SEA HOUSE	their grandson
Brooks, Abbie	THE PIGEON PAIR	Mrs. Clem
Brooks, Clem	THE PIGEON PAIR	live at Tidewater Farm
Burgess, Miss Lettie	THE FABULOUS YEAR	Tracy's aunt

C

Cade, Damon	A DANCER IN YELLOW	troublemaker
Cade, Elmer	A DANCER IN YELLOW	father of Damon and Parris
Cade, Parris	A DANCER IN YELLOW	troublemaker
Cady, Capt. and Mrs.	TURN AROUND TWICE	owners of New Ocean House
Cady, Mont	MASQUERADE AT SEA HOUSE	their son
	TURN AROUND TWICE	Port George lobsterman
Caldwell, Caleb	STORM TIDE	newcomers
Caldwell, Joey	STORM TIDE	son of Caleb and Vinnie
	HOW WIDE THE HEART	Ellen's 21-year-old friend
	CEILING OF AMBER	
Caldwell, Vinnie	STORM TIDE	Mrs. Caleb
	HOW WIDE THE HEART	
Cameron, Barth	ROWAN HEAD	head of Cameron family
Cameron, David	ROWAN HEAD	youngest, artist
Cameron, Douglas	ROWAN HEAD	deceased
Cameron, Felice	ROWAN HEAD	widow of Douglas
Cameron, Genie	COME ABOARD AND BRING YOUR DORY!	14 years old
Cameron, Geordie	COME ABOARD . . .	20 years old
Cameron, Giles	ROWAN HEAD	troublesome brother
Cameron, Jean	TOO YOUNG TO KNOW	Kenneth Morgan's interest
Cameron, Lucy	COME ABOARD AND BRING YOUR DORY!	oldest girl
Cameron, Penn	COME ABOARD . . .	17 years old
Cameron, Peter	COME ABOARD . . .	one twin
Cameron, Phillip	COME ABOARD . . .	other twin
Campion, Amy	HOW WIDE THE HEART	grandniece of Asenath and Suze

Campion, Asanath	THE DAWNING OF THE DAY	brother to Foss
	HOW WIDE THE HEART	
	THE YOUNG ISLANDERS	
Campion, Binnie	THE DAWNING OF THE DAY	Mrs. Sky
Campion, Cindy	THE SEASONS HEREAFTER	daughter of Kathy and Terence
	AN ANSWER IN THE TIDE	
	THE SUMMER OF THE OSPREY	
Campion, Danny	THE SEASONS HEREAFTER	Foss and Helen's son
	THE DAY BEFORE WINTER	
Campion, Davey	THE SEASONS HEREAFTER	Kathy and Terence's son
Campion, Dorrie	THE DAY BEFORE WINTER	Binnie and Sky's child
Campion, Foss	THE DAWNING OF THE DAY	brother to Asanath
	THE SEASONS HEREAFTER	
	STRAWBERRIES IN THE SEA	
	AN ANSWER IN THE TIDE	
	THE SUMMER OF THE OSPREY	
	CEILING OF AMBER	
	THE YOUNG ISLANDERS	
Campion, Helen	THE DAWNING OF THE DAY	Mrs. Foss
	AN ANSWER IN THE TIDE	
	HOW WIDE THE HEART	
Campion, Johnny	THE SEASONS HEREAFTER	son of Kathy and Terence
	STRAWBERRIES IN THE SEA	
	THE DAY BEFORE WINTER	eighth grade
Campion, Kathy	THE SEASONS HEREAFTER	Mrs. Terence
	THE SUMMER OF THE OSPREY	
Campion, Peggy	THE DAWNING OF THE DAY	daughter of Foss and Helen
Campion, Perley	THE DAWNING OF THE DAY	Helen's 17-year-old son
Campion, Schuyler (Sky)	THE DAWNING OF THE DAY	son of Foss and Helen
Campion, Stuart	THE DAY BEFORE WINTER	son of Binnie and Sky
Campion, Suze	THE DAWNING OF THE DAY	Mrs. Asanath
	HOW WIDE THE HEART	
Campion, Terance	THE DAWNING OF THE DAY	Sky's first cousin
	THE SEASONS HEREAFTER	nephew of Foss
	STRAWBERRIES IN THE SEA	
	AN ANSWER IN THE TIDE	
	THE SUMMER OF THE OSPREY	
	THE DAY BEFORE WINTER	
Carradine, Claire	THERE MAY BE HEAVEN	Mag's grandniece
Carradine, Nancy	THERE MAY BE HEAVEN	Claire's daughter
Carter, Mavis	A DANCER IN YELLOW	Dorri's friend
Chapman, Ella	NO EVIL ANGEL	Fordyce's hired girl
Chase, Miriam	ROWAN HEAD	Felice Cameron's companion
Chisholm, Ewen	THE SILENT ONES	writer (as Finlay Gordon)
Christie, Martin	MASQUERADE AT SEA HOUSE	15 years old

Christie, Monica	MASQUERADE AT SEA HOUSE	7 years old
Clement, Rodina	THE ROAD TO NOWHERE	servant
Clements, Lucy	JENNIE GLENROY	Jennie's first American friend
Clements, Phyllis	BEAUTIFUL GIRL	classmate from Ohio
Conrad, Don	BECKY'S ISLAND	father
Conrad, Georgie	BECKY'S ISLAND	age 17, debutante
Conrad, Laurence	BECKY'S ISLAND	13 years old
Conrad, Maude	BECKY'S ISLAND	10 years old
Conrad, Pip	BECKY'S ISLAND	youngest
Conrad, Sam	BECKY'S ISLAND	Vicky's uncle
Conrad, Vicky (Victoria)	BECKY'S ISLAND	first cousin to Georgia and Laurence
Converse, Ned	WHISTLE FOR A WIND	recluse
Coombs, Jim	HIGH TIDE AT NOON	Margaret's husband
Coombs, Margaret Douglass	HIGH TIDE AT NOON	Alec's sister
Craine, Steven	THE DREAMING SWIMMER	painter, knew Cory
Crowell, Phyllis	STRAWBERRIES IN THE SEA	Mrs. Adam C.; Con's lady
Cruikshank, Clement, Jr.	WHEN THE MUSIC STOPPED	lawyer
Cruikshank, Clement, Sr.	WHEN THE MUSIC STOPPED	lawyer
Curtis, Betsy	THERE MAY BE HEAVEN	Nancy's friend
Curtis, Bonny	THERE MAY BE HEAVEN	Nancy's friend
Curtis, Josie	THERE MAY BE HEAVEN	Mrs. Larry
Curtis, Larry	THERE MAY BE HEAVEN	Finn's friend
Curtis, Marnie	THE FABULOUS YEAR	runs Capurnia's

D

Dallas, Jock	JENNIE ABOUT TO BE	outlaw family
Dallas, Kristy	JENNIE ABOUT TO BE	Mrs. Jock
Danton, Leslie	THE FACE OF INNOCENCE	artist
Deming, Alice	WEEP AND KNOW WHY / THE DREAMING SWIMMER	mother of Bett and Ronnie
Deming, Bett	WEEP AND KNOW WHY	15-year-old friend
Deming, Ronnie	WEEP AND KNOW WHY / THE DREAMING SWIMMER	17-year-old friend
Deverell, Caroline	THE ROAD TO NOWHERE	Mrs. Scott, Jean's mother
Deverell, Francesca	THE ROAD TO NOWHERE	Jean's cousin
Deverell, Jean (Roz)	THE ROAD TO NOWHERE	Deverell's daughter
Deverell, Piers	THE ROAD TO NOWHERE	Francesca's brother
Deverell, Scott	THE ROAD TO NOWHERE	Jean's father
Dinsmore, Diane	THE SEASONS HEREAFTER / ANSWER IN THE TIDE / THE SUMMER OF THE OSPREY	daughter of Rob and Maggie
Dinsmore, Maggie	THE SEASONS HEREAFTER / STRAWBERRIES IN THE SEA	Mrs. Rob

(Dinsmore, Maggie, cont.)	AN ANSWER IN THE TIDE	
	THE SUMMER OF THE OSPREY	
	THE DAY BEFORE WINTER	
Dinsmore, Rob	THE SEASONS HEREAFTER	islander
	STRAWBERRIES IN THE SEA	
	AN ANSWER IN THE TIDE	
	THE SUMMER OF THE OSPREY	
	THE DAY BEFORE WINTER	
Dinsmore, Tammie	THE SEASONS HEREAFTER	daughter of Rob and Maggie
	STRAWBERRIES IN THE SEA	
	THE DAY BEFORE WINTER	eighth grade
Dodge, Harriet	THE WITCH DOOR	Mrs. Markie
Dodge, Markie	THE WITCH DOOR	sold home to Megan
Douglass, Alec	HIGH TIDE AT NOON	marries Joanna Bennett
	HOW WIDE THE HEART	Ellen's dead father
Douglass, Ellen	HIGH TIDE AT NOON	daughter of Alec and Joanna
	STORM TIDE	
	THE EBBING TIDE	12 years old
	THE SEASONS HEREAFTER	
	STRAWBERRIES IN THE SEA	
	THE SUMMER OF THE OSPREY	married Robert
	HOW WIDE THE HEART	
Douglass, Joanna	HIGH TIDE AT NOON	Mrs. Alec
Drake, Felix	THE SUMMER OF THE OSPREY	rich newcomer
Drummond, Andrew	IMAGE OF A LOVER	Miranda's cousin
Drummond, Ian	IMAGE OF A LOVER	Miranda's cousin
Drummond, Patrick	IMAGE OF A LOVER	Miranda's cousin
Dunnett, Paulie	THE DAY BEFORE WINTER	Jo's childhood friend
Dunton, Ed	WHERE THE LOST APRILS ARE	Barstow's driver
Dunton, Mrs.	BECKY'S ISLAND	housekeeper
Dyer, Jeff	WATERS ON A STARRY NIGHT	Lettie's father
Dyer, Joab	BECKY'S ISLAND	set children ashore
Dyer, Lettie	WATERS ON A STARRY NIGHT	daughter of Jeff and Rita
Dyer, Rita	WATERS ON A STARRY NIGHT	Mrs. Jeff

E

Eastman, Harve	THERE MAY BE HEAVEN	hires herring seiners
Elliot, Tony	A THEME FOR REASON	artist friend from Illinois
Eloise	BLUEBERRY SUMMER	Adam's cousin
	THE FABULOUS YEAR	
Emerson, David	THE FACE OF INNOCENCE	Susan's former boyfriend
Erskine, Meg	WHISTLE FOR A WIND	Mrs. Dougal
Erskine, Old Dougal	WHISTLE FOR A WIND	Scotsman
Esmond, Emma	WHEN THE MUSIC STOPPED	violinist
Esmond, Mary Ann	WHEN THE MUSIC STOPPED	(see Rigby, Marianne)

F

Fordyce, Viola	NO EVIL ANGEL	Mrs. John
Forrester, Roger	AN ANSWER IN THE TIDE	Linnie's interest
Foss, Milford	WATERS ON A STARRY NIGHT	Dina's friend
Foster, Leah	HIGH TIDE AT NOON	Mrs. Ned
Foster, Ned	HIGH TIDE AT NOON	newcomers
Fowler, Lewis	THE YOUNG ISLANDERS	grandson of Mary and Randolph
Fowler, Randolph	STORM TIDE	owns Brigport store/post office
Fowler, Randy	STORM TIDE AN ANSWER IN THE TIDE	Brigport lobsterman
Fowler, Winslow	STORM TIDE	Brigport lobsterman
Fraser, Rory	THE FABULOUS YEAR	diversion for Cass
Freddy	AN ANSWER IN THE TIDE	Phoebe's husband
French, Mr.	THE ROAD TO NOWHERE	schoolteacher
Frye, Septimus	JENNIE GLENROY	notary, J.P., insurance agent

G

Gage	HOW WIDE THE HEART	young Donna's husband
Galbraith, Fritz	HOW WIDE THE HEART	from Stonehaven
Gardner, Kip	THERE MAY BE HEAVEN	Paul's son
Gardner, Paul	THERE MAY BE HEAVEN	tries to purchase Mag's land
Garland, Dr. Dennis	THE EBBING TIDE	bought Aunt Mary's place
Geoffrey, Lady	JENNIE ABOUT TO BE	Nigel's mother
Gerrish, May	THE DAWNING OF THE DAY	former teacher
Gerrish, Willy	THE SUMMER OF THE OSPREY THE DAY BEFORE WINTER	Drake's friend Owen's helper
Gibson, Annie Laurie	THE EBBING TIDE THE SEASONS HEREAFTER	teacher from Aroostook Cty. married Owen
Gibson, Rich	WHISTLE FOR A WIND	fish buyer
Gilchrist, Alexander (Sandy)	WHERE THE LOST APRILS ARE	Rory's good friend
Gilchrist, Alick	JENNIE ABOUT TO BE	Nigel's cousin (see Glenroy, Alick)
Gilchrist, Archie	JENNIE ABOUT TO BE	Nigel's half-brother
Gilchrist, Christabel	JENNIE ABOUT TO BE	Mrs. Archie
Gilchrist, Nigel	JENNIE ABOUT TO BE	officer, Jennie marries
Gina (Willy's wife)	THE SEASONS HEREAFTER	distraught neighbor
Glenroy, Alexander (Sandy)	JENNIE GLENROY	Carolus's twin brother
Glenroy, Alick	(all 3 Jennie books)	aka Alick Gilchrist
Glenroy, Andrew	JENNIE ABOUT TO BE	bought their way to America
Glenroy, Bell Ann	JENNIE GLENROY	7-year-old daughter
Glenroy, Carolus	JENNIE GLENROY	15-year-old twin
Glenroy, Elspeth	JENNIE ABOUT TO BE	Mrs. Andrew

H

(Hall, Link, cont.)	AN ANSWER IN THE TIDE	
	HOW WIDE THE HEART	
Hallam, Jess	NO EVIL ANGEL	Marty's sister
Hallam, Marty	NO EVIL ANGEL	fisherman
Hallam, Rory	NO EVIL ANGEL	Jess's son
Hallowell, Jonas	A THEME FOR REASON	rented home camp
Hardy, Albion	THE WORLD OF JENNIE G.	deputy director of customs
Hardy, Julian	WHEN THE MUSIC STOPPED	Fee's lover
Harmon, Cluny	THE DAY BEFORE WINTER	daughter of Myles and Nan
Harmon, Myles	THE DAY BEFORE WINTER	newcomers
Harmon, Nan	THE DAY BEFORE WINTER	Mrs. Myles
Harmon, Shannon (Shannie)	THE DAY BEFORE WINTER	son of Myles and Nan
Harmon, Tracy Lynn	THE DAY BEFORE WINTER	daughter of Myles and Nan
Harper, Bruce	CALL HOME THE HEART	island couple
Harper, Josie	CALL HOME THE HEART	Mrs. Bruce
Harpies, The	WHEN THE MUSIC STOPPED	(C. Fitton, D. Sayers, and S. Barron)
Hawley, Tib	THE FABULOUS YEAR	outspoken classmate
Hawthorne, Carolus	JENNIE ABOUT TO BE	Jennie's father
Hawthorne, Eugenia (Jennie)	JENNIE ABOUT TO BE	orphaned at 21
Hawthorne, Ianthe	JENNIE ABOUT TO BE	Jennie's sister
Hawthorne, Isabel	JENNIE ABOUT TO BE	Mrs. Carolus, Jennie's mother
Hawthorne, Sophie	JENNIE ABOUT TO BE	Jennie's 15-year-old sister
Hawthorne, Sylvia	JENNIE ABOUT TO BE	Jennie's sister
Hendries, Richard	THE WITCH DOOR	family friend
Heriot, Fiona (Fee)	WHEN THE MUSIC STOPPED	Glen's twin sister
Heriot, Glenroy (Glen)	WHEN THE MUSIC STOPPED	Eden's good friend
Higham, Aunt	JENNIE ABOUT TO BE	Jennie's aunt
Higham, Uncle	JENNIE ABOUT TO BE	Jennie's uncle
Holgerson, Bodine (Dina)	WATERS ON A STARRY NIGHT	Thora's mother
Holgerson, Thor	WATERS ON A STARRY NIGHT	Thora's father
Hopkins, Alec	TURN AROUND TWICE	founder of Hopkins Island
Hopkins, Hugh	TURN AROUND TWICE	Alec's grandson
Horne, Alexia (Alix)	A THEME FOR REASON	children's portraitist

I

Innes, Iain	JENNIE ABOUT TO BE	Scottish servant
Irene (Renie)	CALL HOME THE HEART	Ruel's woman

J

Jarrett, Earl	WHEN THE MUSIC STOPPED	Guy's father-in-law
Jarrett, Kitty	WHEN THE MUSIC STOPPED	married Guy Rigby, Sr.
Jason	BELLWOOD	Morgan's manservant

Jason, Becky	WEEP AND KNOW WHY	daughter
Jason, Ede	WEEP AND KNOW WHY	mother of boys
Jason, Hubie	WEEP AND KNOW WHY	Ede's son
Jason, Ikey (Isaac)	WEEP AND KNOW WHY	Ede's son
Jason, Ruel	WEEP AND KNOW WHY	Ede's son
	THE DREAMING SWIMMER	clammer
Jason, Simmy	WEEP AND KNOW WHY	Ede's son
	THE DREAMING SWIMMER	Ruel's brother
Jenkins, Bronwen	AN ANSWER IN THE TIDE	new lobster buyer
Jess, Aunt	WEEP AND KNOW WHY	Mirabell's aunt
	THE DREAMING SWIMMER	
John	BLUEBERRY SUMMER	Sheila's husband
	THE FABULOUS YEAR	
Johnson, Cindy	THERE MAY BE HEAVEN	Nell's daughter
Johnson, Elmer	THERE MAY BE HEAVEN	Finn's fisherman friend
Johnson, Marshall	THERE MAY BE HEAVEN	Nell's son
Johnson, Nell	THERE MAY BE HEAVEN	mother of two boys
Johnson, Timmy	THERE MAY BE HEAVEN	Nell's young son
Jones, Emlyn	THE DAY BEFORE WINTER	Owen's new sternman
Jones, Tracy	THE FACE OF INNOCENCE	Amy's classmate
Judson, Cleon	THERE MAY BE HEAVEN	childless
Judson, Danny	THERE MAY BE HEAVEN	son of Roy and Helen
Judson, Dolly	THERE MAY BE HEAVEN	widow of Jud
Judson, Finn	THERE MAY BE HEAVEN	youngest and single
Judson, Helen	THERE MAY BE HEAVEN	Mrs. Roy
Judson, Hester	THERE MAY BE HEAVEN	Mrs. Rafe
Judson, Onni	THERE MAY BE HEAVEN	Mrs. Cleon
Judson, Jud	THERE MAY BE HEAVEN	killed in war
Judson, Rafe	THERE MAY BE HEAVEN	childless
Judson, Roy	THERE MAY BE HEAVEN	oldest son
Jury, Marshall	THE FACE OF INNOCENCE	art museum director

K

Kalloch, Dill	IMAGE OF A LOVER	Ethan's cousin
Kalloch, Ethan	IMAGE OF A LOVER	fisherman
Kemper, Max	THE DREAMING SWIMMER	writer, painter
Kemper, Priscilla	THE DREAMING SWIMMER	Max's sister
Kendrum, Angus	THE DEVIL IN TARTAN	produces documentaries
Kendrum, Calum	THE DEVIL IN TARTAN	twin of Ross (16)
Kendrum, Hector	THE DEVIL IN TARTAN	owner of Bain Place
Kendrum, Jamesy	THE DEVIL IN TARTAN	son of Len and Stuart
Kendrum, Janet	THE DEVIL IN TARTAN	Mrs. Archie
Kendrum, Len	THE DEVIL IN TARTAN	Mrs. Stuart
Kendrum, Munro	THE DEVIL IN TARTAN	in Sidney
Kendrum, Priscilla	THE DEVIL IN TARTAN	widow of Alec

Kendrum, Robert Bruce (Robbie)	THE DEVIL IN TARTAN	Virginia's son (14)
Kendrum, Ross	THE DEVIL IN TARTAN	twin of Calum (16)
Kendrum, Rowan	THE DEVIL IN TARTAN	Priscilla's daughter
Kendrum, Stuart	THE DEVIL IN TARTAN	Len's husband
Kendrum, Virginia	THE DEVIL IN TARTAN	widow of Robert Sr.

L

Laroque	NO EVIL ANGEL	the woods boss
Larry	HIGH TIDE AT NOON	returned Joanna to island
Larssen	NO EVIL ANGEL	woodcutter
Larsson, Eric	THE PIGEON PAIR	Larsson's son
Larsson, Mr. and Mrs.	THE PIGEON PAIR	woodcutter and wife
Larsson, Nils	THE PIGEON PAIR	Larsson's son
Larsson, Rolf	THE PIGEON PAIR	Larsson's son
Larsson, Signe	THE PIGEON PAIR	Larsson's daughter
Learoyd, Quint	STRAWBERRIES IN THE SEA	washed ashore
Levenson, Mark	ROWAN HEAD	artist, David's friend
Leverett, Mark	BECKY'S ISLAND	Georgie's crush
Levine, Aaron	NO EVIL ANGEL	inter-island peddler
Linden, Amy	THE FACE OF INNOCENCE	15 years old
Linden, Barry	THE FACE OF INNOCENCE	12 years old
Linden, Richard	THE FACE OF INNOCENCE	Susan's husband
Linden, Susan	THE FACE OF INNOCENCE	Mrs. Richard, formerly Leslie Danton
Loomis, Trudy	HIGH TIDE AT NOON	running after Owen

M

MacArthur, Mr.	THE WORLD OF JENNIE G.	settlers' leader
Macaulay, Charlie	THE SILENT ONES	befriends Alison
MacDonald, Hank	WATERS ON A STARRY NIGHT	lobster buyer
MacIvor, Mrs.	JENNIE ABOUT TO BE	cook
MacKenzie, Anna Kate	THE WORLD OF JENNIE G. JENNIE GLENROY	Mrs. Hector
MacKenzie, Anthony (Tony)	THE WORLD OF JENNIE G.	son of Colin and Lydia
MacKenzie, Bruce	THE YOUNG ISLANDERS AN ANSWER IN THE TIDE THE SUMMER OF THE OSPREY	Emmie's eldest son
MacKenzie, Calum	THE WORLD OF JENNIE G.	swept overboard
MacKenzie, Colin	THE WORLD OF JENNIE G.	employer of Jennie and Alick
MacKenzie, Dougal	THE WORLD OF JENNIE G.	eldest settler
MacKenzie, Emmie	THE YOUNG ISLANDERS	Mrs. Niall
MacKenzie, Fiona (Fee)	TOO YOUNG TO KNOW	neighbor, friend

MacKenzie, Frances (Frank)	THE WORLD OF JENNIE G.	age 7, Jennie's student
MacKenzie, Hannah	THE SUMMER OF THE OSPREY	Mrs. Bruce
MacKenzie, Hector	THE WORLD OF JENNIE G.	married to Anna Kate
MacKenzie, Jeannie	THE YOUNG ISLANDERS	Robbie's twin
MacKenzie, Laddie	THE YOUNG ISLANDERS AN ANSWER IN THE TIDE	Emmie's 6-year-old son
MacKenzie, Lydia	THE WORLD OF JENNIE G.	Mrs. Colin
MacKenzie, Mairi	THE WORLD OF JENNIE G.	widow of Calum
MacKenzie, Niall	THE YOUNG ISLANDERS	in prison
MacKenzie, Paulina Revere	THE WORLD OF JENNIE G.	born on board ship
MacKenzie, Robbie	WHEN THE MUSIC STOPPED THE YOUNG ISLANDERS	determined pianist Jeannie's twin
MacKenzie, Rory	JENNIE GLENROY	piper
MacKenzie, Susanna (Sukey)	THE WORLD OF JENNIE G.	age 9, Jennie's student
MacKenzie, Tormod	THE WORLD OF JENNIE G.	works at shipyard
MacLeod, Donald	THE SILENT ONES	befriends Alison
MacLeod, Hugh	CALL HOME THE HEART	son-in-law of Leslie and Giles
MacLeod, Jean	CALL HOME THE HEART	Mrs. Hugh
MacLeod, Martin	WATERS ON A STARRY NIGHT	Thora's grandfather
MacNichol, Nancy	JENNIE ABOUT TO BE	Mrs. Niall
MacNichol, Niall	JENNIE ABOUT TO BE	owned Ft. William rooming house
Mannering, Bunny	A THEME FOR REASON	Shane's daughter
Mannering, Cathleen	A THEME FOR REASON	Shane's wife
Mannering, Shane	A THEME FOR REASON	love of Alix's life
Manning, Laura	A DANCER IN YELLOW	Roxie's mother
Manning, Roxie	A DANCER IN YELLOW	Dorri's classmate
Marchant, Victoria (Vic)	STRAWBERRIES IN THE SEA	Holly's friend
Markham, Emmie	THE YOUNG ISLANDERS	married Niall MacKenzie
Marriot, Capt.	WHISTLE FOR A WIND	in War of 1812
Marriot, Pleasance	WHISTLE FOR A WIND	Captain's wife
Marshall, Eric	THE DAWING OF THE DAY THE SUMMER OF THE OSPREY HOW WIDE THE HEART THE YOUNG ISLANDERS	Philippa's son now the Rev. E. J. Jamie's 12-year-old cousin Jamie's 13-year-old cousin
Marshall, Jeff	BLUEBERRY SUMMER THE FABULOUS YEAR	rents Bradford place
Marshall, Philippa	THE DAWNING OF THE DAY THE SUMMER OF THE OSPREY THE DAY BEFORE WINTER	new teacher from Boston marries Stevie Bennett
Marshall, Toby	BLUEBERRY SUMMER THE FABULOUS YEAR	rents Bradford place

Matthews, May	ROWAN HEAD	housekeeper
Mayfield, Chet	THE WORLD OF JENNIE G.	crew of *Paul Revere*
	JENNIE GLENROY	
Mayfield, Elder	THE WORLD OF JENNIE G.	pastor
Mayo, Albee	NO EVIL ANGEL	hired man
Mayo, Ida	NO EVIL ANGEL	Mrs. Albee
Meads, Jeffery	THE FABULOUS YEAR	Alicia's father
Merrill, Bella	STORM TIDE	Mrs. George
Merrill, Forest	HIGH TIDE AT NOON	Thordis's husband
Merrill, George	STORM TIDE	Capt. Merrill's cousin
Merrill, Tim	AN ANSWER IN THE TIDE	owns lobster car
Merrill, Toby	STORM TIDE	from Brigport
Micah	THE SUMMER OF THE OSPREY	Selina's baby
Michaels, Soren	A THEME FOR REASON	Danish artist
Monica	BLUEBERRY SUMMER	music teacher
	THE FABULOUS YEAR	
	BECKY'S ISLAND	
Moore, Cora	MY SUMMER LOVE	Diana's mother
Moore, Diana	MY SUMMER LOVE	problem student
Moore, Faye	WHERE THE LOST APRILS ARE	Barstow's hired help
Moore, Nanty	NO EVIL ANGEL	Mrs. Timmy
Moore, Timmy	NO EVIL ANGEL	fisherman
Morag	JENNIE ABOUT TO BE	Scottish servant
Moreton, Juliet (Jule)	THE ROAD TO NOWHERE	Scott Deverell's daughter
Moreton, Beatrice (Mummie)	THE ROAD TO NOWHERE	twins' stepmother
Morey, Ralph	COME ABOARD AND BRING YOUR DORY!	Genie's friend
Morgan, Kenneth	TOO YOUNG TO KNOW	Mary Kate's father
Morgan, Lucy	TOO YOUNG TO KNOW	Mrs. Mark
Morgan, Mark	TOO YOUNG TO KNOW	married to Lucy
Morgan, Mary Kate	TOO YOUNG TO KNOW	Kenneth's "little girl"
Morgan, Sheila	TOO YOUNG TO KNOW	editorial job in NY city
Morgan, Rees	BELLWOOD	Tim's father
Morgan, Tim	BELLWOOD	Caroline's charge
Morley, Jake	WHEN THE MUSIC STOPPED	plumber
Morley, Jane	WHEN THE MUSIC STOPPED	daughter of Edith and Jake
Morse, Greta	THE FABULOUS YEAR	classmate
Mr. Johnny	NO EVIL ANGEL	head of family
Muir, Miranda	IMAGE OF A LOVER	raised by uncle
Munroe, Robin Angus (Rob)	TOO YOUNG TO KNOW	orphan, Mary Kate's interest
Murray, Hattie Salisbury	THERE MAY BE HEAVEN	Mag Abbot's sister

N

Naomi, Aunt	MASQUERADE AT SEA HOUSE	guardian
Neville, Dr. Carlotta	JENNIE GLENROY	doctor from Connecticut
Neville Jr., Ira (Sonny)	WHEN THE MUSIC STOPPED	Janine's boyfriend
Nickerson, Aunt Alice	THE PIGEON PAIR	Kitty's sister
Northrup, Clyde	BLUEBERRY SUMMER	Jay's father
	THE FABULOUS YEAR	
Northrup, Jay	BLUEBERRY SUMMER	Peter's friend
	THE FABULOUS YEAR	

O

O'Dowda, Mr.	THE WORLD OF JENNIE G.	Irishman, started school
Orissa (Rissie)	CALL HOME THE HEART	Hugh's aunt

P

Paige, Noel	THE DEVIL IN TARTAN	fourth-grade teacher
Paisley, Eloise	AN ANSWER IN THE TIDE	wed Darrell Robey
Parmenter, Eunice	WHERE THE LOST APRILS ARE	Kitty's choice for Rory
Pearse, Enos	THE YOUNG ISLANDERS	from Brigport
Pease, Erline	IMAGE OF A LOVER	servant
Pease, Faustina	IMAGE OF A LOVER	islander
Pepperell, Luke	BECKY'S ISLAND	senator's son, helped teach
Percy, Clare	THE DAWNING OF THE DAY	daughter of Ella and Randall
Percy, Ella	THE DAWNING OF THE DAY	Mrs. Randall
Percy, Fort	THE DAWNING OF THE DAY	son of Ella and Randall
	AN ANSWER IN THE TIDE	
Percy, Frances	THE DAWNING OF THE DAY	daughter of Ella and Randall
Percy, Marjorie	STRAWBERRIES IN THE SEA	Mrs. Ralph
	AN ANSWER IN THE TIDE	
	THE SUMMER OF THE OSPREY	
	THE DAY BEFORE WINTER	
	CEILING OF AMBER	
Percy, Ralph	STRAWBERRIES IN THE SEA	islander
	THE DAWNING OF THE DAY	seventh grader
	AN ANSWER IN THE TIDE	
	THE SUMMER OF THE OSPREY	
	THE DAY BEFORE WINTER	
	CEILING OF AMBER	
Percy, Randall	THE DAWNING OF THE DAY	islander
Perrin, Joan	NO EVIL ANGEL	Mrs. Perrin's daughter
Perrin, Mrs.	NO EVIL ANGEL	schoolmistress
Perth, Vivian	WATERS ON A STARRY NIGHT	Lyle's lady from away
Peter Rabbits, The	WEEP AND KNOW WHY	Otto and Daphne Bains

Phillips, Capt.	BLUEBERRY SUMMER	Cass's father
	THE FABULOUS YEAR	
Phillips, Cass (Catherine)	BLUEBERRY SUMMER	16 years old
	THE FABULOUS YEAR	
Phillips, Mrs.	BLUEBERRY SUMMER	Cass's mother
	THE FABULOUS YEAR	
Phillips, Peter	BLUEBERRY SUMMER	Cass's 8-year-old brother
	THE FABULOUS YEAR	
Phoebe (Mrs. Freddy)	AN ANSWER IN THE TIDE	daughter of Dave and Alice
Pierce, Jonas	STORM TIDE	Pierce boys' father
Pierce, Leona	STRAWBERRIES IN THE SEA	Rosa's friend
Pierce, Raymie	STRAWBERRIES IN THE SEA	Leona's eldest son
Pierce, Theron	STORM TIDE	Jonas's brother
Pinkham, Darius	NO EVIL ANGEL	Enos's son
Pinkham, Enos	NO EVIL ANGEL	fisherman
Pinkham, Sukey	NO EVIL ANGEL	Enos's daughter
Polly, Madame President	THE DREAMING SWIMMER	pres. of historical society
Price, Astrid	A DANCER IN YELLOW	Mrs. Graham
Price, Cam	A DANCER IN YELLOW	Gray's brother
Price, Christian	A DANCER IN YELLOW	Astrid and Gray's son
Price, Fletcher (Fletch)	A DANCER IN YELLOW	Gray's brother
Price, Graham (Gray)	A DANCER IN YELLOW	married to Astrid
Price, Harriet	A DANCER IN YELLOW	Mrs. Cam, Carrie Sears's cousin
Price, Hughie	A DANCER IN YELLOW	son of Fletch and Nora
Price, Peter Graham	A DANCER IN YELLOW	son of Astrid and Gray
Price, Nora	A DANCER IN YELLOW	Mrs. Fletcher
Pulsifer, Joseph	THE WORLD OF JENNIE G.	Zeb's father
Pulsifer, Zeb	THE WORLD OF JENNIE G.	"trouble"

R

Raeburn, Alix	A FORGOTTEN GIRL	17 years old
Raeburn, Myra	A FORGOTTEN GIRL	Mrs. Richard
Raeburn, Richard	A FORGOTTEN GIRL	father of girls
Raeburn, Val	A FORGOTTEN GIRL	15 years old
Raintree, Nick	WHEN THE MUSIC STOPPED	area's mysterious stranger
Ransom, Lucy	THE FABULOUS YEAR	classmate
Ricky	HOW WIDE THE HEART	baby son of Donna and Gage
Rideout, Paul	BELLWOOD	Caro's former fiancée
Rigby, Edith	WHEN THE MUSIC STOPPED	married Jake Moreley
Rigby, George	WHEN THE MUSIC STOPPED	married Naomi Wells
Rigby, Guy	JENNIE G. LENROY	general's clerk
Rigby, Guy, Jr.	WHEN THE MUSIC STOPPED	married to Beth
Rigby, Guy, Sr.	WHEN THE MUSIC STOPPED	married to Kitty Jarrett

Rigby, Kenneth	WHEN THE MUSIC STOPPED	Guy Jr. and Beth's son
Rigby, Marianne	WHEN THE MUSIC STOPPED	83-year-old pianist, widow of Guy Sr.
Ritchie, Ann-Marie	WATERS ON A STARRY NIGHT	12 years old
Ritchie, Bethany (Bethie)	WATERS ON A STARRY NIGHT	8 years old
Ritchie, Christine	WATERS ON A STARRY NIGHT	10 years old
Ritchie, Lyle	WATERS ON A STARRY NIGHT	father of four daughters
	THE ROAD TO NOWHERE	Saltberry Point fisherman
Ritchie, Rosalind (Nod)	WATERS ON A STARRY NIGHT	6 years old
Ritchie, Thora	WATERS ON A STARRY NIGHT	Mrs. Lyle
Robert	THE SUMMER OF THE OSPREY	Ellen's husband
Robey, Darrell	AN ANSWER IN THE TIDE	from Brigport
Robey, Earl	STORM TIDE	Tom's nephew
Robey, Eloise	AN ANSWER IN THE TIDE	married, but looking
Robey, Milt	HIGH TIDE AT NOON	from Brigport
Robey, Phillida	THE SUMMER OF THE OSPREY	from Brigport
	THE DAY BEFORE WINTER	
	HOW WIDE THE HEART	
Robey, Pooch	MASQUERADE AT SEA HOUSE	lobsterman/thief
Robey, Tom	HIGH TIDE AT NOON	Brigport lobster buyer
	STORM TIDE	
	CEILING OF AMBER	
Robey, Whit	STORM TIDE	uncle of Tom and Milt
	AN ANSWER IN THE TIDE	
Rollins, George	A DANCER IN YELLOW	constable
Ross, Adam	BLUEBERRY SUMMER	medical student
	THE FABULOUS YEAR	
Ross, Miss Daisy	THE DEVIL IN TARTAN	Rowan's aunt
Roz	THE ROAD TO NOWHERE	aka Jean Deverell
Ruskin, Myra	A THEME FOR REASON	Mrs. Pete
Ruskin, Pete	A THEME FOR REASON	artist
Ruskin, Pete Jr.	A THEME FOR REASON	son of Myra and Pete
Ryder, Paul	CEILING OF AMBER	Claire's ex-boyfriend

S

Sainsbury, Thomas	WHEN THE MUSIC STOPPED	Fee's criminal lawyer
Salminen, Kathie	THE DAWNING OF THE DAY	Helmi's niece
Salminen, Rob	THE DAWNING OF THE DAY	Helmi's nephew
Sam, Uncle	BECKY'S ISLAND	Vicky's uncle
Sanborn, Lydia	MASQUERADE AT SEA HOUSE	Mrs. Tom
Sanborn, Simon Peter	MASQUERADE AT SEA HOUSE	Tom and Lydia's son
Sanborn, Uncle Theo	MASQUERADE AT SEA HOUSE	heir to Sanborn estate
Sanderson, Cory	THE DREAMING SWIMMER	purchases Darby Place
Saunders, Beatrice	THE ROAD TO NOWHERE	Mummie
Saunders, Crispin	THE DREAMING SWIMMER	Cory's real name

Saunders, Jondy (John)	THE ROAD TO NOWHERE	Mummie's husband
Saunders, Jule	THE ROAD TO NOWHERE	Roz's twin
Sayers, Dora	WHEN THE MUSIC STOPPED	one of The Harpies
Sears, Carrie	A DANCER IN YELLOW	Mrs. Rupert, Harriet Price's cousin
Sears, Doris (Dorri)	A DANCER IN YELLOW	Prices' teenage sitter
Sears, Martin	COME ABOARD AND BRING YOUR DORY!	Shelley's father
Sears, Rupert	A DANCER IN YELLOW	Carrie's husband
Sears, Shelley	COME ABOARD AND BRING YOUR DORY!	marries Penn
Seastrom, Einar	A THEME FOR REASON	Karen's father
Seastrom, Karen	A THEME FOR REASON	Goodwins' granddaughter
Seastrom, Thelma	A THEME FOR REASON	Karen's mother
Seavey, Francis (Franny)	THE EBBING TIDE	islander with problems
Seavey, Thea	THE EBBING TIDE	Mrs. Francis
Sheila	BLUEBERRY SUMMER THE FABULOUS YEAR	Cass's older sister
Snow, Brendan	BEAUTIFUL GIRL	April's cousin
Snow, Claire	BEAUTIFUL GIRL	April's cousin
Snow, Elizabeth (Bethie)	THE PIGEON PAIR	daughter
Snow, Gregory (Greg)	THE PIGEON PAIR	son
Snow, Ingrid (Inger)	THE PIGEON PAIR	daughter
Snow, Kathleen	BEAUTIFUL GIRL	April's friend
Snow, Kitty Nickerson	THE PIGEON PAIR	mother
Snow, Montgomery (Monty)	THE PIGEON PAIR	son
Snow, Rock	THE PIGEON PAIR	son
Snow, Steve	THE PIGEON PAIR	father
Sorensen, Alice	AN ANSWER IN THE TIDE	Mrs. David
Sorensen, Anna	HIGH TIDE AT NOON	Nils's grandmother
Sorensen, David	HIGH TIDE AT NOON AN ANSWER IN THE TIDE THE SUMMER OF THE OSPREY THE DAY BEFORE WINTER	Nils's brother
Sorensen, Eric	STORM TIDE	Nils's uncle, lives in Camden
Sorensen, Gunnar	HIGH TIDE AT NOON	Nils's grandfather
Sorensen, Karl	HIGH TIDE AT NOON	Nils's father
Sorensen, Jamie	THE EBBING TIDE THE DAWNING OF THE DAY STRAWBERRIES IN THE SEA AN ANSWER IN THE TIDE THE SUMMER OF THE OSPREY THE DAY BEFORE WINTER HOW WIDE THE HEART THE YOUNG ISLANDERS	baby son of Joanna and Nils 8 years old 12 years old 13 years old

(Sorensen, Jamie, cont.)	CEILING OF AMBER	19 years old
Sorensen, Joanna	STORM TIDE	Joanna Douglass becomes
	THE EBBING TIDE	Mrs. Nils
	THE DAWNING OF THE DAY	
	THE SEASONS HEREAFTER	
	STRAWBERRIES IN THE SEA	
	AN ANSWER IN THE TIDE	
	THE SUMMER OF THE OSPREY	
	THE DAY BEFORE WINTER	
	HOW WIDE THE HEART	
	THE YOUNG ISLANDERS	
Sorensen, Karin	STORM TIDE	Mrs. Eric, Nils's aunt
Sorensen, Kristi	HIGH TIDE AT NOON	Nils's sister
Sorensen, Linnea	STORM TIDE	daughter of Joanna and Nils
	THE EBBING TIDE	
	THE DAWNING OF THE DAY	
	THE SEASONS HEREAFTER	
	STRAWBERRIES IN THE SEA	
	AN ANSWER IN THE TIDE	
	THE SUMMER OF THE OSPREY	
	THE DAY BEFORE WINTER	traveling in Sweden
	HOW WIDE THE HEART	7 years old
	CEILING OF AMBER	14 years old
	THE YOUNG ISLANDERS	8 years old
Sorensen, Nils	HIGH TIDE AT NOON	islander
	STORM TIDE	marries Joanna Bennett
	THE EBBING TIDE	age 37, returns from WWII
	THE DAWNING OF THE DAY	
	THE SEASONS HEREAFTER	
	STRAWBERRIES IN THE SEA	
	AN ANSWER IN THE TIDE	
	THE SUMMER OF THE OSPREY	
	THE DAY BEFORE WINTER	
	HOW WIDE THE HEART	
	CEILING OF AMBER	
Sorensen, Rosa	THE DAY BEFORE WINTER	Mrs. Jamie
Sorensen, Sara Joanne	THE DAY BEFORE WINTER	Jamie and Rosa's daughter
Sorensen, Sigard	THE EBBING TIDE	Nils's brother
	THE DAY BEFORE WINTER	
Sorensen, Thea	HIGH TIDE AT NOON	Nils's cousin
Sorensen, Thordis	HIGH TIDE AT NOON	Mrs. Forest Merrill
Stewart, Uncle	WEEP AND KNOW WHY	Mirabell's uncle
	THE DREAMING SWIMMER	
Swenson, Hugh	IMAGE OF A LOVER	Jennie's brother
Swenson, Jennie	IMAGE OF A LOVER	Hugh's sister

Sylvester, Bill	COME ABOARD AND BRING YOUR DORY!	uncle to Cameron children
Sylvester, Nora	COME ABOARD …	Mrs. Bill, aunt

T

Taggart, Barnaby	WEEP AND KNOW WHY	Mirabell's friend
	THE DREAMING SWIMMER	Mirabell's husband
Taggart, Lois	WEEP AND KNOW WHY	Seth's wife
	THE DREAMING SWIMMER	
Taggart, Seth	WEEP AND KNOW WHY	Barnaby's brother
	THE DREAMING SWIMMER	
Tanner, Brian	CEILING OF AMBER	15 years old
Tanner, Clarissa (Claire)	CEILING OF AMBER	19 years old
Tanner, Ed	CEILING OF AMBER	deceased father
Tanner, Margaret	CEILING OF AMBER	Mrs. Ed, mother of Claire and Brian
Teague, Allegra	CALL HOME THE HEART	Edith Whitney's sister
Teague, Hamlin (Ham)	CALL HOME THE HEART	store owner
Teague, Josh	CALL HOME THE HEART	Ham's brother
Teague, Marcia	CALL HOME THE HEART	Mrs. Roger. Allegra's sister-in-law
Teague, Roger	CALL HOME THE HEART	island man
Teague, Troy	CALL HOME THE HEART	inherited Barney Teague place
Temple, Amy	WHEN THE MUSIC STOPPED	mother of Ben and Will
Temple, Ben	WHEN THE MUSIC STOPPED	Amy's son
Temple, Will	WHEN THE MUSIC STOPPED	Amy's son
Thatcher, Henry	WATERS ON A STARRY NIGHT	shipwrecked on Jethro's
Thatcher, Roy	WHEN THE MUSIC STOPPED	Fox Point caretaker
Thorne, Cap'n Jeremy	WHISTLE FOR A WIND	Roger's brother
Thorne, Roger	WHISTLE FOR A WIND	schoolmaster
Thornton, Mac	MY SUMMER LOVE	Madge's son
Thornton, Madge	MY SUMMER LOVE	Cora's friend
Thornton, Roger	MY SUMMER LOVE	Madge's young son
Thornton, Tabby	MY SUMMER LOVE	Madge's young daugther
Todd	WEEP AND KNOW WHY	Irenie's fiance
Tolman, Dr. Rich	ROWAN HEAD	Cameron's family doctor
Tolman, Selina	ROWAN HEAD	Dr. Cameron's sister
Trudeau, Jake	HIGH TIDE AT NOON	Mateel's father
Trudeau, Mateel	HIGH TIDE AT NOON	married Charles Bennett
	HOW WIDE THE HEART	
Trudeau, Maurice	HIGH TIDE AT NOON	Mateel's brother
Trudeau, Pierre	HIGH TIDE AT NOON	Mateel's brother
Trudeau, Rose-Marie	HIGH TIDE AT NOON	Mateel's sister
Tuttle, Amy	WATERS ON A STARRY NIGHT	Mrs. Cheever

Tuttle, Cheever	WATERS ON A STARRY NIGHT	Lyle's best friend
Tuttle, Oram	WATERS ON A STARRY NIGHT	son of Amy and Cheever
Tyler, Christian	THE WORLD OF JENNIE G.	Mrs. Royall
Tyler, Royall	THE WORLD OF JENNIE G.	married Colin's daughter

U

Ursula	WEEP AND KNOW WHY	Ronnie's girlfriend

V

Villiers, Robert	HOW WIDE THE HEART	mysterious summer complaint
Vinton, George	JENNIE ABOUT TO BE	Aunt's choice for Jennie

W

Wadsworth, Sam	BLUEBERRY SUMMER THE FABULOUS YEAR	local game warden
Webster, Daniel	THE DAWNING OF THE DAY	Lucy and Jude's son
Webster, Edwin	THE DAWNING OF THE DAY STRAWBERRIES IN THE SEA THE SUMMER OF THE OSPREY	Lucy and Jude's son married, with son
Webster, Faith	THE DAWNING OF THE DAY	Lucy and Jude's daughter
Webster, Helen	BELLWOOD	Mrs. Mark
Webster, Jude	THE DAWNING OF THE DAY STRAWBERRIES IN THE SEA THE SUMMER OF THE OSPREY	reclusive island family Rosa's cousin
Webster, Lucy	THE DAWNING OF THE DAY STRAWBERRIES IN THE SEA THE SUMMER OF THE OSPREY	Mrs. Jude
Webster, Mark	BELLWOOD	Eric's friend
Webster, Rue	THE DAWNING OF THE DAY	Lucy and Jude's daughter
Weir, Irenie	WEEP AND KNOW WHY THE DREAMING SWIMMER	Mirabell's sister
Weir, Jon	WEEP AND KNOW WHY	Mirabell's brother
Weir, Linda	WEEP AND KNOW WHY	Mrs. Jon
Weir, Mirabell	WEEP AND KNOW WHY THE DREAMING SWIMMER	lost job and boyfriend
Wells, Capt.	THE WORLD OF JENNIE G.	Capt. of *Paul Revere*
Wells, Naomi	WHEN THE MUSIC STOPPED	married George Rigby
Wells, Stephen	THE WORLD OF JENNIE G. JENNIE GLENROY	first mate on *Paul Revere* Jennie's first American
Whitcomb, Cyrus	HIGH TIDE AT NOON	Alec's grandfather
Whitcomb, Martha	HIGH TIDE AT NOON	Alec's grandmother
Whitehouse, Celia	A DANCER IN YELLOW	Kevin's mother
Whitehouse, Kevin	A DANCER IN YELLOW	Dorri's 18-year-old friend

Whitney, Aaron	CALL HOME THE HEART	Giles's cousin
Whitney, Edith	CALL HOME THE HEART	Mrs. Aaron
Whitney, Giles	CALL HOME THE HEART	island family
Whitney, Felice	CALL HOME THE HEART	Mrs. Simon
Whitney, Leslie Curtis	CALL HOME THE HEART	Mrs. Giles
Whitney, Noah	CALL HOME THE HEART	son of Leslie and Giles
Whitney, Ruel	CALL HOME THE HEART	Giles's first cousin
Whitney, Simon	CALL HOME THE HEART	son of Leslie and Giles
Wilder, Burnley (Bun)	TURN AROUND TWICE	16 years old
Wilder, Jean	TURN AROUND TWICE	11 years old
Wilder, Mr. and Mrs. Mark	TURN AROUND TWICE	parents
Wilder, Ronnie	TURN AROUND TWICE	13 years old
Wilder, Stuart	TURN AROUND TWICE	15 years old
Wiley, Tommy	THE SUMMER OF THE OSPREY	Owen's helper
	AN ANSWER IN THE TIDE	
	THE DAY BEFORE WINTER	
William	JENNIE ABOUT TO BE	Jennie's brother-in-law
Williamson, Beniah (Ben)	BECKY'S ISLAND	sells seafood
Williamson, Faustina	BECKY'S ISLAND	Mrs. Beniah
Williamson, Jude	BECKY'S ISLAND	child of Faustina and Ben
Williamson, Tamar	BECKY'S ISLAND	child of Faustina and Ben
Willy	THE SEASONS HEREAFTER	Gina's husband
Willy, Garfield (Garf)	THE DREAMING SWIMMER	family founders
Willy, Raymie	THE DREAMING SWIMMER	Garf's grandson
Winstead, Nick	THE ROAD TO NOWHERE	Scott Deverell's attorney
Winter, Eden	WHEN THE MUSIC STOPPED	novelist
Winter, Stormy	WHEN THE MUSIC STOPPED	Eden's father
Winter, Vinca (Gram)	WHEN THE MUSIC STOPPED	Eden's grandmother
Wolcott, Janine	WHEN THE MUSIC STOPPED	Lucas's abused daughter
Wolcott, Lucas	WHEN THE MUSIC STOPPED	alcoholic
Wreckers, The	WHISTLE FOR A WIND	Tim and Izzy Boyd

Y

Yetton, Annie	HIGH TIDE AT NOON	daughter of Susie and Marcus
Yetton, Julian	HIGH TIDE AT NOON	son of Susie and Marcus
Yetton, Marcus	HIGH TIDE AT NOON	poor fisherman
Yetton, Susie	HIGH TIDE AT NOON	Mrs. Marcus

❧ GLOSSARIES

MAINE TERMS

a-flukin'	in a great hurry
arse in a sling	in a difficult position
aye-up	yes; variations include *eyah, ayuh*
backing and filling	going back and forth in short spurts with little accomplishment
bannock	food wasn't that good, fit for a dog
beamy	sturdy and wide
blackback	a very large gull
both oars in the water	competent mentally
bound	where you are going
buoy	wooden float marking location of lobster trap
call	reason or permission
chop	slight roughness to the water
chowderhead	a lout, but a likable one
clip 'n clean	entirely, wholly
conniptions	fits, seizures
coot	a bird given to erratic behavior
crawl under the kelp	go home and go to bed
crawling	if lobsters are crawling, it means the catch is good
cunning	cute, sweet
de-ah	dear; many men use this instead of a woman's actual name
dite	a small amount, a trifle
dreen	Maine pronunciation of drain
drier than a cork leg	thirsty
dub	tinker with
dunnage	baggage or luggage
failings	behavior
featherwhite	pale with anger or fear
finest kind	the very best
fishing shags	cormorants
fog mull	long spell of fog
funny-eye	holds open the traphead hole through which lobsters crawl
gaff	long pole with a hook on the end, used in lobstering
gaffle	to grab hold of, to nab
gorm (n.), gormy (adj.)	awkward, clumsy person
gorry	expression like "gosh," ordinarily part of a resounding cussword

gowels (v.)	bores in
hackles (v.)	angers
hails	greets
heft	lift
high fantods	noisy upset, hysterics
high-liner	one who is getting the most lobster
holding turn	substituting
hosey	to reserve
keeper	a lobster that meets the required measured size
lallygag	waste time; act indecisively
lashings	bindings used to hold pieces together; food
lobster car	float with water-filled compartments where lobsters are stored
loppy	the water is a little rougher than choppy
money cat	a calico cat whose fur shows a least three or four colors
muckled	to grab, grasp, get hold of
mug-up	a lunch or snack that includes a hot drink; from the fisherman's habit of drinking tea or coffee from a mug. Fishermen often tie their boats together to share a mug-up.
old fub	old man
parted your fasts	lost your mind
port side	the left side
pot	lobster trap
potwarp	cordage used on lobster traps
rank cards	school report cards
rote	sound of waves breaking on the shore
rugged	rough
shedder	lobster just after the biological shedding of the old shell
shorten your sails	moderate your speech, behavior, judgment; calm down
sly besom	person tainted with witchiness, a little minx
smarmy	ingratiating, flattering
some	"very"; to strengthen the intensive, add "old," as in "some old good."
spider	frying pan
spleeny	peevish, easily bothered, also hypochondriac
stavin'	remarkably well
sternman	working on a lobster boat, a lobsterman's helper
storm-stayed	saying bad weather prevented completing a journey
summer complaint	summer visitors, tourists; also an intestinal upset
three sheets to the wind	drunk
touse	a row, a rumpus, rather noisy but not necessarily fatal
traphead	twine net filling each end of lobster trap
tunk	a solid tap or hit
turn in	go to bed
warp	rope leading from buoy to trap
williwaws	nervousness

winged out	carrying sail and making a beautiful picture
wivvey	wavering, uncertain of balance
yarn (v.)	tell stories, talk

GAELIC TERMS

beannachid leat, mo coraid	blessings on you, my friend
cock-a-leekie	Scottish soup with lots of onions, leeks, chicken, and rice
croft	farm
Feros ferio	I am fierce with the fierce—clan motto
Fir Bhreige, the	the False Man
grianaig	at the sunny knoll
iolaire	eagle
kerfuffle	a touse (rumpus) of some kind
laird	landlord
mah'a seo!	let's go!
Mairi Ceit	Mary Kate
Meall na Gobhar Mor	the Hill of the Great Goat
Mile Dorcha	Dark Mile
mo graidh	my beloved
mohaggled	worn to a frazzle by harassment
sgian dubh	small knife traditionally carried in the Highlander's sock
'shean trubhais	ragged trousers
strupach	mug-up
tha gradh agam ort-sa	I love thee
plaid, the	tartan; serves as a blanket, cloak, tent, or to do up your possessions in
Torsaig	Thor's Bay, the land of the forever young
uisge-baugh	whiskey
uisge-iolaire	water eagle

❧ LOCATIONS IN OGILVIE NOVELS

Alec's Cove	CALL HOME THE HEART
Allan Swan and Son Store	THE DEVIL IN TARTAN
Algnish	THE SILENT ONES
Amity Bay	THE WITCH DOOR
Amity Point	A DANCER IN YELLOW
Andrews Cove	IMAGE OF A LOVER
Applecross Center	THE DREAMING SWIMMER
Applecross Harbor	WEEP AND KNOW WHY
Appleton Ridge	THERE MAY BE HEAVEN
Ardgour Hills	JENNIE ABOUT TO BE
Arey House	THE EBBING TIDE
Armadale	THE SILENT ONES
Augusta	WHERE THE LOST APRILS ARE
	THE ROAD TO NOWHERE
	THE PIGEON PAIR
	MASQUERADE AT SEA HOUSE
	THERE MAY BE HEAVEN
Back Cove	STRAWBERRIES IN THE SEA
Bain Place	THE DEVIL IN TARTAN
Ballard's Island	THERE MAY BE HEAVEN
Banff	JENNIE ABOUT TO BE
Bangor	THE ROAD TO NOWHERE
Bannock Island	IMAGE OF A LOVER
	BELLWOOD
Barlow Mills	WHEN THE MUSIC STOPPED
Barney Teague Place	CALL HOME THE HEART
Barstow and Cady Lobster Company	COME ABOARD AND BRING YOUR DORY!
Barque Cove	THE EBBING TIDE
	THE SEASONS HEREAFTER
	STRAWBERRIES IN THE SEA
	THE SUMMER OF THE OSPREY
Bath	TURN AROUND TWICE
Beacon Heights	THE FACE OF INNOCENCE
Becky's Island	BECKY'S ISLAND
Belfast	A DANCER IN YELLOW
	STRAWBERRIES IN THE SEA

Camden Hills	STORM TIDE
	WHISTLE FOR A WIND
Cameron Cove	COME ABOARD AND BRING YOUR DORY!
Cameron Yard	WHISTLE FOR A WIND
	ROWAN HEAD
Cape Silver	WEEP AND KNOW WHY
Casco Bay	IMAGE OF A LOVER
Castine	HOW WIDE THE HEART
Chip Cove	STORM TIDE
	CEILING OF AMBER
Clean Sweep	THE ROAD TO NOWHERE
Cliff Island	CALL HOME THE HEART
Clubhouse	HIGH TIDE AT NOON
	AN ANSWER IN THE TIDE
	THE DAY BEFORE WINTER
Coates Cove	THE SUMMER OF THE OSPREY
Crandall Island	WATERS ON A STARRY NIGHT
Cree Ridge	AN ANSWER IN THE TIDE
Crit's Cove	THE WORLD OF JENNIE G.
Crow's Nest	COME ABOARD AND BRING YOUR DORY!
	THE SEASONS HEREAFTER
	CEILING OF AMBER
Damariscotta	TURN AROUND TWICE
	A THEME FOR REASON
Dan Whitney Place	CALL HOME THE HEART
Darby Homestead	THE DREAMING SWIMMER
Dartmouth	THE DEVIL IN TARTAN
David's, The	WHEN THE MUSIC STOPPED
Deadman's Bluff	THE YOUNG ISLANDERS
D. E. Drummond and Sons Store	IMAGE OF A LOVER
Deep Cove and Deep Wood	WEEP AND KNOW WHY
Devil's Den	STRAWBERRIES IN THE SEA
	WEEP AND KNOW WHY
Drummond's Island	IMAGE OF A LOVER
Dunbar's Island	BEAUTIFUL GIRL
Dunvegan Lodge	THE FABULOUS YEAR
Eastern End	THE YOUNG ISLANDERS
	HIGH TIDE AT NOON
	THE DAWNING OF THE DAY
	THE SEASONS HEREAFTER
	STRAWBERRIES IN THE SEA
	AN ANSWER IN THE TIDE

Gib's Cove	A THEME FOR REASON
Glenroy Boatyard	WHEN THE MUSIC STOPPED
	JENNIE GLENROY
Goose Cove	(All 9 Bennett's Island Books)
	CEILING OF AMBER
	HOW WIDE THE HEART
Goose Cove Ledge	STORM TIDE
Grange Hall	ROWAN HEAD
Grant's Point	THE EBBING TIDE
Grayrocks	BECKY'S ISLAND
Great Harry Shoal	CEILING OF AMBER
Green Ledge	STORM TIDE
Griffin's Island	A THEME FOR REASON
Gypsy Field	WEEP AND KNOW WHY
Halifax	THE DEVIL IN TARTAN
Harbor Ledge	STRAWBERRIES IN THE SEA
Harbor Point	WEEP AND KNOW WHY
Harborview Hotel	THE SEASONS HEREAFTER
Harborview Motel	BELLWOOD
Harnden College	IMAGE OF A LOVER
for Women	
Harper's Cove	A DANCER IN YELLOW
Harris, Isle of	THE DEVIL IN TARTAN
Hawthorne Farm	A SUMMER LOVE
Haypenny Island	WHEN THE MUSIC STOPPED
Head, The	HOW WIDE THE HEART
Herbert's Funeral Home	A DANCER IN YELLOW
Heriot's Island	WHEN THE MUSIC STOPPED
Heron Cliff	WEEP AND KNOW WHY
Herring Gut	IMAGE OF A LOVER
Highlands	JENNIE ABOUT TO BE
High Ledge	WHEN THE MUSIC STOPPED
Hillside Farm	THE SEASONS HEREAFTER
	STRAWBERRIES IN THE SEA
	THE SUMMER OF THE OSPREY
	THE DAY BEFORE WINTER
	CEILING OF AMBER
Hix's Hill	WATERS ON A STARRY NIGHT
Hollowell	THERE MAY BE HEAVEN
Home Cove	IMAGE OF A LOVER
Homestead Point	THE DAY BEFORE WINTER
Hopkins Island	TURN AROUND TWICE
Hospital Point	THE WORLD OF JENNIE G.
Huckleberry Cove	ROWAN HEAD
Indian Beach	WEEP AND KNOW WHY
Inverness	JENNIE ABOUT TO BE

Tiree Ledge	A THEME FOR REASON
Torsaig	THE SILENT ONES
Tremaine	THE ROAD TO NOWHERE
Tuckanuck	HIGH TIDE AT NOON
Twobush	HOW WIDE THE HEART
Two-Horse Light	WEEP AND KNOW WHY
Viking Camp	WEEP AND KNOW WHY
Vinalhaven	HOW WIDE THE HEART
	THE YOUNG ISLANDERS
Wainwright Hotel	BELLWOOD
Waldoboro Shipyard	WHISTLE FOR A WIND
Water Street	THE SEASONS HEREAFTER
Wawenock Bay	WATERS ON A STARRY NIGHT
Weir Cove	IMAGE OF A LOVER
Wells Corner Church	A DANCER IN YELLOW
Western End	HIGH TIDE AT NOON
	CEILING OF AMBER
Western Harbor Point	STRAWBERRIES IN THE SEA
	THE SUMMER OF THE OSPREY
	THE YOUNG ISLANDERS
Weymouth Cove	WATERS ON A STARRY NIGHT
Whaleback	STRAWBERRIES IN THE SEA
Whitcomb House	STORM TIDE
Whitehead	HOW WIDE THE HEART
Whittier, North, South,	THE WORLD OF JENNIE G.
and Center	WHEN THE MUSIC STOPPED
Willis Inn	A DANCER IN YELLOW
Williston	A DANCER IN YELLOW
	THE ROAD TO NOWHERE
	THE PIGEON PAIR
	THERE MAY BE HEAVEN
	WEEP AND KNOW WHY
Williston High School	A DANCER IN YELLOW
	THE ROAD TO NOWHERE
	THE PIGEON PAIR
	THERE MAY BE HEAVEN
Windward Point	THE SEASONS HEREAFTER
	STRAWBERRIES IN THE SEA
	AN ANSWER IN THE TIDE
	HOW WIDE THE HEART
	THE DAY BEFORE WINTER
Winter Head	WHEN THE MUSIC STOPPED
Wiscasset	TURN AROUND TWICE
Wood Cove	THE SEASONS HEREAFTER

❧ COMFORTS AND PASTIMES

FOOD SERVED IN OGILVIE NOVELS

Mug-ups

apple pie and coffee	(The Bennett books)
crackers and cheese and hot chocolate	THE DREAMING SWIMMER
blackberry tarts and tea	WHEN THE MUSIC STOPPED
blueberry bread	CALL HOME THE HEART
cinnamon toast and tea	WHEN THE MUSIC STOPPED
doughnuts and coffee or milk	THE DREAMING SWIMMER
	(The Bennett books)
	THE PIGEON PAIR
	THE YOUNG ISLANDERS
	BLUEBERRY SUMMER
	COME ABOARD AND BRING YOUR DORY!
Finnish coffee bread and coffee	THERE MAY BE HEAVEN
gingerbread and coffee or milk	THE DREAMING SWIMMER
	COME ABOARD AND BRING YOUR DORY!
	(The Bennett books)
	THE FACE OF INNOCENCE
	MASQUERADE AT SEA HOUSE
	THE ROAD TO NOWHERE
graham loaf and cocoa	THE DEVIL IN TARTAN
hermits and milk	WEEP AND KNOW WHY
	(The Bennett books)
lemon loaf cake and tea	WHERE THE LOST APRILS ARE
lemon meringue pie and coffee	WHERE THE LOST APRILS ARE
marmalade cookies	THE DEVIL IN TARTAN
mincemeat tarts	WHISTLE FOR A WIND
mince squares, Mrs. Cady's	TURN AROUND TWICE
molasses cookies and coffee	THE DREAMING SWIMMER
molasses cookies and lemonade	WATERS ON A STARRY NIGHT
	BLUEBERRY SUMMER
molasses cookies and tea	CALL HOME THE HEART
molasses cookies and spiced tea	NO EVIL ANGEL
	THE DEVIL IN TARTAN
peanut butter sandwiches and milk	COME ABOARD AND BRING YOUR DORY!

raisin cookies and milk	BECKY'S ISLAND
spice cake and coffee	(The Bennett books)
sultana scones (warm) and shortbread	(The Jennie books)
sugar cookies and raspberry shrub	IMAGE OF A LOVER
Swedish coffee bread	(The Bennett books)

Breakfast

bacon, eggs, and toast	THE DREAMING SWIMMER
	(The Bennett books)
	THE DEVIL IN TARTAN
bacon (home-cured) sandwich	THE DEVIL IN TARTAN
blackberry muffins	BLUEBERRY SUMMER
cinnamon rolls and coffee	WHERE THE LOST APRILS ARE
cranberry coffeecake	WEEP AND KNOW WHY
eggs, scrambled, and coffee	WHERE THE LOST APRILS ARE
French toast and Postum	WATERS ON A STARRY NIGHT
huckleberry fool	(The Jennie books)
oatcakes	THE SILENT ONES
oatmeal with raisins and brown sugar	WHEN THE MUSIC STOPPED
porridge and smoked ellwives (alewives)	NO EVIL ANGEL
porridge, Highland	(The Jennie books)
raisin muffins and coffee	(The Jennie books)

Meals

beef stew	WHERE THE LOST APRILS ARE
	THE DEVIL IN TARTAN
cheese nightmares	THE DREAMING SWIMMER
chicken pot pie	WEEP AND KNOW WHY
	THE ROAD TO NOWHERE
clam chowder	THERE MAY BE HEAVEN
	TURN AROUND TWICE
	A DANCER IN YELLOW
clam pie	THE DREAMING SWIMMER
clams, fried	THE FABULOUS YEAR
clams, steamed	TURN AROUND TWICE
corned beef and onion sandwiches	THE DREAMING SWIMMER
	WATERS ON A STARRY NIGHT
corned beef (mashed with mayonnaise and chopped pickle) sandwiches	WATERS ON A STARRY NIGHT
corn fritters	THE SEASONS HEREAFTER
egg (fried) sandwich; instant coffee	THE DREAMING SWIMMER

eggs (scrambled) with mushrooms and chives; salad of greens with vinegar-and-celery-seed dressing; wild strawberry pie	MASQUERADE AT SEA HOUSE
fish cakes	CALL HOME THE HEART
fish chowder	(The Bennett books)
	IMAGE OF A LOVER
	WHEN THE MUSIC STOPPED
	NO EVIL ANGEL
fish hash	THE DREAMING SWIMMER
	(The Bennett books)
goose (wild), roast	WHISTLE FOR A WIND
haddock (baked stuffed); fresh cukes and tomatoes; apple cobbler	IMAGE OF A LOVER
haddock chowder	(The Jennie books)
	(The Bennett books)
halibut; coconut custard pie	THE DEVIL IN TARTAN
"Island picnic lunch"	THE WITCH DOOR
"Island supper"	THE WITCH DOOR
lobster (baked stuffed)	(The Bennett books)
	COME ABOARD AND BRING YOUR DORY!
lobster chowder	(The Bennett books)
	CEILING OF AMBER
	IMAGE OF A LOVER
	MASQUERADE AT SEA HOUSE
pea soup and johnnycake	(The Bennett books)
	WHISTLE FOR A WIND
	JENNIE GLENROY
	A DANCER IN YELLOW
pollock, dried, with pork scraps, boiled potatoes, mashed squash, laced together with green tomato piccalilli	THERE MAY BE HEAVEN
salmon casserole	A DANCER IN YELLOW
seafood casserole	BELLWOOD
seafood paella	A THEME FOR REASON
spaghetti sauce	(The Bennett books)
	TOO YOUNG TO KNOW
spaghetti with clam sauce	WEEP AND KNOW WHY
squash pie	(The Bennett books)
	ROWAN HEAD
	BEAUTIFUL GIRL
steamed clams	TURN AROUND TWICE
steak kabobs; garlic bread; coconut custard pie	WEEP AND KNOW WHY
turkey sandwiches (hot); apple pie	COME ABOARD AND BRING YOUR DORY!

Desserts

apple cake	THE DREAMING SWIMMER
apple cobbler	IMAGE OF A LOVER
apple pie	COME ABOARD AND BRING YOUR DORY!
apple pudding	WHISTLE FOR A WIND
apple turnover	(The Bennett books)
applesauce cake	THERE MAY BE HEAVEN
	CEILING OF AMBER
	IMAGE OF A LOVER
blackberry fool	IMAGE OF A LOVER
blackberry tarts	(The Jennie books)
Boston cream pie	COME ABOARD AND BRING YOUR DORY!
brownies	HOW WIDE THE HEART
chocolate bread pudding with meringue topping	(The Tide Trilogy)
chocolate jumbles	BECKY'S ISLAND
chocolate layer cake	MY SUMMER LOVE
	MY WORLD IS AN ISLAND
chocolate mousse	THE ROAD TO NOWHERE
chocolate squares, frosted	TOO YOUNG TO KNOW
coconut custard pie	THE DEVIL IN TARTAN
	WEEP AND KNOW WHY
cranachan	THE WORLD OF JENNIE G.
custard pie	THE DREAMING SWIMMER
Dutch apple cake	WEEP AND KNOW WHY
eclairs	WEEP AND KNOW WHY
	(The Bennett books)
fritters, fancy, with hot cranberry sauce	WEEP AND KNOW WHY
gingerbread (warm) with applesauce	WATERS ON A STARRY NIGHT
Indian pudding	(The Bennett books)
	(The Jennie books)
	NO EVIL ANGEL
lemon sponge pudding	IMAGE OF A LOVER
mincemeat filled cookies	WATERS ON A STARRY NIGHT
mincemeat squares	(The Bennett books)
mincemeat turnovers	THE DREAMING SWIMMER
	WATERS ON A STARRY NIGHT
	THERE MAY BE HEAVEN
	CEILING OF AMBER
	WHEN THE MUSIC STOPPED
petits fours	THE FABULOUS YEAR
rhubarb pies	A DANCER IN YELLOW
Rhubarb tart with thick yellow cream	(The Jennie books)
strawberry pie (wild strawberries)	A FORGOTTEN GIRL

(strawberry pie, continued)	MASQUERADE AT SEA HOUSE
trifle	(The Jennie books)
	IMAGE OF A LOVER
upside-down cake of applesauce and peaches	CEILING OF AMBER
venison mincemeat pies	THE PIGEON PAIR

Beverages (see *also* Mug-ups)

raspberry shrub	WHISTLE FOR A WIND
	BECKY'S ISLAND
	THE WORLD OF JENNIE G.
switchel	WHISTLE FOR A WIND
	(The Bennett books)

MUSIC IN OGILVIE NOVELS

"Aura Lee"	IMAGE OF A LOVER
"Barnyards of Delgatie"	THE DREAMING SWIMMER
"Beautiful Dreamer"	IMAGE OF A LOVER
"Black Watch Leaving for Flanders, The"	(The Jennie books)
"Blue Danube Waltz"	(The Bennett books)
"Bonnie Lass of Fyvie, The"	THE DREAMING SWIMMER
"Boston Fancy"	(The Bennett books)
	THE FABULOUS YEAR
	CALL HOME THE HEART
Calum Kennedy's recordings	THE DREAMING SWIMMER
Chopin's nocturnes	THE DREAMING SWIMMER
Chopin's preludes	ROWAN HEAD
"Come, Thou Fount of Every Blessing"	(The Bennett books)
"Danny Boy"	THE ROAD TO NOWHERE
"De'il's Awa' wi' the Exciseman, The"	(The Jennie books)
"Devil's Dream, The"	IMAGE OF A LOVER
	(The Jennie books)
	(The Bennett books)
	THE DREAMING SWIMMER
"Drink to Me Only With Thine Eyes"	(The Jennie books)
"Farmer in the Dell, The"	(The Bennett books)
"Flower of Portencross, The"	(The Bennett books)
"Flowers of the Forest, The"	(The Bennett books)
"Foggy, Foggy Dew, The"	THERE MAY BE HEAVEN
"Free America"	(The Jennie books)
"Frog and the Crow, The"	A DANCER IN YELLOW

"Garryowen"	NO EVIL ANGEL
"Gin (if) I Were a Baron's Heir"	THE DREAMING SWIMMER
"Girl with the Hole in Her Stocking, The"	(The Bennett books)
"Going to Jerusalem"	(The Bennett books)
"Good Night, Ladies"	(The Bennett books)
"Green Grow the Rashes, O"	(The Jennie books)
"Home Sweet Home"	IMAGE OF A LOVER
"Hull's Victory"	(The Bennett books)
	CALL HOME THE HEART
"If You Were the Only Girl in the World"	THE ROAD TO NOWHERE
"I'll Sing Thee Songs of Araby"	NO EVIL ANGEL
"Jesu, Joy of Man's Desiring"	THE DEVIL IN TARTAN
"Jesus Loves Me"	A DANCER IN YELLOW
"Juanita"	THE FABULOUS YEAR
"Lady of the Lake"	IMAGE OF A LOVER
	(The Bennett books)
	THE FABULOUS YEAR
"Let Me Call You Sweetheart"	(The Bennett books)
"Liberty Waltz"	(The Bennett books)
"Life on the Ocean Wave, A"	(The Bennett books)
"Little Brown Jug"	WATERS ON A STARRY NIGHT
"Loch Lomond"	(The Bennett books)
"March and Circle"	(The Bennett books)
"Meeting of the Waters, The"	(The Bennett books)
"Merry Widow"	NO EVIL ANGEL
"Minstrel Boy"	IMAGE OF A LOVER
"Moon and I, The"	NO EVIL ANGEL
"My Days Have Been So Wondrous Free"	(The Jennie books)
"My Love Is but a Lassie Yet"	(The Bennett books)
"My Money Is All Spent and Gone"	(The Bennett books)
"Oak and the Ash and the Bonny Ellum Tree, The"	THE PIGEON PAIR
"Oh, Mama, How Pretty the Moon Looks Tonight"	WATERS ON A STARRY NIGHT
"Onward, Christian Soldiers"	(The Bennett books)
"Over the Waves"	(The Bennett books)
"Owl and the Pussycat, The"	NO EVIL ANGEL
"Passing By"	(The Jennie books)
"Portland Fancy"	IMAGE OF A LOVER
	(The Bennett books)
	CALL HOME THE HEART
"Put Your Little Foot Right Out"	(The Bennett books)
"Rakes of Mallow, The"	(The Bennett books)
"Red River Valley"	(The Bennett books)
"Remember Me, Love, in Your Dreams"	NO EVIL ANGEL

"Road to Dundee, The"	WATERS ON A STARRY NIGHT
"Road to the Isles, The"	(The Bennett books)
"Roses of Picardy"	ROWAN HEAD
"Shall We Gather at the River"	THERE MAY BE HEAVEN
"Soldier's Joy"	(The Bennett books)
"Song to Celia"	(The Jennie books)
"Stack of Barley"	(The Bennett books)
"Strathbuie MacKenzies Arrive in America, The"	(The Jennie books)
"Strawberries in the Sea"	STRAWBERRIES IN THE SEA
"Sweet Afton"	(The Jennie books)
"Take Me Out to the Ballgame"	(The Bennett books)
"Tavern in the Town, The"	(The Bennett books)
"Tennessee Waltz, The"	CALL HOME THE HEART
"Twinkle, Twinkle, Little Star"	(The Jennie books)
"Vienna Blood"	ROWAN HEAD
"Waltzing Matilda"	THE PIGEON PAIR
"We Shall Return No More"	(The Jennie books)
"When I Grow Too Old to Dream"	(The Bennett books)
"White Cockade, The"	(The Jennie books)
	(The Bennett books)
"Yankee Doodle"	(The Jennie books)

GAMES PLAYED IN OGILVIE NOVELS

backgammon	THE ROAD TO NOWHERE
baseball	A DANCER IN YELLOW
basketball	A DANCER IN YELLOW
cards	(The Bennett books)
	THE ROAD TO NOWHERE
checkers	(The Bennett books)
chess	IMAGE OF A LOVER
	THE ROAD TO NOWHERE
Chinese checkers	(The Bennett books)
cribbage	(The Bennett books)
	THE PIGEON PAIR
	WATERS ON A STARRY NIGHT
	WEEP AND KNOW WHY
	THE DREAMING SWIMMER
	A DANCER IN YELLOW
croquet	NO EVIL ANGEL
	THE PIGEON PAIR

❧ BOATS IN OGILVIE NOVELS

NAMES OF BOATS

(* = Bennett's Island series; + = Jennie Series)

Andromeda
Annie-Elmira*
Ariel+
Artemis+
Astarte*
Aurora B*
Beautiful Dreamer*
Bel Fiore+
Blue Jay+
Bonnie Eloise*
Brianna*
Cecile*
Centurion*
Clarice Hall*
Conqueror*
Corsair
Cynthia*
Donna*
Dovekie*
Drake's Pride*
Eaglet
Edith and Maude*
Elaine*
Eleanora*
Ella Vye*
Elsie R*
Enoch Lincoln+
Finest Kind*
Floam-Flower
Gemini*
Girl Kate*
Golden-Eye
Gull*
Gypsy Queen*
Hannah Mac*
Helen*

IBEX
Iolaire+
Island Magic
Janet F*
Jean-Felice
Jemima C
Joanna S*
Julia May*
Juno
Kestrel*
Kingfisher
Lady Grace
Lady Lydia+
Laura
Linnea*
Liza*
Liza Jane*
Louis*
Lucy Foster*
Marianne*
Marietta
Marmion+
Marjorie C
Mary C
Mateel*
Minerva*+
Miranda
Miss Alice
Monster
Moonlight
Morag
Nanette Harmon*
Nereid
Nerita
Ocean Pearl
Omni J

Old Girl*
Paul Revere+
Peregrine*
Pet
Philippa*
Phoebe
Phoebe Ann*
Princess
Princess Pat
Priscilla*
Ripper*
Robin B*
Sea Dancer*
Sea Gypsy*
Sea Pigeon*
Sea Rover*
Sea Star*
Sheila-Catherine
Sunbeam*
Susan C*
Sweet Helen*
Tahiti
The Basket*
The Blue Streak
The Four Brothers
The Gardner Girl
The Maid of All Work+
The Tilson Girls*
Triton*
Undine
Valkyrie*
We Two*
White Lady*
Wind Dancer*

Types of Watercraft

barkentine

cabin cruiser

canoe

Chebacco boat

cockleshell dinghy

cutter

dinghy

dory* (*also* decked-over dory; outboard
    dory; Grand Banks dory; seine dory)

double-ender* *A rowboat or sailboat
    shaped exactly the same at both ends.*

dragger, two-man (*also* small dragger)

Johnny wood boat. *A small boat used to
    transport wood for the lime kilns.*

ketch

lapstrake *Overlapping planks or strakes on a
    boat's frame.*

lobster boat

mailboat (*also* mail packet)

motorboat

peapod*

pink; pinky. *A distinctive small schooner with
    sharp or "pinked" stern.*

powerboat

punt

sailing yacht (tall-masted; two-masted)

schooner (two-masted schooner; five-
    masted schooner; barrel-bottomed
    schooner; coasting schooner)

seiner (*also* broad-beamed seiner)

shad

skiff

sloop. *A sailboat with a single mast.*

smack (*also* lobster smack)

square-rigger

square-sterned Dogbody

steamer

steam yacht

tender

trawler, two-man (*also* diesel trawler)

wherry

yawl

*A note about peapods, dories, and double-enders: A peapod is a round-bottomed, double-ended rowboat, sometimes rigged for sailing. (The Maine way to row a peapod is to stand up, facing forward, pushing oars in wooden tholepins rather than metal oarlocks.) A peapod is a double-ender, but a double-ender isn't necessarily a peapod; lots of canoes and canoe-hulled sailboats are double-enders. Peapods are almost always round-bottomed, whereas dories are usually flat-bottomed with flaring sides.

✿ FLORA AND FAUNA IN OGILVIE NOVELS

TREES & PLANTS

* = Bennett's Island novels   + = Jennie novels   ^ = young adult novels

alders+*
alyssum
apple trees*^
    Astrakhan
    Greening
    red^
    wild
Arethusa bulbosa+
asters
    deep lavender*
    purple*
    wild*
barberry*
bayberries*^ (*also* bay *and*
    bay bushes+*)
beach peas*^
beets*
bindweed*
birches+*^
    white
    yellow*
birdsong*
blackberries*^
black-eyed Susans
bluebells*
blueberries *^
blue flag* (iris)
boneset*
bunchberries*
    red^
    white-blossoming
buttercups+*^

Caledonian pines+
caraway, wild*
catnip
cherry trees*
chicory*
chrysanthemums*
    white*
chokecherry
cinquefoil+
clover, red & white*
columbines*
cormeille+
cosmos
cranberries+*^
crocuses*
cucumber
currants+
Cypripedium calceolus (yellow
    moccasin flower)+
daffodils+
dahlias*
daisies+*^
dandelions
delphiniums*
devil's paint brush*
elms*^
evening primrose*
ferns+^
    bracken+
    curling
    fern roots*
fire bushes*
firs

forget-me-nots*
forsythia
geranium, red*
gill-over-the-ground, purple+
goldenrod*
goose tongue
hackmatack^ (larch)
hardhack (meadowsweet)
hawthorn+
heather+
herbaceous border+
highland cranberries
hollyhocks*^
honeysuckle+^
huckleberries^
hyacinths*
gorse+
Indian, or ghost, pipes
Indian paintbrush*
iris
Jack-in-the-pulpit
Johnny-jump-ups
juniper+*
lady slippers, white
lambkill (sheep laurel)
larkspur^
lichens, scarlet+
lilacs+*^
    purple*
    white*
lily-of-the-valley*+
linden
lupine^

maple*
   red flowered
   swamp
marigolds
   dwarf
marsh rosemary
mayflowers*^
monkshood
moosewood
morning glories+
   pink^
   wild^
moss
   green+
   silvery+
mountain ash
mushrooms
narcissus, white
nicotiana
oak+
pansies
   deep blue
   miniature
pear trees
pear trees, wild
peonies*
periwinkles, yellow
petunias, scarlet *
pine, virgin +

poplar*^
popple tree (aspen)
primroses+
Queen Anne's lace*
quince, Japanese
raspberries+*^
reindeer moss (lichen)
rhododendrons+
rockweed*
roses
   ever blooming
   lavender*
   old fashioned
   red^
   rugosa*
   scarlet ramblers^
   white*
   wild*^
rowan tree+*
seaweed
seven-sisters bush
shadbushes
shore greens
snapdragons
snowball bushes
snow bedstraw*
snowdrops
spruce*^
   blue

sawtooth
squirreltail grass
starflowers
Stars of Scilla, azure*
stocks, night scented *
strawberries, wild *
swamp buttercup
swamp candles*
sweet William^
syringa
tansy*
thistles+*^
toadstools
tomato plants
tormentil+
trout lilies+
tulips, Red Emperor
violets+*
   African^
   blue
   flaming red
   white
watercress+
weigela
whortleberry+
wild flowers*
wintergreen
wood sorrel
zinnias

MARINE LIFE

bluefish
catfish
clams
codfish
crabs
cunners
dogfish
flounders
haddock

hake
harbor pollock
hermit crabs
herring
jellyfish
lobsters
mackerel
mussels
pollock

porpoises
salmon
scallops
seals
sea urchins
shrimp
starfish
whales

Birds

blackbird, red-winged
bluebirds
bluejays
buzzards
catbird
chickadees
cormorants (shags)
crossbills
crows
cuckoo
curlew
dove, mourning
ducks
    black ducks
    blue-winged teal
    buffleheads
    eiders
    mallards
    medricks
    oldsquaws
    sheldrakes
eagles
finches
    goldfinches
    purple finches
fish hawks (osprey)
flickers
flycatchers
fowl
    bantam chicks; banty
        roosters

(fowl, *continued*)
    guinea hens
    Rhode Island Reds
geese
    brant geese
    Canada geese
grackles
grebes
grosbeaks
grouse, spruce
gulls (seagulls)
    black-back gulls
    herring gulls
    mackerel gulls
hawk, red-shouldered
herons
    great blue heron
    night heron
hummingbirds
juncoes
kingfisher
kinglets
loons
nuthatches
oriole, Baltimore
osprey
owl, saw-whet
partridge
pheasants
phoebes
pigeons

plovers
raven
redstarts
robins
sandpipers
sea pigeons (puffins)
sparrows
    fox sparrows
    ground sparrows
    red fox sparrows
    song sparrows
    white-throated sparrows
starlings
swallows
    barn swallows
    tree swallows
terns, arctic
thistle birds, yellow-and-black
thrushes
veeries
vireo
varblers
    chestnut-sided warbler
    green-throated warbler
    magnolia warbler
    myrtle warbler
    wood warbler
whaups (European curlews)
woodcock
woodpecker, downy

Other Animals

bobcat
chipmunk
deer
donkey
frogs
goats

mice
moose
peepers; tree frogs
pig
pine marten
porcupine

rabbits
raccoon
squirrels
woodchuck

PETS AND DOMESTIC ANIMALS

Adam, gray horse	JENNIE ABOUT TO BE
Aphrodite, red hen	AN ANSWER IN THE TIDE
Apollo, bull	WHERE THE LOST APRILS ARE
Argo, long-haired dog	THE SEASONS HEREAFTER
Babby, border collie	WEEP AND KNOW WHY
Babe, dog	MASQUERADE AT SEA HOUSE
Beebee, basset-beagle	THE DREAMING SWIMMER
Bianca, pony	A DANCER IN YELLOW
Blackie, hen	THE YOUNG ISLANDERS
Blanchard, horse	JENNIE GLENROY
Bobby Shafto, cat	AN ANSWER IN THE TIDE
Bosun, black dog	STORM TIDE
Bounce, terrier	JENNIE GLENROY
Brisky, pony	JENNIE GLENROY
Britton Gwinnett, kitten	BLUEBERRY SUMMER
Bruce, border collie	WEEP AND KNOW WHY
Bruno, dog	THERE MAY BE HEAVEN
	STRAWBERRIES IN THE SEA
Chad, a black Labrador	WHEN THE MUSIC STOPPED
Champ, dog	THE SUMMER OF THE OSPREY
Charlie, Skye terrier	IMAGE OF A LOVER
Clover, cow	WHISTLE FOR A WIND
Damon, ox	WHISTLE FOR A WIND
Dandy, gray horse	JENNIE GLENROY
Darroch, black Newfoundland dog	JENNIE GLENROY
Deirdre, horse	TOO YOUNG TO KNOW
Diamond, horse	JENNIE GLENROY
Diana, horse	JENNIE GLENROY
Dick, dog	THE EBBING TIDE
	THE DAWNING OF THE DAY
Digger, red Australian terrier	WEEP AND KNOW WHY
	THE DREAMING SWIMMER
Dolly, sorrel pony	JENNIE GLENROY
Dora, chestnut mare	JENNIE ABOUT TO BE
Duke, beagle dog	THE PIGEON PAIR
Ebony, sheep	JENNIE ABOUT TO BE
lamb	JENNIE GLENROY
Elfie, pony	A DANCER IN YELLOW
Fritz, fox	WEEP AND KNOW WHY
Garnet, gray tabby cat	JENNIE GLENROY
George, dog	MASQUERADE AT SEA HOUSE
Girl, red Australian terrier	WEEP AND KNOW WHY
Gretchen, dog	BEAUTIFUL GIRL

Gretel, dachshund	BLUEBERRY SUMMER
Gromyko, rooster	THE DAWNING OF THE DAY
Hank (Prince Henry the Navigator),	THE SUMMER OF THE OSPREY
herring gull	THE DAY BEFORE WINTER
Hansel, dachshund	BLUEBERRY SUMMER
Hector, horse	WHISTLE FOR A WIND
Heidi, dog	BEAUTIFUL GIRL
Henry, buck	WEEP AND KNOW WHY
Hero, black Newfoundland dog	IMAGE OF A LOVER
Hodge, cat	CEILING OF AMBER
	THE ROAD TO NOWHERE
Hugo, German shepherd	THE DREAMING SWIMMER
Inkie, black cat	MY SUMMER LOVE
Jack, rooster	THE WORLD OF JENNIE G.
James, gray-and-white cat	WHEN THE MUSIC STOPPED
Jason, black-and-white border collie	WHERE THE LOST APRILS ARE
Joe, duck	THE EBBING TIDE
Joey, terrier	THE ROAD TO NOWHERE
John Peel, cock pheasant	WEEP AND KNOW WHY
Jones, terrier	BEAUTIFUL GIRL
Jonquil, cow	IMAGE OF A LOVER
Judy, duck	THE EBBING TIDE
Juno, horse	JENNIE ABOUT TO BE
Justin, Morgan horse	THE WORLD OF JENNIE G.
Leo, large yellow cat	THE SUMMER OF THE OSPREY
Lissa, dog	BEAUTIFUL GIRL
Louis, large gray-striped cat	THE SEASONS HEREAFTER
big gray tiger store cat	THE SUMMER OF THE OSPREY
	STRAWBERRIES IN THE SEA
	THE DAY BEFORE WINTER
Louisa, cow	JENNIE GLENROY
Maggie, lamb	TOO YOUNG TO KNOW
cat	BLUEBERRY SUMMER
Max, small brown dog	THE DAWNING OF THE DAY
Michael, horse	JENNIE GLENROY
Missy, cat	WATERS ON A STARRY NIGHT
Nelson, pony	JENNIE ABOUT TO BE
Nicodemus, black-and-white cat	A FORGOTTEN GIRL
Nixie, pony	THE WORLD OF JENNIE G.
Old Bobby, boatyard cat	THE DAY BEFORE WINTER
Old Lady Henrietta, hen	THE YOUNG ISLANDERS
Oliver, black Newfoundland dog	THE WORLD OF JENNIE G.
Orion, rooster	NO EVIL ANGEL
Peggy, cow	JENNIE GLENROY
Penny, golden retriever	THE DREAMING SWIMMER

Perry, horse	JENNIE GLENROY
Peter, big mongrel shepherd dog	STORM TIDE
black Lab	CEILING OF AMBER
Philip, cat	HOW WIDE THE HEART
	THE YOUNG ISLANDERS
Phronsie, lamb	WHERE THE LOST APRILS ARE
cat	CEILING OF AMBER
sculptured money cat	WHEN THE MUSIC STOPPED
Phythias, ox	WHISTLE FOR A WIND
Pickwick (Pickie), collie-Siberian husky	THE DAY BEFORE WINTER
Pip, black and white cat	THE SUMMER OF THE OSPREY
cat	THE DAY BEFORE WINTER
Polly, silver-striped tabby cat	WHEN THE MUSIC STOPPED
Poochie, wooly mongrel terrier	A DANCER IN YELLOW
Prince, pony	THE WORLD OF JENNIE G.
dog	THE DREAMING SWIMMER
Priscilla, cat	THE EBBING TIDE
Puss, cat	WHISTLE FOR A WIND
Ralph, pony	A DANCER IN YELLOW
Rip, black-and-white collie	TOO YOUNG TO KNOW
Rob, dog	ROWAN HEAD
Robey, collie	AN ANSWER IN THE TIDE
Rolfe, dog	BEAUTIFUL GIRL
Rory Mar (Rory)	STRAWBERRIES IN THE SEA
	AN ANSWER IN THE TIDE
Sam, tiger cat	MY SUMMER LOVE
Newfoundland dog	NO EVIL ANGEL
gull	A DANCER IN YELLOW
Sancho, dog	BEAUTIUFL GIRL
Sheena, dog	JENNIE ABOUT TO BE
Shonnie, horse	JENNIE GLENROY
Sidney, wooly gray-black mongrel dog	A THEME FOR REASON
Snow, white cat	MY SUMMER LOVE
Snowflake, sheep	TOO YOUNG TO KNOW
Tabby, cat	THE DAY BEFORE WINTER
Tad, beagle dog	CALL HOME THE HEART
Theresa, tiger cat	HIGH TIDE AT NOON
Tiger, dog	THE SEASONS HEREAFTER
shaggy red terrier	AN ANSWER IN THE TIDE
terrier dog	THE SUMMER OF THE OSPREY
Titus, gray cat	THE FABULOUS YEAR
Tom, yellow cat	THE DAWNING OF THE DAY
Tommy, beagle	BLUEBERRY SUMMER
	THE FABULOUS YEAR
Tray, dog	THE DAY BEFORE WINTER

Tristan, cat	BELLWOOD
Victor, horse	JENNIE ABOUT TO BE
Walter, German shepherd "monster-dog"	MY SUMMER LOVE
William, 15-lb. gray tiger cat	A THEME FOR REASON
Winnie, collie-spaniel	HIGH TIDE AT NOON
Young Dog Tray, large, hairy, black-and-brown	THE DAY BEFORE WINTER
Young Joshua, horse	JENNIE GLENROY

LIST OF PUBLISHED WORK

Fiction

Adult Novels

* = Bennett's Island series + = Jennie series

****High Tide at Noon.*** New York, Crowell, 1944; London, Harrap, 1945.
****Storm Tide.*** New York, McGraw-Hill, 1945; London, Harrap, 1947.
****The Ebbing Tide.*** New York, Crowell, 1947; London, Harrap, 1948.
Rowan Head. New York, McGraw-Hill, 1949; London, Harrap, 1950.
****The Dawning of the Day.*** New York, McGraw-Hill, 1954.
No Evil Angel. New York, McGraw-Hill, 1956; London, Harrap, 1957.
The Witch Door. New York, McGraw-Hill, 1959; London, W. H. Allen, 1961.
Call Home the Heart. New York, McGraw-Hill, 1962.
There May Be Heaven. New York, McGraw-Hill, 1966.
****The Seasons Hereafter***. New York, McGraw-Hill, 1966.
Waters on a Starry Night. New York, McGraw-Hill, 1968.
Bellwood. New York, McGraw-Hill, 1969.
The Face of Innocence. New York, McGraw-Hill, 1970.
A Theme for Reason. New York, McGraw-Hill, 1970.
Weep and Know Why. New York, McGraw-Hill, 1972.
****Strawberries in the Sea.*** New York, McGraw-Hill, 1973.
Image of a Lover. New York, McGraw-Hill, 1974.
Where the Lost Aprils Are. New York, McGraw-Hill, 1975.
The Dreaming Swimmer. New York, McGraw-Hill, 1976.
****An Answer in the Tide.*** New York, McGraw-Hill, 1978.
A Dancer in Yellow. New York, McGraw-Hill, 1979.
The Devil in Tartan. New York, McGraw-Hill, 1980.
The Silent Ones. New York, McGraw-Hill, 1981; Bath, Chivers, 1983.
The Road to Nowhere. New York, McGraw-Hill, 1983.
+***Jennie About to Be.*** New York, McGraw-Hill, 1984.
+***The World of Jennie G.*** New York, McGraw-Hill, 1986.
****The Summer of the Osprey.*** New York, McGraw-Hill, 1987.
When the Music Stopped. New York, McGraw-Hill, 1989.
+***Jennie Glenroy.*** Camden, Maine, Down East Books, 1993.
****The Day Before Winter.*** Camden, Maine, Down East Books, 1997.

Young Adult / Juvenile Novels
* = Young Bennetts series + = Scholastic/Wildfire Young Love series

Whistle for a Wind: Maine 1820 (illus. by Charles H. Geer), New York, Scribners, 1954.
Blueberry Summer (illus. by Algot Stenbery), New York, McGraw-Hill, 1956.
The Fabulous Year. New York, McGraw-Hill, 1958.
How Wide the Heart. New York, Whittlesey House/McGraw-Hill, 1959; republished as *A Steady Kind of Love,* Scholastic Book Service, 1979.
The Young Islanders (illus. by Robert Henneberger), New York, McGraw-Hill/Whittlesey House, 1960.
Becky's Island. New York, McGraw-Hill, 1961.
Turn Around Twice. New York, McGraw-Hill, 1962;
Ceiling of Amber. New York, McGraw-Hill, 1964; published as *Until the End of Summer* by Scholastic Book Service, 1981.
Masquerade at Sea House. New York, McGraw-Hill, 1965.
The Pigeon Pair. New York, McGraw-Hill, 1967.
Come Aboard and Bring Your Dory! New York, McGraw-Hill, 1969; published as *Nobody Knows About Tomorrow,* London, Heinemann, 1971.
+*Beautiful Girl.* New York, Scholastic Book Services, 1980.
+*A Forgotten Girl ... and a Forgotten Time.* New York, Scholastic Book Services, 1982.
+*Too Young to Know.* New York, Scholastic Book Services, 1982; London, Hippo, 1983.
+*My Summer Love.* New York, Scholastic Book Services, 1985.

Film Novelization

Honeymoon. Elisabeth Ogilvie's novelization of screenplay by Michael Kanin, based on a story by Vicki Baum, 1947. New York, Bartholomew House, 1947.

Short Stories

"And Then It Will Be Spring," *Everywoman,* New York, date unknown.
"Summer Girl," *Woman's Day,* July 1944.
"Eighteenth Summer," *Woman's Day,* July 1947.
"Hubert and the Eternal Feminine," *Woman's Day,* March 1950.
"Scobie," *Woman's Day,* August 1951 and reprinted as a selection in *Maine Speaks: An Anthology of Maine Literature,* The Maine Literature Project, 1989.
"A Weekend with Ebony," *Woman's Day,* August 1952.
"A Woman's Reputation," *Redbook,* October 1962.
"Island of Shadows," *Good Housekeeping,* November 1969.
"Reach for the Dawn," *Good Housekeeping,* February 1981.

Film Adaptation

High Tide at Noon. Film by J. Arthur Rank, The Rank Organisation, Pinewood Studios, London, England, 1957. An 80-minute black-and-white production filmed at North West Cove, Queensland, Nova Scotia, starring Betta St. John, William Sylvester, and Flora Robeson. Produced by Julian Wintle; screenplay by Neil Paterson; directed by Philip Leacock.

Early Stories from *The Manet*

"A Case of Mistaken Identity," 1930.
"Davey's Pirate," 1931.
"Legs for Ruport," 1931.
"Night Errant," 1933.
"The Power and the Glory," 1934.
"Mon Meilleur Noel," 1934.
"The Delightful Guest," 1934
"Meet Mr. King," 1934.

NONFICTION

Articles about Maine Island Life

"The Lobsterman's Wife," *Boston Transcript,* June 1946.
"Last Waltz on Criehaven," *Island Journal,* vol. 13, 1996.

Autobiography

My World Is an Island. Illus. by Paul Galdone, Whittlesey House/McGraw-Hill, 1950. Second edition with epilogue and photos, Camden, Maine, Down East Books, 1990.

Professional Articles

"Background—the Most Important Character," *The Writer,* July 1966.
"Suspense in Fiction," *The Writer,* January 1970.
"Suspense and a Sense of Place," *The Writer,* September 1976.
"Speaking of Magic Carpets," *The Writer,* September 1981.
"The Practice and the Passion," *The Writer,* April 1985.

✼ BIBLIOGRAPHY AND RESOURCES

BOOKS

Acheson, James. *The Lobster Gangs of Maine*. Univ. Press of New England, Hanover, N.H., 1988.

Commire, Anne, ed.. *Something About the Author,* vol. 40. Gale Research Company, 1985.

Digby, Ian. *Scotland*. Mayflower Books, Inc. New York, 1980.

Fillmore, Robert B. *Gems of the Ocean.* Opinion Print, Rockland, Me., 1914.

Finlay, Ross. *Journey Through Scotland.* Gallery Books, New York, 1986.

Fischer, Jeff, ed. *Maine Speaks: An Anthology of Maine Literature*. Maine Writers and Publishers Alliance, 1989.

Formisano, Ron. *The Great Lobster War.* Univ. of Massachusetts Press, Amherst, Mass., 1997.

Henderson, Lesley, ed. *Twentieth-Century Romance and Historical Writers*. St. James Press, London, 1990.

Kunitz, Stanley. *Twentieth-Century Authors: A Biographical Dictionary of Modern Literature,* 1st Supplement. H.W. Wilson Co., New York, 1955.

Long Charles A.E. *Matinicus Isle: Its Story and its People. Lewiston Journal* Printshop, Me., 1926.

McLane, Charles B. *Islands of the Mid-Maine Coast: Muscongus Bay and Monhegan Island.* Tilbury House, Gardiner, Me. and The Island Institute, Rockland, Me., 1992.

Martin and Lipfert. *Lobstering and the Maine Coast.* Maine Maritime Museum, Bath, Me, 1985.

Morton, H.V. *In Search of Scotland.* The Vail-Ballou Press, Inc., Binghamton, N.Y., 1929.

Rogers, D. K. *Tales of Matinicus Island: History, Lore and Legend—A Visitor's Guide.* Offshore Publishing, 1990.

Simpson, Dorothy. *Island in the Bay.* J. B. Lippincott Co., 1956. Reprinted by Blackberry Books, Nobleboro, Me., 1993.

Simpson, Dorothy. *The Maine Islands in Story and Legend.* J. B. Lippincott Co., 1960. Reprinted by Blackberry Books, Nobleboro, Me., 1987.

Vickers, Daniel. *Farmers & Fishermen: Two Centuries of Work in Essex County, Massachusetts.* Chapel Hill Press, 1994.

ARTICLES

Anderson, David. "Author Finds Inspiration on Maine Coast." *Lewiston "Sunday,"* April 16, 1989.

Barnes, Jack C. "Elisabeth Ogilvie: Maine's Prolific Writer," *New Hampshire Sunday News,* April 23, 1989.

Barnes, Jack C. "Sweep of Nature Fills Novelist Ogilvie's Life and Books." *Maine Sunday Telegram*, April 26, 1989.

———. "Ogilvie's Fans Can Smile Again." *Maine Sunday Telegram*, September 12, 1993.

———. "Maine Novels by Old Friends Back in Print." *Maine Sunday Telegram*, July 17, 1994.

———. "A Love for the Island That Never Grew Old." *Maine Sunday Telegram*, February 14, 1999

Barry, William David. "*Day Before Winter* Keeps Eye on Island Life." *Maine Sunday Telegram*, January 18, 1998.

Beston, Henry. "Brontë-like Maine." *Saturday Review*, September 17, 1949.

"Blueberry Summer: A Review." *Christian Science Monitor*, May 10, 1956.

Brown, Ron. "An Answer in the Tide will evoke many emotions." *Bangor Daily News*, October 8, 1991.

Cakouros, Jeanette. "Elisabeth Ogilvie: Tides of Change." *Maine in Print*, June 1991, vol. VI, no. 5.

———. "The Jennie Trilogy." *Maine in Print*, October 1994.

Caldwell, Bill. "Two Salty Authors Season Our Coast." *Portland Press Herald*, 1978.

Crie, Ethel. "The 'Air Mail' of Yesterday and Today." 1945.

Davis, Georgeanne. "Maine's Most Uncommon Book Club." *The Free Press*, May 6, 1999.

———. "Criehaven Reunion." *The Free Press*, May 4, 2000.

"Elisabeth May Ogilvie." Gale Literary Database. Contemporary Authors Online, The Gale Froup, 2000.

Haldane, Gina and Dara. "Author Profile: Elisabeth Ogilvie." *Gothic Journal*, December/January 1996, Vol. 5, No. 4: 10–14.

Kontos, Carol. "Review of *When the Music Stopped* by Elisabeth Ogilvie." *Kennebec: A Portfolio of Maine Writing*, vol. XIV, Univ. of Maine, Augusta, 1990.

Lau, Edie. "On Criehaven, Visitors Worthy of Big Welcome." *Maine Sunday Telegram*, September 1, 1996.

Lincoln, Nan. "Love Affair with an Island." *Bar Harbor Times*, June 7, 1990.

McCallum, Nancy. "Life as It Ought to Be: Maine Author Ogilvie Spins Another Winner." York County *Journal Tribune*, August 21, 1993.

McWilliams, Margot. "The Scriveners." *Down East*, October 1994.

Marsh, Pamela. "A Good Read for Mystery Buffs: *The Silent Ones*, by Elisabeth Ogilvie." *Christian Science Monitor*, October 21, 1981.

Mather, Karen. "Ogilvie's Third 'Jennie' Novel Wraps Up Her Scottish Series." Brunswick, Me. *Times Record*, August 20, 1993.

Mayo, Bob. "Island Lore Dominates Lives, Writings of Maine Authoresses." *Bangor Daily News*, October 12, 1961.

Morgan, Patricia Griffith. "Returning to Elisabeth Ogilvie's Bennett's Island." *Down East*, November 1985.

Moses, Tim. "Profile: Elisabeth Ogilvie, Novelist." Down East Books profile, December 18, 1992.

Parker, Mary Ann. "Jennie Glenroy." *Library Journal*, June 15, 1993.

Perry, Katy. "Award to Elisabeth Ogilvie Highlights Spring Conference." *The Maine Line*, Maine Media Women newsletter. May/June 1998.

"Profile: Grand Dames of Criehaven, Dorothy Simpson and Elisabeth Ogilvie." *Island Journal*, vol. 2, 1985.

Putz, George. "This New England: Criehaven, Maine." *Yankee*, May 1987: 68–77, 138–142.

Sanders, Estelle Watson. "Interview: Elisabeth Ogilvie." Windham High School, Windham, Me.. *Kennebec: A Portfolio of Maine Writing*, vol. XIV, Univ. of Maine, Augusta, 1990.

Sher, Joan Lear. "*The Pigeon Pair*: A Review." *The New York Times Book Review*, May 7, 1967.

Stothart, Betta. "Elisabeth Ogilvie: True-Life Romance with a Shake of Pain." *Maine Times*, November 15, 1991.

Taylor, Helene Scherff. "Elisabeth Ogilvie." *Wilson Library Bulletin*, September 1951.

Tirrell-McLaughlin, Anne. "A Profile of Maine Author Elisabeth Ogilvie." *Maine Life*, December 1980.

Wallace, Margaret. "Salt and Seaweed." *The New York Times Book Review*, April 16, 1944.

TELEVISION AND RADIO INTERVIEWS

Interview for *Chronicle* with Peter Mehegan, WCVB-TV (Boston, Mass.), in Cushing, Maine (mainland house), April 19, 1992.

Interview for CPTV Production (Connecticut Public Television), "Islands of New England," on Gay's Island, 1992. Also includes interview with Dot Simpson.

Interview by Tim Sample, "Postcards from Maine," for *Sunday Morning with Charles Osgood*, CBS-TV, on Gay's Island, May 22, 1994.

Interview by Amy Sinclair, "Where's Amy?" for 6:00 News, WGME-TV (Channel 13, Portland, Maine), on Gay's Island, August 24, 1998.

Interview by Mary Margaret McBride, at a New York City radio studio, following publication of *High Tide at Noon*, early 1945.

Interview by Paul Warren, (telephone interview with Elisabeth Ogilvie at her Cushing home) "Typewriter Repairman," for *Maine Things Considered*, Maine Public Radio, February 24, 2000.

NEWSLETTER

A Mug-up with Elisabeth. Editors Melissa Hayes and Marilyn Westervelt. Quarterly newsletter. For subscription information, contact Marilyn Westervelt, HC 35 Box 430, Tenants Harbor, ME 04860. Send SASE to same address for index of published articles.

WEBSITE

www.mugup.com

INDEX

Authors **Marilyn Westervelt** and **Melissa Hayes** (left to right) are the publishers of *A Mug-Up with Elisabeth, The Newsletter for Readers of Elisabeth Ogilvie.*

Melissa "discovered Ogilvie by chance" at her local library in the early 1990s, and loved her work so much that within just a few years she'd collected all the Ogilvie novels. She and her husband are the creators of the www.mugup.com website.

Marilyn has been enjoying Elisabeth's writings for more than forty years, and she credits the novels with inspiring her to visit the Maine coast and eventually make it her home.